Our Forest, Your Ecosystem, Their Timber

Nicholas K. Menzies

Our Forest, Your Ecosystem, Their Timber

Communities, Conservation, and the State
in Community-Based Forest Management

Columbia University Press
New York

Columbia University Press
Publishers Since 1893
New York   Chichester, West Sussex
Copyright © 2007 Columbia University Press
All rights reserved

Library of Congress Cataloging-in-Publication Data
Menzies, Nicholas K.
Our forest, your ecosystem, their timber : communities, conservation, and the
    state in community-based forest management / Nicholas K. Menzies.
    p.   cm.
Includes bibliographical references and index.
ISBN-13: 978-0-231-13692-1 (cloth : alk. paper)
ISBN-10: 0-231-13692-7 (cloth : alk. paper)
1. Community forestry—Case studies. 2. Forest management—Case studies.
    3. Forest policy—Case studies. I. Title.
SD561.M46   2007
333.75—dc22
    2006018948

Columbia University Press books are printed on permanent and durable
    acid-free paper.
This book was printed on paper with recycled content.
Printed in the United States of America
c 10 9 8 7 6 5 4 3 2 1

Designed by Lisa Hamm
References to Internet Web sites (URLs) were accurate at the time of writing.
Neither the author nor Columbia University Press is responsible for URLs that
may have expired or changed since the manuscript was prepared.

As we progressively understood the causes of environmental degradation, we saw the need for good governance. Indeed, the state of any country's environment is a reflection of the kind of governance in place, and without good governance there can be no peace.

—WANGARI MAATHAI, NOBEL LECTURE, 2004

Contents

Acknowledgments

I HAD no idea when I arrived three years ago in California from East Africa what I was embarking on. My plan was to write some papers on community forestry for publication in relevant journals and professional publications. As I worked, I found the issues proliferating, while at the same time they surfaced and resurfaced in different places and guises but were still recognizably the same issues. The papers that I had expected to write turned into several thematic papers, possibly to be included in an edited volume. These in turn evolved into this one book, still focused on current issues in community forestry but reflecting at the same time on past trajectories to the present and on where community-based forest management might find its place in a future, wider picture of forests and communities.

In the process of turning a vast topic into something manageable, I have had to make difficult choices about what to include and what to leave out. Perhaps the most difficult decision was to concentrate this analysis on places where communities and state resource management agencies are cautiously moving toward a new dispensation, which includes communities as forest managers, in contrast to past policies of exclusion. Inevitably, this decision means that there is little here about the rich legacy of indigenous and local forest management systems or forest management systems devised and implemented by communities themselves on their own land. For centuries, communities from

New England to Switzerland to Borneo and countless other places have cared for and maintained forestland to provide for their material needs and to enrich their cultures and spiritual lives. Much still needs to be written about these communities and their forests, but it will have to wait for another opportunity. In this book, I have chosen to look at how communities, states, civil society, and commercial interests are inching their way to accommodations over the utilization of land that they variously perceive as being forest, endangered and vulnerable ecosystems, or valuable timber resources.

I have been able to work on this book thanks to a generous grant from the Ford Foundation to the Division of Society and Environment in the Department of Environmental Science, Policy, and Management at the University of California, Berkeley. I would like to thank my former colleagues in Ford Foundation offices around the world who had enough confidence in me to support my idea of trying to capture at least some of what has been happening over the last twenty or thirty years in community forestry. I have benefited from their trust and from many opportunities to talk and exchange ideas with a remarkable group of peers.

The lengthy reference list at the end of this book testifies to the work of many professionals and scholars who have been involved in the emergence of community-based forest management and in analyzing what it means both for communities and for forests. I am indebted to all who have carried out the case studies, theory-building, and syntheses that have shaped the field and without which I would not have been able to even start this study.

I have built this book on four snapshots of communities managing forests and on four longer stories from around the world. Many dedicated community leaders, researchers, and representatives of government agencies and NGOs made my own visits to communities described here easier and more productive than they would otherwise have been. A far from exhaustive list of those who assisted me must include Chief Edwin Ogar of Ekuri, Nigeria; Louis Lesage of the Conseil de la Nation Huronne-Wendat in Québec; Leticia Merino-Pérez and David Bray in Oaxaca, Mexico; He Jun and Xu Jianchu of CBIK in Kunming, China; Thabit Masoud and the staff of DCCFF and of CARE International in Zanzibar; Amália's family in Mazagão and Miguel Pinedo-Vazquez in New York; and Rajeev Ahal, Vasant Saberwal, Mark Baker, Kim Berry, and members of the forest cooperatives in the Kangra valley. In other places that did not become snapshots or stories in the book but that were essential to my thinking about communities and forests, I would particularly like to thank Harry May and the staff of the Surplus People Project in Namaqualand, South Africa; Marilyn Hoskins, formerly of FAO; Lin Ostrom and members of the IFRI network, especially in Uganda and Kenya; and John Watkin, formerly of the African Conservation Centre in Nairobi. Thanks also to the very many people who are not listed here by name but who have helped me throughout this project.

During the year and a half that it took me to write this text, I had the unique pleasure and honor to be part of a book group at Berkeley with Louise Fortmann and Nancy Peluso, who were working on their own books at the same time. Time after time, they reminded me that even if I thought I knew what I was trying to say, I had not communicated my meaning with sufficient clarity. They helped me to rethink, rewrite, and look afresh at what others have already worked on and written. I can only hope in return that they have both found at least a little value in having me in the group with them.

Finally, while I embarked on this book alone, I could not possibly have stayed with it and completed it without the strength and support of my wife and closest companion, Melinda. She kept me going even on those days when I struggled to write just one or two sentences, knowing that I would probably have to erase them the next day because they were not quite right. Without her, I could not have done it.

Introduction

A GLOBAL review of forest ownership published in 2002 estimated that approximately 11 percent of all the world's forested land is under some form of community-based ownership (White and Martin 2002). In the eighteen developing countries in a sample of the top twenty-four of thirty forested countries, the same survey found an even higher total of 22 percent of land to be under community ownership. The statistics are impressive, but they reduce to simple numbers the rich diversity of experience and the many pathways that have brought communities to a point at which they are accorded the recognition that is their due as important players in the stewardship of the world's forests. Four brief snapshots of different communities managing forests will illustrate the diversity of people, practices, and institutions behind the statistics:

- In 1989 one Chinantec and three Zapotec communities in the Juarez Oaxaca mountains of central Mexico formed the Unión Zapoteca-Chinanteca (UZA-CHI) after years of struggle to regain control over their collectively owned forest, where a timber company had been operating under a twenty-five-year concession from the central government. UZACHI now manages more than 26,000 hectares of forestland remarkable for its high level of biodiversity. The union operates a sawmill, processing logs from its land and earning income

PLATE 1. Dancers at New Ekuri village welcome visitors to a celebration of the community's forest.   PHOTO: AUTHOR

from the timber, which is certified by the Forest Stewardship Council (FSC) as sustainably produced. It is also experimenting with other forest activities, such as orchid cultivation and harvesting and cultivating mushrooms, including the export of matsutake mushrooms to Japan (Anon. 2000).

- The six thousand residents of the villages of Old and New Ekuri in Nigeria's Cross River State resisted a state forestry department decision in the early 1990s to sell permits to commercial logging companies to harvest timber from communally owned village land. In the early 1990s, with assistance from local NGOs and international donors, the two villages collaborated with the nearby Cross River National Park to conduct their own forest inventory and develop a management plan with permanent transects monitoring forest condition. The state forestry authorities have now accepted the plan, ensuring that the two communities will control how the forest is used in the future (Anon. 1999).[1]

- In 1897 the Huron-Wendat people of Canada's Québec Province lost their hunting and fishing rights to an extensive area of forest with the creation of the Réserve Faunique des Laurentides—a forest reserve where the province currently grants twenty-five-year concessions to commercial timber companies. By the 1980s the Huron-Wendat concluded that their survival as a First Nation depended on the restoration of their rights and on developing forestry-based employment opportunities. In 1987 they entered into negotiations with the province and with Gestofor, the company that held the concession to the Tourilli area of the reserve. The Huron-Wendat Nation now co-manages a 400-square-kilometer area with the province and has an agreement with Gestofor for the remaining years of its current concession and expects to negotiate an expanded co-management agreement over a larger area during the period of the next concession.[2]

- Lakeview is a small community in eastern Oregon that grew around a timber mill processing logs from the Fremont-Winnema National Forest. In 1996 the U.S. Forest Service halted logging in the area in response to lawsuits from environmental groups concerned about the threat to wildlife habitat. Faced with the likely closure of the mill, the citizens of Lakeview invited environmentalists, scientists, and Forest Service officials to join them in an effort to break through the deadlock of entrenched interests and to come to a consensus on a way forward. By 2001 the Forest Service approved a management plan devised by what had become known as the Lakeview Stewardship Group. The plan's goal is the restoration of the forest, allowing logging to continue, with scientists monitoring forestry activity for its environmental impacts and with contractors from the community receiving preference for work in the area. The stewardship group is now preparing a longer-term management plan, and the timber mill continues to operate and to employ local people (Hanscom 2004).

These four sketches portray different people and places: an association of indigenous communities in Mexico, forest villages under the authority of traditional rulers in West Africa, one of Canada's First Nations looking to a revitalized cultural and economic future, and a small economically threatened rural community in the United States. In each of these places, people are acting together and following distinctive strategies to assert their claims in forests over which they feel they have lost control in the course of the last century or more. They and many others around the world are taking steps to protect their forests in order to secure long-term benefits from the products and services that flow from the forests in which they live. While the differences between them are as important as the similarities, they are all representative of what has come to be known as "community-based forest management" (CBFM).[3]

The four snapshots give a glimpse of the many histories that have led to communities becoming forest managers and of the range of activities that they are involved in. Each of the next four chapters tells a longer and more detailed story of people struggling to secure their interests in forests on which they depend or of a community that is becoming an active player in caring for forests. The stories—from China, Zanzibar, Brazil, and India—are each unique in their ecological setting, their history and politics, and the way the communities live with the forest. The four snapshots and these four stories all share a common narrative, however, which highlights questions about how and why CBFM has entered the agenda of both conservation and development, how communities face the challenges of managing forests, and the difficult process of negotiating partnerships between communities and others claiming an interest in forest resources.

Chapters 6–10 take up these questions to consider them in the light of a growing body of experience from around the world in order to situate CBFM in the context of the different expectations converging on forests and to consider where it fits in the repertoire of possible different management regimes in forests.

Forest management in any one location brings together a constellation of people and institutions whose differences may overwhelm their common interest in the forest. Actors claiming a stake in the present and future condition of forests include governments, the private sector, communities living in or near the forest, and other interested parties such as urban environmental and recreational organizations or seasonal users such as nomadic pastoralists. In the past, governments and state resource management agencies have declared a public interest in the forest and regulated all uses, often favoring industrial and commercial interests to the detriment of local people. CBFM breaks with this exclusionary pattern to include forest communities both in managing the forest and in benefiting from at least a share of the income or services flowing from management. After twenty or more years of experimentation, forest communities and their partners are counting the costs and the benefits of participating in CBFM. This book examines the challenges they face in reconciling the different local, national, and global interests in forests and considers the present and future roles of CBFM in the sustained use and conservation of forests around the world.

Conservation and Utilization of Forest Resources

Historically, humans have continually modified their habitat, usually with forests and woodlands giving way to agriculture, livestock grazing, and urbanization. Changing patterns of subsistence and livelihoods make some degree of change in land use inevitable and acceptable in the interests of social progress. Nevertheless, from earliest times, philosophers and other observers of changing landscapes distinguished between necessary utilization of natural resources and abusive exploitation and degradation of the environment, conceptualizing conservation in the context of use. The sacred texts of Hinduism distinguished three kinds of forest: Mahāvana, Tapovana, and Śrīvana. Mahāvana were untouched forests, the abode of the gods. Tapovana were accessible to humans, places of spiritual sustenance and retreat that provided fruit and fodder. And Śrīvana were primarily sources of sustenance for humans and could be natural or cultivated forests (Banwari 1992:31–40). Over two thousand years ago the Chinese philosopher Mencius[4] formulated what has become a famous statement of the rationale for wise stewardship—as opposed to destructive exploitation—of forests, fisheries, and wildlife:

> If the seasons of husbandry be not interfered with, the grain will be more than can be eaten. If close nets are not allowed to enter the pools and ponds, the fishes and turtles will be more than can be consumed. If the axes and bills enter the hills and forests only at the proper time, the wood will be more than can be used.
>
> —MENG-TZU, *LIANG HUI WANG* 1.1.3.3 (TRANSLATED IN LEGGE 1960:130)

At almost the same time that the teachings of Mencius were being compiled in China, Plato drew a link between deforestation and soil erosion in Greece. Telling a story that has been retold in countless adaptations to other times and places, he contrasted a mythical ancient era of plenty to the hardships that farmers of his time endured to extract harvests from soils exhausted by deforestation and soil erosion (Glacken 1967:121).

By the time of the Industrial Revolution in Europe and North America, observers recognized a relationship between environmental disasters such as floods or drought and the exploitation of forests for fuel and timber to feed the new industries, calling for state intervention to control the use of forests (Marsh 1864). More recent scholarship has mapped the webs of relationships that tied states to the very interests that consumed the timber and other products from the forests and described the political dynamics that drove the demarcation, allocation, and disposal of the forest estate. During the twentieth century, in particular, forest clearance for conversion to agricultural or urban uses, large-scale commercial timber harvesting in concessions allocated to the politically powerful at rates well below economic values, and colonization schemes to bring strategic border areas under central government control have been just some of the many actions that have contributed to continuing losses of forested land (Barraclough and Ghimire 1996; Geist and Lambin 2001; Hecht and Cockburn 1989; Kaimowitz 2003; Xu et al. 1999).

States have intervened to assert control over the forest estate, claiming that only the state is able to engage in scientific, long-term management of a resource whose environmental services and economic benefits extend well beyond the area immediately under the control of forest communities (Fernow

1913). The model of forest management that state forest agencies and the forestry profession adopted has involved the manipulation of blocks of forestland to meet a planned objective, usually the production of wood or fiber, over a period of time measured in decades or more. Management objectives were determined by a professionalized institution responsible for planning, making decisions, and implementing the plan; and forests were legally designated areas of land owned by an individual or a clearly identified single legal property owner (which was often the state).

Assuming a public interest in forest products and services extending beyond the limits of the forest itself, state authorities have regulated access to and utilization of forest resources. They have demarcated boundaries to bring into existence an administrative category of land known as "forest," created agencies to implement preferred management regimes on that land, and policed the forests to exclude and punish offenders against the declared public interest. Peluso and Vandergeest have described how colonial state administrations during the late nineteenth and early twentieth centuries invented the "political forest . . . that was either demarcated by the state for permanent reservation or . . . that was claimed by the state" and "Customary Rights, which in many cases led to a racialization of the landscape" (2001:801). In partitioning the landscape between forest and other land uses, states divided the rural population into categories of legal and illegal residents, usually conforming to ethnic and cultural stereotypes of (legally) settled agrarian people and (illegal) squatters—mobile nomadic forest dwellers persisting in their customary way of life.

While Peluso and Vandergeest based their "genealogies of the political forest" on the histories of three southeast Asian countries, the story of government demarcation and control of forested lands was common to most colonized countries (Anderson and Grove 1987; Ghai 1991:13–14; Sivaramakrishnan 1999), nominally independent countries such as China, and other states in formation such as the United States, Italy, and the Scandinavian countries (Gaunitz 1984:137–44). The dominant pattern of government intervention has been one of increasing central control over forest resources, the denial of access to forest resources by groups that have traditionally or historically depended on them, and control over trade in (and thus the ability to benefit from) forest species and products (Peluso and Vandergeest 2001:768).

In practice, the record of state management of forest resources in the public interest is mixed. As a strategy for furthering the economic development of rural areas, large-scale forest management for timber production has been shown to be subject to severe cycles of expansion and collapse. The timber economy has most often left a legacy of "boom and bust"—often due to exhaustion of commercially accessible trees to harvest—with short-term gains undermined by the economic and social collapse of forest communities (Cook 1995; Lee, Field, and Burch 1990; Marchak 1983; Pinedo-Vasquez et al. 2001).

In countries with indigenous populations, resource management agencies have purportedly acted on behalf of "native peoples," while they have often left a legacy of impoverishment and cultural deprivation instead. Even Gifford Pinchot, the first chief of the U.S. Forest Service who was otherwise a strong advocate of scientific management of forests by a federal agency, was shocked at the fraud and mismanagement that characterized the administration of Native American forests by the then Indian Office of the Department of the Interior (precursor of the present Bureau of Indian Affairs). Looking back to the early years of the twentieth century, he wrote in his autobiography that "no one in the Indian Office, or on the ground was capable of handling these forests, and the result was what you might expect" (Pinchot 1947:411–12; C. Miller 2000). In more modern times, countries as diverse as South Africa, Australia, Indonesia, and Brazil are still wrestling with the social, cultural, and economic deprivation that has been the legacy of policies centered on state claims to natural resources that privilege specific racial groups.

Globally, there has been little evidence of improved forest condition in environmental terms—on the contrary, the last century has witnessed continuing and extensive losses of forest cover. During the second half of the twentieth century, in particular, the data indicate that forest cover was decreasing dramatically, often related to national policies favoring agricultural development (Repetto and Gillis 1988; Hecht and Cockburn 1989) or to the allocation by government agencies of forest concessions to state or privately owned industrial interests and the lack of monitoring of harvesting and regeneration (Bryant, Nielsen, and Tangley 1997; Richards and Tucker 1988; Tucker and Richards 1983; Weiss 2001). An oral history told by an elderly man in a village near Yongning in Yunnan Province of the forests surrounding Lugu Lake on the border between Sichuan and Yunnan provinces in southwestern China tells not only of the effects on local people of the loss of access to resources claimed by a succession of state agencies, but also of the environmentally devastating consequences of their mismanagement:

When I was about twelve years old, there were a lot of fish in the lake and we wove cloth for our clothing from hemp.

During the 1940s this area was mostly forested. The village chiefs prohibited cutting trees. There were so many tigers that we had to blow horns to frighten them away when we went into the forest.

In the 1950s we began to open up some fields for agriculture along the lake.

In the 1960s the government set up a fish-processing factory. The army came and used hand grenades to get fish out of the water. Then they tried to introduce fingerlings into the lake to increase the numbers of fish again, but they put in the wrong species, and the new fish ate all the eggs of the native fish.

Later on, the Sichuan government built a small hydropower dam where the river comes out of the lake, and no more fingerlings could come into the lake. So now we hardly have any fish.

In the late 1960s and into the 1970s the provincial department of forest industries came and harvested nearly all the trees around the lake. It was officially organized and people were brought in from Sichuan and Yunnan to harvest. Sometimes they used explosives to clear the roads.

In 1983 during the agricultural reforms, we were allocated land including freehold land. But now we need permits to cut any wood. Later on, that land was put into the conservation area and now we are not allowed to cut anything.

—AUTHOR'S FIELD NOTES, NOVEMBER 1992

More alarmingly, tensions between forest management agencies, the commercial forest products sector, environmental activists, and communities surrounding the forests appeared to be increasing. National parks and other protected areas around the world reported increasing encroachment and poaching. Popular movements such as the Chipko movement in India were taking direct action to prevent commercial enterprises from harvesting timber on land that communities considered to be theirs and a source of products vital to their own well-being (Guha 1990; Rangan 2000). In Thailand, Buddhist monks ordained trees in timber concessions to protect them (Darlington 1997, 1998). Meanwhile, in some wealthier industrialized countries, such as the United States, Canada, and Australia, activist groups such as Earth First! or Greenpeace engaged in controversial and well-publicized acts of civil disobedience to press their demands for more stringent protection of forests. Through peaceful acts such as the two years that Julia Butterfly spent perched on a platform in a tree to protect a grove of old-growth redwood trees in California (*San Francisco Examiner* 1999) and more confrontational blockades to prevent logging at Clayoquot Sound in Canada (*Toronto Globe and Mail* 1993; *Environment News Service* 1999) or in Tasmania and New South Wales in Australia (*Sidney Morning Herald* 1998), organized, vocal groups signaled their rejection of forest policies that they claimed were determined by government agencies and commercial interests in disregard of the public interest. In less dramatic but equally determined ways, public pressure was growing in the form of legal appeals challenging state forest management agencies to reconsider their policies and to reorient them from commercial timber production to management strategies more respectful of local communities' interests and conservation values (Baker and Kusel 2003:55–77).

An Invitation to Forest Communities

By the 1970s some professionals working on forest management in developing countries began to question the effectiveness of the conventional model of management in plantations and enclosed, protected areas of forest. Faced with strong evidence that existing regimes of state-administered forest management were not realizing their own mandates, some foresters, representatives of international aid agencies, and researchers began to question the traditional orientation of forest policies and of the profession toward commercial exploitation, particularly of timber. Developing countries where the scale and intensity of both conflict and forest loss were perhaps most acute were the site of intense questioning of established practices and of tentative moves to open the closed preserve of forestry to those who had been excluded.

In the 1970s Jack Westoby, a New Zealand forester nearing the end of his career with the United Nations' Food and Agriculture Organization (FAO), was among the most vocal of these critics, urging in his reports and public addresses that forestry should "serve the people." In 1978, as the guest speaker at the Eighth World Forestry Congress in Jakarta, Westoby denounced the ongoing loss of tropical forests and the failure of forest policies and practice to provide for social needs (1987:241–54). His speech and the declaration adopted at the end of the congress gave legitimacy, if not substance, to the contention that excluding local people from the forest and from the planning and implementation of management programs does not work. Forest resources are critical to the survival and vitality of neighboring communities, and managers would have to take account of broader social interests in the forest resource if forests were to survive.

At this time, the term *social forestry* emerged in India to describe programs supported by the Indian Forestry Department to plant trees on hillsides, roadsides, and other so-called wastelands in order to provide a range of forest products of importance to neighboring communities (Ballabh and Singh 1988; Pankaj-Khullar 1992; Romm 1982). The concept of social forestry evolved to encompass a range of management strategies in many developing countries, which considered social functions of forests in addition to timber and other commercial products (Poffenberger 1990). Within a decade, social forestry itself was criticized as being too state-directed, excluding local participants from decision-making, and not addressing conflicts on existing forested lands.

During the 1980s in West Bengal, some district forest officers began to experiment with partnerships involving village committees in formulating and implementing management plans to regenerate degraded forests and monitoring forest users. In return for their participation, communities received a share of income from timber and other forest products. The success of their efforts demonstrated the potential for joint management of forests, and the model began to spread to other states. In 1988 the Indian Forestry Department adopted joint forest management (JFM) as a national policy, marking perhaps the first time that communities formally and legally reclaimed at least some of the rights of access to forests that they had lost in the course of the creation of a national forest estate (Poffenberger and C. Singh 1996).

Interest in reconfiguring the relations between state natural resource administrations and forest communities has been widespread and in no way limited to the developing countries in Africa, Asia, and Latin America. The proliferation of experiments, policies, and projects has generated a varied terminology as it has been applied to different geographical regions, to different ecosystems, and to a changing understanding of the complexity of relations between individuals, communities, society, and natural resources. Community management, co-management, participatory forestry, forest stewardship, collaborative management, community-based conservation, and others have been added to an ever richer—and sometimes confusing—lexicon to describe a vision of resource management in which resource-dependent people are recognized as having a stake in the condition of the natural resource. From a focus on forests, the concept has broadened in scope to include water and wetlands, fisheries, wildlife, and pasture under the term *community-based natural resource management* (CBNRM) (perhaps the most inclusive term).

While it may not be desirable to draw sharp boundaries among the mosaic of different ecosystems that make up a landscape, this study will focus on forests—ecosystems dominated by trees—in rural areas, and it will use the term CBFM, recognizing that wildlife, fungi and mushrooms, water, carbon sequestration, and a wide range of other goods and services are at least as important as trees and wood in forested ecosystems. I will center the discussion on "forest communities," referring to the people living in and around forests, whose lives are directly affected by the condition of the forest and by legislation, policies, and practices that control access to and use of all or part of the forest ecosystem. This working definition does not preclude consideration of the interests in forests of physically more remote actors such as timber companies or urban-based environmental groups, but it does distinguish between interests rooted in particular places, rather than interests in the forest as an economic or ecological category.

Different Interests in Forest Resources and CBFM

Communities have managed forests for centuries before the contemporary prominence of CBFM. Colonial settlements in New England set aside community woodlots to ensure a supply of timber and fuelwood. Clans in prerevolutionary rural China managed forests for construction timber and to generate income for schools and clan welfare. Long-established systems such as these tell of the resilience and ecological viability of carefully crafted community forest management institutions. I have, however, focused here on newer regimes where state control over forested land is giving way to the inclusion of user communities. It is in these places that a public interest in sustainable use and environmental protection intersects with ethical concerns for human rights and social justice and with local interests in improved livelihoods. It is in this intersection that a realignment of priorities, rights, and responsibilities is taking place that will determine where CBFM fits in a spectrum of resource management systems extending from strictly enforced preservation through protection by the state to private ownership constrained only by the individual's responses to market forces and personal preference.

One definition of community forestry is that it is a process whereby specific community forest users protect and manage state forests in some form of partnership with the government (Hobley 1996). This definition assumes that if forest communities are partners in decision-making, implementation, and monitoring of activity in the forest, there will be long-term benefits both in terms of the ecological health of the forest and in terms of the benefits accruing to forest communities and the larger society of which they are a part. This simple statement, however, encompasses and obscures widely divergent visions, goals, and institutional regimes. Different interests view CBFM through the lens of their own concerns and their own visions of an equilibrium between states, people, and the environment. In the United States, many CBFM advocates consider themselves to be part of a social movement to reverse the injustice and exclusion that they see as marking the history of forestry (Baker and Kusel 2003:190). India's Forestry Department, by contrast, describes the goals of its JFM program in a more limited way as a mechanism to share responsibilities for managing forestland between the government and village (RUPFOR 2002).

The literature on development commonly refers to people and institutions as stakeholders representing different interests. The cast of stakeholders varies in different fields of development, but in the case of natural resource management, the most prominent actors identified tend to be the state, private enterprise, communities, indigenous people, and conservationists or environmentalists.

These actors pursue a diversity of interests that converge on forests, including—without being limited to—the following:

- the livelihoods and subsistence of forest communities
- the ecological health of forested ecosystems and maintenance of biodiversity
- global markets for forest products
- state or national security
- labor and employment
- social justice through land redistribution
- social justice through reparations for past injustice and dispossession
- contested claims to spiritual and cultural values embodied in forests
- urban interests in water and hydroelectric energy
- competition over the allocation of decision-making authority between different levels of authority, from the household to the international or global

Different individuals and groups of people have different interests at different times, and in many cases, the same person—or institution—may be pursuing several, possibly conflicting, interests at the same time. In the analysis that follows, then, I will refer to the interests of the diverse actors who are represented in CBFM, rather than the less helpful, though widely used, term *stakeholders.*

Contestation over the balance between economic development and biodiversity conservation and over rights and responsibilities between the state and citizens, devolution and decentralization, gender equity, and social justice constitute the topography of debate about the concept and practice of CBFM. With different visions of community, of the functioning of forest ecosystems, and of the allocation of rights and responsibilities over natural resources in the governance of modern nation states, these overlapping and contradictory constructions of CBFM generate different expectations and assessments among different actors of the validity of CBFM as a model for forest management.

CBFM in the Discourse of Development

Terms such as "sustainable development" and "redressing inequity and social injustice" are common to the various definitions of CBFM. The language used indicates that CBFM touches on many of the themes central to the global undertaking known as "development," which has mobilized people and financial resources on an unprecedented scale since the end of the Second World War in an effort to improve people's lives in the poorer countries of Africa, Asia, and Latin America.

The pursuit of development has generated bureaucracies and institutions at the global, national, and local levels through which planning takes place, funding is channeled, and information flows and is processed. In such a crowded arena, local voices and initiatives struggle to make themselves audible or visible. Despite shifts in rhetoric favoring participation and "people-centered development," it would still be accurate to describe the role of poor and disadvantaged people as onlookers at the party rather than the hosts or even invited guests.

Development discourse has created the category of "underdeveloped" or "developing" people and regions to which assistance is targeted (Escobar 1991; Peet and Watts 1993). The priorities of development and the channels of its delivery have, from the outset, been determined by "developed" people and countries, and targets of development assistance are to be found within developed countries as well as in whole countries and regions in Africa, Asia, and Latin America. The forest communities involved in CBFM find themselves the targets or recipients of development efforts, but these efforts have set up a scenario where it is necessary to create mechanisms or institutions to include in forest management the people who are in fact those most directly concerned with the state of the forest—forest communities.

A cursory review of the history of development reveals the ahistoric nature of the rise to prominence of different development strategies. New strategies emerge as solutions with little reference to past experience, often ignoring current efforts. Analyzing the preamble to the United Nations Declaration of the New International Economic Order (NIEO) in 1974, one scholar states:

> The preamble seeks to suggest a "messianic" novelty through its use of the expression "for the first time." . . . In keeping with the religious structure of declarations on "development," it first describes the present situation in dramatic terms ("inequalities," "widening gap"), then contrasts it to a future of peace, justice, equity, co-operation and social well-being, and finally sets out the measures that need to be taken to achieve these objectives.
>
> —RIST 1997:146

CBFM has found a place on the development agenda in concert with the rise of a discourse of sustainable development and improved governance. In practice, in the search for "messianic" new solutions, there are few opportunities and even fewer incentives to build on existing experience, to engage in consultation, and to make the small adjustments that might, over time, build the skills, resilience, and flexibility to address a problem as complex as the management of forest resources.

Reviewing CBFM and Its Role in Forest Management

This study contends that, in view of the different goals and interests involved in CBFM, little is gained in asking whether CBFM has succeeded or failed or whether it is a good thing or a bad thing. Instead, it reviews the landscape of CBFM practice and experiences to ask how and under what circumstances CBFM can contribute to reconciling the multiple and often conflicting demands of the many interests in forested landscapes. Rather than selecting and weighing the evidence to reach a judgment on whether the many paths and trajectories taken by CBFM have successfully reached a single goal, the study seeks to situate CBFM within the larger ecological, social, economic, and political systems that shape the landscapes in which forests and forest communities are embedded.

Taking account of the many models of CBFM around the world, this study follows three lines of enquiry:

- What are the dynamics that have caused states to move from excluding communities from forest resources in the name of the public interest to invoking communities in the name of more effective sustainable forest management?
- How do different expressions of the goals of CBFM shape the partnerships in CBFM and their outcomes?
- What conditions strengthen communities' capacities to improve their livelihoods and to maintain or improve the health of forest ecosystems through the management of forest resources?

The snapshots that opened this chapter are anecdotes that hint at the many ways in which CBFM is taking root around the world. An exhaustive catalog and critique of all the known examples of activities referred to as CBFM would be impossible to accomplish and tedious to read. In the four chapters that follow, I have chosen instead to tell four stories from China, Zanzibar, India, and Brazil. Each of these stories is an account of the people who live and work in a unique place. Their present circumstances and distinct histories give each story its own voice and perspective. Together, they illustrate different episodes of a common narrative of the loss of resources, of negotiations and action to reclaim some form of access, and of the many twists and turns on the paths along which communities and others are journeying through constantly changing forest landscapes.

The stories are the starting point for a discussion of some important issues—features punctuating the common narrative of their journeys. My concluding remarks revisit these issues to suggest that in many places CBFM is showing communities to be more capable and concerned stewards of forestland than states or commercial interests have been. In projecting their own goals and agendas onto CBFM, however, different partners often have different expectations of what an ideal outcome would look like. Fear of adverse outcomes can lead to a counterproductive imposition of regulatory frameworks constraining the role of community institutions to the extent that the perceived extra burden of forest management outweighs the benefits to the community, undermining the incentive to care for the resource as a valuable community asset.

This study proposes that the time has come to ensure that community management equips communities with the tools and the authority to manage, not just to provide their labor in exchange for a modest percentage of revenue. It does not offer further messianic solutions to the complexities of managing forested land. Instead, it concludes with an appeal to governments, resource management agencies, and NGOs to make the transition from collaboration and partnership as an experimental exception or concession to collaboration and partnership as the norm.

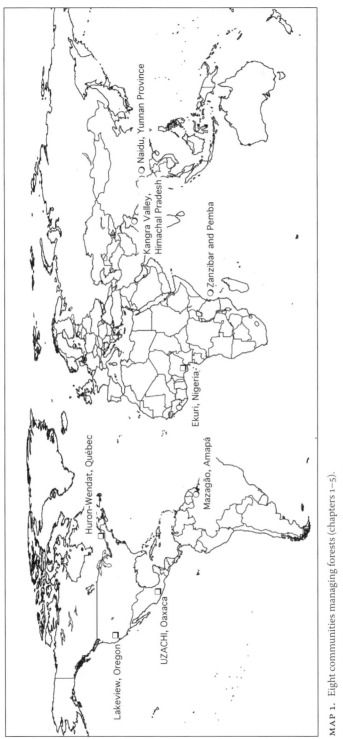

MAP 1. Eight communities managing forests (chapters 1–5).

Chapter 1: Four Snapshots

UAZCHI, Oaxaca, Mexico
Ekuri, Cross River State, Nigeria
Nation Huronne-Wendat, Québec, Canada
Lakeview, Oregon, USA

Four Stories

Chapter 2: Naidu, Yunnan Province, China
Chapter 3: Zanzibar and Pemba, Tanzania
Chapter 4: Mazagão, Amapá State, Brazil
Chapter 5: Kangra Valley, Himachal Pradesh State, India

Labels on map:

Huron-Wendat, Québec
Lakeview, Oregon
UZACHI, Oaxaca
Mazagão, Amapá
Ekuri, Nigeria:
Zanzibar and Pemba
Kangra Valley, Himachal Pradesh
Naidu, Yunnan Province

Naidu Village, Yunnan Province, China

> For generations we have looked after these mountains and forests. The state
> forest has now been ruined. We can't understand why they won't let us look
> after that forest. We have looked after it for such a long time.
>
> —VILLAGER IN NAIDU, YUNNAN PROVINCE
> (AUTHOR'S FIELD NOTES, NAIDU, AUGUST 2003)

NAIDU VILLAGE is set in lush forested hills overshadowed by the
peaks separating Yunnan Province from Tibet. The intricately carved
woodwork on the window frames and in the main living spaces inside the large
houses are witness to the modest prosperity of this Tibetan community, located
little more than one hour's drive from the county town, officially renamed
Shangri-la recently in a bid to attract tourists to what had formerly been the
remote county of Zhongdian in the Diqing Tibetan Autonomous Prefecture.
One recent source of prosperity is the summer harvest of matsutake mushrooms (*Tricholoma matsutake*) gathered in the community's mixed oak and
pine forests and sold through a chain of traders and entrepreneurs stretching
from the forest to the supermarkets and gourmet shops of Osaka and Tokyo
in Japan. The community is proud that it has succeeded in maintaining the
quantity and the quality of mushrooms from its collectively owned forest, while
the neighboring state-owned forest yields fewer and smaller mushrooms from
one year to the next. Since 1999 Naidu has developed and enforced its own
regulations to control harvesting and marketing of matsutake, and few villagers
doubt that this village initiative has spared their forest from experiencing what
they consider to be the free-for-all occurring on the state forest.

The 140 residents of Naidu practice a mixed farming and pastoral system,
producing barley and potatoes in the valley bottom surrounding the village

and grazing yaks and cattle to produce milk, butter, and cheese and occasionally to sell for slaughter. In common with other Tibetan communities and other mountain communities around the world, they practice transhumance, grazing their livestock in pastures close to the village during the winter and taking them higher up the mountains to pastures above the tree line during the summer months. The combination of agriculture and livestock ensures that people in the village rarely go hungry, but it is the forest surrounding the village that is the source of the cash income that allows them to buy the carved household altars that enrich their spiritual lives and material comforts such as a television, a DVD player, and even, for some families, a small motorbike, making access to the market easier than it had been in the past. Through the summer months, nearly every family in the village is involved in a daily search for mushrooms to sell to buyers from the cities, who sell them on to the Japanese market from the provincial capital of Kunming.

Since the early 1980s Yunnan has become one of the major sources for matsutake sold in Japan.[1] Market demand has expanded rapidly and highlighted many difficult questions concerning access to forests and forest products, sustainable management of a resource about whose ecology and reproduction little is known, and the risks of dependence on just one cash crop subject to frequent unpredictable price changes where market demand is determined by the tastes of luxury consumers in one country. Naidu and the sixteen other villages or hamlets (*she*) under the jurisdiction of Jidi Village Committee[2] are not immune to these unsettling forces in their lives, but they have taken action to regain some element of control by developing their own rules and practices for managing their forest and the harvest and sale of matsutake. Their story tells of their determination to keep some control over forestland claimed by the state and of the patient crafting of rules and monitoring systems to avoid the loss of a valuable source of income for individuals, families, and the community as a whole.

Village and State Forest Management in Naidu

Until the 1950s the Tibetan borderlands of what is now Yunnan were administered by representatives of the Chinese central government together with a Tibetan local chieftain (*tusi*).[3] For the following twenty years, agricultural production and the administration of rural areas in the region were merged in the process of collectivization of the Chinese countryside, which led to the People's Communes. The communes were, in turn, formally disbanded in 1982 and gave way to smallholder production under new policies known as the household responsibility system. During the collective period, land and all the nation's resources were deemed to be owned by "the people," with the state and the Communist Party of China exercising jurisdiction in the name of the people. While the people of Naidu say that they resented the state taking over forests that they had traditionally perceived as theirs, the government allowed no discussion or negotiation over land and resource ownership. With no forum in which any contested claims over ownership or utilization of resources could be articulated or addressed, resentment simmered without erupting into violence.

In 1983 nonagricultural land in Naidu was divided into state-owned forest (*Guoyou Lin*) under the jurisdiction of national forest and land-management agencies, collective forest (*Sheyou Lin*) under the jurisdiction of local government ("the collective"), and freehold forest (*Ziliu Shan*) for which individual households have management responsibilities (Grinspoon 2002:27–63; Menzies and Peluso 1992). The allocation of state-owned forest in particular did not go unchallenged. Responsibility for forests and forest products was at the time shared between the Ministry of Forestry (*Linye Bu*), with a mandate to manage, protect, and expand China's forested lands, and the Ministry of Forest Industries (*Linye Gongye Bu*).[4] The Ministry of Forestry feared that its industrial and commercially oriented counterpart would move quickly to grant logging concessions for any remaining timber in state-owned forests to timber companies (which were all owned by agencies of the government or the military). In Naidu, representatives of the Ministry of Forestry succeeded in getting a section of state-owned forest redesignated as collective forest to prevent it being logged. Twenty years later, villagers remember the support they received from the Ministry of Forestry and consider that they still have a good working relationship with local forest officials, though intense resentment remains over the actions of the logging company that operated in the state-owned forest. While the company employed able-bodied villagers as loggers and paid them daily wages for their labor, all the income from timber sales went to the timber company, with no royalties or fees of any kind accruing to the village or local governments. Villagers were also acutely aware of the damage caused to the forest, not only by logging, but also by the destructive behavior of company employees:

> Timber company employees used to shoot animals in the forest. They used to shoot several hundred monkeys at a time. They would eat some of them, but they were shooting them just for fun. They would also shoot bears and other larger animals. We would never harm monkeys. Tibetans cannot harm monkeys because they are so close to humans. Traditionally, we used to do some hunting in the forest, but only what we needed for food.
>
> —AUTHOR'S FIELD NOTES, NAIDU, AUGUST 2003

At one point in 1985 the timber company attempted to encroach on Naidu's collective forest. Several men from the village took bedding with them and camped for two days in the path of the bulldozers moving in from the state-owned forest. Others from the village appealed for assistance from the nearby office of the forest department, which had already demonstrated its intent to prevent logging by having the area designated as collective forest. After ten days of a tense standoff between villagers and the bulldozers, the forest department finally intervened in favor of the village:

> On the tenth day, the forest department came and told the company that they could not push peasants around in their own forest. They would have to get permission and they would have to pay the village it they wanted to harvest in the collective forest. The forest department helped us to demarcate the boundary between the state forest and the collective forest.
>
> —AUTHOR'S FIELD NOTES, NAIDU, AUGUST 2003

Since this confrontation, the two ministries have merged and in 1998 became a department within a new Ministry of Land and Resources (Xu and Ribot 2004:156). The tension between forestry-as-environmental-protection and forestry-as-timber-production has persisted, however. In 1998 the central government responded to extensive flooding with a logging ban in the whole of the Upper Yangtze watershed (which includes Zhongdian), deciding in effect that the primary function of the forestry administration is conservation, leaving timber production to the commercial sector (although many of the timber companies continue to be owned by the state or military interests). In principle, the ban affected only state-owned forestland, but in practice, provincial and local authorities have extended it to cover all land regardless of ownership, exacerbating the sense of insecurity felt by collective and individual forest managers. While logging has been halted, the people of Naidu contrast what they perceive to be continuing destruction of non-timber resources in the state-owned forest—for the benefit of outsiders—with the careful system of rules and monitoring that the village has put in place to govern the use of the collective forest. Unhappiness at state management is aggravated by a lingering sense that all the forestland surrounding the village, regardless of its official designation, is really village forest taken over by the state within the lifetimes of many residents.

State Concessions and Village Rules

The ecology of *Tricholoma matsutake* is still poorly understood. It appears to grow best in mixed oak and pine forests. While many commercially valuable fungi regenerate from spores released when the fruiting body (the cap of the mushroom) opens, matsutake seems to regenerate from the mycelium, which stretches like a web between individual fungi below the surface of the forest floor. The mycelium is very sensitive to light and drying, so that it is important in harvesting not to disturb the duff (dried needles and leaves) on the forest floor (Hosford et al. 1997). A provincial multiagency body has developed harvesting guidelines that are widely publicized through a poster and education campaign supported by international conservation agencies such as the Worldwide Fund for Nature (WWF) and the Nature Conservancy (TNC) (China CITES Office 2002). The guidelines include suggestions for the minimum size of matsutake to be harvested, a prohibition on the use of pointed metal implements for digging up matsutake, and recommendations to carefully replace the duff layer after harvesting. The guidelines are simple—by design—but their enforcement is a challenge in the steep and remote terrain where the remaining forests are located and where the resource is available to anyone able to devote the time and the effort needed to search for matsutake.

The rapid extension during the late 1980s of the Japanese market for matsutake into the forests of northern Yunnan turned a formerly worthless fungus into a valuable commodity easily harvested by anyone physically able to walk into the forest during the season (June to August in the higher elevation areas around Zhongdian) to search in the dried pine needles and fallen oak leaves covering the ground.[5] The right to gather non-timber forest products (NTFPs) such as mushrooms from state and collective forests was transformed from a gesture acknowledging people's subsistence needs into a commercial opportunity.

As a listed, threatened species, matsutake must receive export permits issued after inspection by the TRAFFIC office for Yunnan, located in and staffed by the provincial department of forestry.[6] Regulations governing harvesting and local marketing, however, are left to the discretion of county and village authorities. By 1989 the county government had already implemented a concessionary system regulating matsutake collection in the state-owned forest—most, if not all of the permits being sold to harvesters from outside the village. At first, the county government sold the concessions themselves. In 2000 Jidi Administrative Village (now Jidi Village Committee) won the right to supervise concessions, although it is still perceived as allocating permits only to outsiders. The village committee now controls the sale of concessions and permits, but does not follow up with any systematic monitoring and supervision of harvesting practices in the concessions. Once again, the residents of Naidu feel that the government has wrested control away from them over a valuable potential source of income, fueling resentment among harvesters in the village, who believe that both the quality and the quantity of matsutake harvested from the state-owned forests are falling: "There is no supervision or monitoring in the state-owned forest. There are fewer mushrooms there every year and soon there won't be any left at all. Last year there were about 500 outsiders with concessions in the forest, now there are only 180" (author's field notes, August 2003).

The outcome of the altercation in 1985 between the village and the timber company had established the right of the village to control the use of its collective forest. The transformation of matsutake into a valuable commodity eventually forced Naidu village to take action in 1999 to translate their right to control forest use into rules and practices—a system of community-based forest management—to ensure the long-term viability of their new source of prosperity. For some ten years, however, villagers were content to allow free access to the forest. Two factors appear to have prompted the shift to controlled harvesting: violence in the forest between matsutake harvesters from different villages and the recognition that matsutake production in the forests was falling while market demand was shifting to place a premium on higher quality matsutake.

Disputes with neighboring villages over access to collective forestland erupted in fighting. In 1997, 1998, and 1999 the Public Security Bureau (police) of Zhongdian county sent a force—known in Naidu as "the mushroom patrol" (*Junzi bing*)—to keep order. The police arrested and jailed several intruders on Naidu forestland and made it clear that outsiders could harvest matsutake only with permits in the state-owned forest.

As this was happening, the county's Foreign Trade Corporation (a government entity that regulates foreign trade originating in the county) had been working with Japanese buyers to improve the quality of matsutake and to develop more effective and transparent marketing structures. In 1999, partly in response to the suggestions of these advisors and partly in response to the fighting between villages, Naidu and other hamlets in Jidi began to craft the rules governing the harvesting and marketing of matsutake that are now being implemented and that have helped, people believe, to ensure a regular harvest of high quality mushrooms at a time when most of the neighboring villages report decreasing harvests compounded by a dramatic drop in the market price for matsutake.[7]

Regulating Matsutake Harvesting in Naidu

Every natural village or hamlet (*she*) under Jidi Village Committee has its own set of rules for collecting matsutake on collectively owned forestland (*Sheyou Lin*). Jidi shares some twenty square kilometers of forest with a neighboring village committee—the outcome of an earlier administrative decision splitting what had formerly been one village into two. The residents of Naidu formulated their rules in open village meetings but have chosen not to write them down "because everyone knows them." Public awareness of the rules is reinforced by frequent meetings during the harvesting season, when offenders are disciplined and enforcement of the rules is discussed. In addition, the village holds one annual meeting shortly before the harvesting season begins to review and make adjustments to the regulations as needed. To maintain interest and active participation over the years, the village makes a celebration of the annual meeting, using income from fines and fees levied over the year to pay for the event: "We make a big occasion of the meeting so that people will come, and there are no other all-village meetings in the year. We sometimes invite the local song and dance troupe to come and give a performance which attracts people. Last year we combined the meeting with the local sports day" (author's field notes, August 2003).

There are open and closed seasons for matsutake collection—in contrast with common practice in other parts of Zhongdian, where harvest starts as soon as the matsutake begin to appear in the forest. In July, as the temperature and humidity begin to favor the growth of matsutake, two village leaders go into the forest together every day. When they find mushrooms that are big enough (greater than five centimeters) they declare that the season has started. The season officially ends on September 14 or 15, when the barley harvest starts, after which there are no restrictions on harvesting matsutake, but most people are busy with the barley harvest at this time and say that there are not many mushrooms to collect anyway (author's field notes, Naidu, August 2003). The open and closed seasons do not apply to other mushrooms, although on the days during the matsutake harvesting season when the hills are closed (see table 2.1, rule 1) no one is allowed into the hills for any reason other than to participate in the patrols monitoring compliance with the closed period (author's field notes, Naidu, August 2003).

The seven rules that govern matsutake harvesting in Jidi (table 2.1) control access to the forest by placing limits on the times of harvesting, restricting who may enter the forest to harvest matsutake, and specifying the tools and techniques that may be used for harvesting. Monitoring and enforcing the rules rely on formal administrative authorities within the village and on social norms and mechanisms backed by sanctions in the form of fines levied on offenders and on villagers who do not have a direct interest in the sustainability of the resource. While the regulations have no formal legal standing, leaders in each hamlet have taken care to embed their regulatory system within the organs of state power by assigning the village committee militia to patrol the forest every day during the harvesting season. The militia has

PLATE 2. A village inspector monitors matsutake harvesting in the village forest near Naidu.

PHOTO: AUTHOR

the power to take action against anyone offending against a broadly defined "public order," bringing them to the hamlet leaders who might choose to fine them or to impose some other punishment. Six of the seventeen hamlets in Jidi, including Naidu, employ a forest guard whose duties and title are modeled on the state-run forest management system—although they are elected by the hamlet, not appointed by the department of forestry.

TABLE 2.1 Naidu Village Harvesting Rules

1. The hills are open to collectors for ten days at a time, after which they are closed for five days. When the hills are closed, all men over the age of thirty in the village are expected to take part in patrols (without any payment) to guard the area from outsiders. Any man who does not go must pay RMB¥5 per day to the village community fund. Businessmen in the village must pay RMB¥50 per day.

   • "Generally everyone goes up [into the forest]. We divide into six groups, and the village head [*shezhang*] goes up with them, which gives them the authority to arrest people, to fine them, or to take whatever measures are necessary."

   • "Everyone in the village is expected to contribute up to twenty-five days every year for community activities [*yiwu laodong*]. Patrolling the mountains during the closed days is considered to be part of your annual contribution. These days of 'voluntary labor' are also used for activities such as maintaining irrigation ditches and so on."

2. On the days when the hills are open for matsutake harvesting, the harvesters must leave the village together, at 6:00 AM. They meet on the flat land at the entrance to the forest. At 6:30, the village head gives a signal, and everyone heads into the forest using whatever transport they have available.

   • "This is so that we can check on who is going. We can make sure that there are no children who are missing school and that there are no outsiders in the group. People in the village think that it is fairer for everyone to go at the same time. Any one family can send as many people as it likes. If anyone in a harvesting group sees an outsider in the hills that day, they report it in the evening when they get back, and a group made up of one person from each family goes to the outsider's village to demand a RMB¥300 fine. They go as a group for safety so that they do not get beaten up."

3. On days when the hills are closed for harvesting, all the women in the village must gather in one place at 8:30 AM. The head of the Women's Committee checks that no one has gone up to harvest. They have to meet again at 1:30 PM, and then at 10:30 PM all the men and the women must gather together to be sure that no one is going into the hills after dark.

   • "The women have to meet because they are busy down in the village on these days and the men are all in the hills on patrol" (see rule 1).

4. Mushroom harvesters must go in groups of at least three people and monitor each other. They must check that they do not disturb the soil and that they do not pick any mushrooms smaller than four centimeters in length. There are also six people, all village heads, who monitor sales in the market every evening. If someone is found to be picking or selling undersize mushrooms, then they are let off with a warning the first time, but if someone does it again, they will be banned from harvesting for a year.

5. People can use only sticks to dig for matsutake. They must not use metal tools or even bamboo sticks. The sticks must be made of the roots of birch trees.

   • "Our village experts [lao zhuan jia] have noticed that matsutake do not grow again when people use bamboo to dig them up. Bamboo seems to have some kind of poison that affects matsutake regeneration."

6. People are not allowed to use plastic bags. They must use moss (Shumao) to wrap up the mushrooms they harvest. This is so that they can be sure that there are no chemicals or pesticides that would affect the quality of the mushrooms. They must carry the mushrooms in a basket they carry on their backs. Those who disobey this rule will be fined RMB¥50.

   • "This is a new rule we introduced in 2002. It was added after the Japanese buyers claimed in October last year that one consignment of matsutake was contaminated with pesticides and the prices immediately dropped."

7. One section of the forest—about half the total area—is closed to all cutting (even for fuel and timber for house building) for ten years at a time to improve the habitat for matsutake.

These rules have been transcribed from my field notes (Naidu, August 2003). Comments following the rules are quotations from residents and matsutake collectors.

Marketing Rules

While each natural village or hamlet has devised its own set of regulations and practices governing matsutake harvesting, rules governing marketing are the outcome of negotiations between representatives of all the communities under the Jidi Village Committee and are jointly monitored and routinely discussed by representatives of all the communities. In order to facilitate monitoring compliance with rules governing the size and quality of harvested matsutake, they have chosen to restrict transactions to a central location, supervised by the heads of all the natural villages.[8] Matsutake may be sold only between 5:00 PM and 6:30 PM on "open days" during the harvesting season (see table 2.1, rule 2) in a market consisting of wooden sheds built around a small square at the side of the main road from Zhongdian running through Naidu. Other mushrooms may be traded outside and at other times. People arrive at the market as early as 4:00 PM and begin to negotiate prices with the stall holders—although no transactions may be made until the market officially opens. At five o clock, one of the supervisors (a village head, *shezhang*) blows a whistle, and selling begins. One and a half hours later the monitor blows the whistle again, and trading must end. The *shezhang* are expected to attend the market and may hold a meeting on the spot, at the end of the day's trading, if they have encountered any problems with public order or with enforcement of the rules.

Unlike the rules for harvesting, which have not been written down, the village committee has printed a sheet with rules for the market, which are prominently posted in each stall. Eight rules are listed, with fines and punishments specified for those who violate the rules. The eight rules address three areas of concern:

1. Maintaining order in the market: three rules (1, 7, 8) prohibit fighting, cheating, and occupying other traders' spaces.
2. Ensuring sustainable production and harvest of matsutake: several rules (2–5)—based on county regulations—specify the size and age at which matsutake may be harvested and regulate open and closed seasons.
3. Entry and participation in the market: two rules (3, 6) limit trading in matsutake to the market set up by the villages and emphasize that traders are there not by right but with permission granted by the village authorities—which may be revoked if they do not follow the rules.

Rule-Making and Implementation

Any institution managing a natural resource is faced with the challenge of how to develop a regulatory regime that is understood and accepted by all users, that is enforceable, and that has the flexibility to adapt to changes over time. Pending more detailed discussion below of ways in which communities around the world are facing this challenge, the story of Naidu tells of a community crafting and refining a process of rule-making and implementation with some important characteristics that bode well for the future.

The rules for harvesting mark out clear boundaries in time and space. They apply only to the village forest, with clear, public procedures for declaring the beginning and end of harvest season and for open and closed periods within the harvesting season. In a similar vein, matsutake may be sold in only one easily monitored location—the market under village supervision.

The process of making rules was participatory—everyone had an opportunity to be involved in working out the rules, and everyone is involved in the annual meeting to monitor and modify rules if necessary. To encourage a high level of attendance, the annual public meeting is associated with a festive event. Systems are in place for monitoring and enforcing the rules, and militia involvement reinforces local rules with a link to the more formal policing authorities of the state. The possibility of free-riding is limited through public and highly visible procedures such as the morning count of villagers before harvesters leave for the forest and through fines and fees levied on those who do not contribute time or labor.

Many of the same practices that build a sense of ownership among the residents of Naidu also play a role in generating an environment of transparency and accountability, which contributes to their willingness to be bound by the regulations: inclusive and public procedures, mutual supervision (no one may go alone into the mountains), accounts that are available to everyone for scrutiny, rules that are printed and posted in the market, and the nondiscretionary use of income from fines, which can be used only to pay the forest guard and to organize the annual community meeting and associated festivities.

International conservation organizations and government agencies in China and Yunnan Province have paid almost exclusive attention to formulating and publicizing guidelines for harvesting, which focus on size and harvesting techniques, but these are not the most important element of the regulatory system crafted by the residents of Naidu. Matsutake markets all over Zhongdian display posters issued by the Nature Conservancy that explain the importance of not disturbing the duff layer on the forest floor and of harvesting mushrooms only between certain size limits. In Shusong village, in another part of Zhongdian prefecture, a program to develop a sustainable matsutake harvesting regime funded by another international conservation agency active in Yunnan focused almost entirely on developing and enforcing rules based on harvesting techniques and the size of harvestable mushrooms. The pilot project left enforcement of the regulatory system in the hands of a management committee, composed only of official village leaders (party secretary and village heads), all of whom are men. There were no mechanisms to keep out or to sanction free-riders, and there was no provision for public access to accounts or any designated procedures for using revenue from fines and fees. A preliminary appraisal of the project made in early 2003 noted that "the impact of the regulations has yet to be seen."[9] In Jidi, by contrast, only three of the eight rules (rules 4–6) specifically address technical aspects of harvesting (size that may be harvested, tools and containers that may be used). Of these, the rule regulating harvestable size (rule 3) is in fact just one element of a rule that focuses on mutual supervision by requiring harvesters to enter the forest and work in groups. It would appear to be the case that where the community itself has crafted a regulatory system, it has paid more attention to monitoring and accountability than to technical rules.

Reflections on the Naidu Story

The residents of Naidu have had to make major adjustments to their land use and livelihoods over the last sixty years due to government decisions and actions over which they have had little or no control—except through occasional acts of local resistance, such as the protest against the logging company's incursion onto village-owned forest. They have had to watch as government agencies granted concessions to state-owned timber companies from outside the area whose destructive practices have left their mark on the forests surrounding the village. They have found themselves designated by the state as the agents of forest degradation and have had to adjust their land use practices to conform to restrictions on forest use imposed by the central government in the name of environmental protection. Under conditions of considerable political and economic uncertainty, they have taken action to protect and maintain control over the extraction and management of matsutake mushrooms, which have become an important source of revenue from the forest.

The communities of Naidu are in the process of putting in place a community-based regime of forest management that is embedded within county and provincial guidelines for harvesting of an NTFP. The regime is built on a set of carefully formulated rules governing the organization and monitoring of harvesting and marketing—although community control does not extend past the village market. Market forces have played an important role in motivating the community to forge a consensus on the need to control harvesting, and it is likely that the implementation of the management regime is facilitated by the overwhelming importance of one single product. It is also clear that the level of supervision and control over people's behavior is high and more intrusive than would be acceptable in communities that have not experienced the level of state and party control that has characterized the last fifty-five years in China.

Taking account of these elements that are specific to Naidu, the story does give credence to some theoretical propositions concerning essential components of effective governance over natural resource systems. Later chapters in this study will pursue the analysis of effective management regimes and institutions in greater detail. This review of the harvesting and marketing regime in Naidu and Jidi does, however, support the validity of Ostrom's proposition (1998:1) that an effective governance system must exert regulatory control over the following elements:

- who is allowed to appropriate products
- who is obligated to contribute resources to provide or maintain the resource
- how appropriation and obligation activities are to be monitored and enforced
- how conflicts over appropriation and obligation activities are to be resolved
- how the rules affecting the above will be changed over time with changes in the extent and composition of the forest and the strategies of participants

A final cautionary note is in order. The sudden emergence of the Japanese market for matsutake gave the people of Naidu the incentive to take action to regulate harvesting and marketing in the forest that they claim as theirs and that they had already struggled to protect from the depredations of the timber company. The unpredictability of the market could, however, mean that market dynamics might prove also to be a critical weakness in the system. The monopsonistic character of the Japanese market makes matsutake harvesting a precarious source of income. Prices have been dropping. Village leaders in Shusong believed that low prices are one of the main reasons for the lack of interest in developing and enforcing a regulatory system there. In Jidi, the introduction of the prohibition against using plastic bags was in response to a market problem—but as of August 2003 it was clearly not being enforced, for many people at the market brought their matsutake wrapped in plastic bags.

3

Jozani Forest, Ngezi Forest, and Misali Island, Zanzibar

It shall be the policy of the Government of Zanzibar to encourage the active involvement of local people in the sustainable planning, management and conservation of forest resources through community forestry programmes.

—POLICY GROUP ONE—COMMUNITY FORESTRY POLICIES

ONLY A few small patches of forest remain on the islands of Zanzibar off the coast of East Africa. This chapter tells the story of the communities that use three of these patches and their experiences since the government of Zanzibar committed itself to a policy of community forestry in 1995. Jozani and Ngezi are two forests surrounded by villages whose residents use them for fuelwood and charcoal burning, poles for construction, and fishing in the mangroves. Misali is an uninhabited forested island used as a fishing camp and believed by the Islamic communities of the nearby villages to be a sacred place.

Before 1995 the few remaining areas of Zanzibar's natural forest were legally designated as reserved forests under the control of the Department of Forestry in the Ministry of Agriculture, Livestock, and Natural Resources and Cooperatives. The department—which has since been renamed the Department of Commercial Crops, Fruits, and Forestry (DCCFF)—rigorously excluded residents of communities surrounding the forests. The new forest policy encouraging local involvement in management appeared in the context of an overall political environment that was emerging from twenty years of a rigid socialist regime under the Cold War patronage of the Soviet bloc, with a planned economy and little commitment to popular participation in resources management or, indeed, in any aspect of government.

By 2004 Jozani forest on Zanzibar's main island of Unguja had been gazetted as a national park under legislation granting the communities rights to participate in determining and demarcating the boundaries, to receive a percentage of the revenue from entrance fees to the park, and to use forest products from certain designated areas of the park. The communities surrounding Ngezi forest on the northern island of Pemba were engaged in negotiations and a planning process to establish new institutions for community-based management. Misali Island had been designated a conservation area under the management of a committee representing the fishing communities on Pemba that use the island—and the communities had offered the island as a "Sacred Gift for a Living Planet" under a global program coordinated by an alliance of international conservation and faith-based NGOs.[1]

The story of Zanzibar's efforts to realize the vision of the 1995 policy paper in these three places tells of many of the same challenges and questions that communities and their partners everywhere face as they move tentatively toward new patterns of utilization and decision-making in the forest. It points to the difficulties in orchestrating the discordant demands of resource utilization and conservation. It highlights the complexity and importance of defining who is the community, of anchoring new institutions and agreements in existing legal and political structures, and of offering real benefits to communities that are being asked to make a sacrifice in the name of conservation. Most importantly, though, it is a reminder that it takes time to break down suspicion and confrontation and to build the confidence and trust without which it is not possible to negotiate new partnerships.

Zanzibar: People, Politics, Forests, and Wildlife

Zanzibar is a semiautonomous entity within the United Republic of Tanzania, consisting of two main islands, Unguja and Pemba, and a number of smaller islands in an archipelago located about fifty kilometers off the coast of East Africa. Long a center for the Indian Ocean trade in slaves, spices, and ivory between India, the Arabian Peninsula, and the coast of East Africa, Zanzibar was the capital of the Sultanate of Oman during the early nineteenth century until it became a British protectorate in 1890. The islands achieved independence from Britain in December 1963. In January 1964 a violent revolution overthrew the sultan. The Afro-Shirazi Party that took power installed a revolutionary government, claiming legitimacy as the inheritors of the "indigenous" African slaves, in a racialized history identifying the sultanate with Arab domination and slavery. Shortly after the revolution, Zanzibar entered into a loose union with mainland Tanganyika in what is now known as the United Republic of Tanzania. For fifteen years, Zanzibar's revolutionary government sought to transform the islands into a socialist society in the image of the Eastern European countries of the former Soviet bloc—in contrast to the mainland, where China was a more direct source of inspiration for the Ujamaa model of African socialism championed by the late President Nyerere. During the late 1970s the regime became less reclusive and more closely integrated into the union with the merging of the two ruling parties in 1977, the adoption of market oriented reforms in 1982, and the reintroduction of multiparty politics in 1992.[2]

Zanzibar has been and remains marked by conflicting memories of the revolution and the islands' earlier history. The political environment remains more partisan and tense than on the mainland. The elections held since the advent of multiparty politics have revealed deep divisions between the two main islands, associated in the popular imagination with the regionally and historically opposed identities of "Arab" and "African." CCM (Chama cha Mapinduzi or Revolutionary Party), the ruling party on both Zanzibar (with its support on the island of Unguja) and the mainland, lays claim to the heritage of the revolt against the sultan, casting the opposition Civic United Front (CUF) with its support on Pemba as the heirs to the old order (Myers 2000). Elections in 1995 and 2000 were marked by violence—quelled in 2000 by the intervention of armed police from the mainland. The vote in both elections was evenly divided between the two parties, aggravating the significance of charges of fraud and prompting CUF to boycott the House of Representatives in protest of CCM's claim of victory. The contested outcomes of the elections led to the suspension of most bilateral international aid to the islands in 1996. International mediation has succeeded in preventing further violence, but the political crisis and the cultural narratives with which it is associated continue to simmer and frame conflicts and divisions at all levels of Zanzibari life.

Against this backdrop of a deeply rooted political rift, there have at the same time been profound changes in Zanzibar, as in Tanzania as a whole. Partly in response to international pressures for economic reform and democratization and partly as a result of stagnation and a failing infrastructure, the country has engaged in wide-ranging economic liberalization, an openness to international exchanges, and a rapid increase in the importance of tourism. In Zanzibar, tourism had become the islands' major source of foreign revenue by the late 1990s, but had itself become a subject of contestation. Accusations of land-grabbing and money-laundering for the construction of resorts swirled around the highest levels of government. Ordinary Zanzibaris worried that large numbers of European visitors showed little sensitivity in their dress and behavior to the Islamic values that permeate all aspects of life in the islands. With most hotel and resort development taking place on the east coast of Unguja, tourism, too, has become a part of the contested politics of Zanzibar.[3]

Traditionally, Zanzibar's economy depended on its position as an entrepôt for trade and on the production of cloves and other spices. The original vegetation has long been cleared for agriculture, with large areas of Unguja covered by an anthropogenic agroforest of fruit trees and palms with spice gardens in the understory.[4] The structure and composition of these agroforests closely resemble the better-studied home gardens and agroforests of Java and Sumatra in Indonesia, reflecting, perhaps, the history of trade and cultural exchange along the monsoon trade routes to Asia. On Pemba, by contrast, the landscape consists of groves and plantations of clove trees interspersed in the flatter areas with fields of maize and rice. On both islands, the indigenous vegetation has been reduced to a few patches of forest and stretches of mangrove along the coast, all of which have been modified by human use for centuries.

The physical extent of Zanzibar's forests is small, intensifying their importance for different reasons to local people, to international conservation interests, and to the Zanzibar government. Local people resent losing the access to building materials and fuelwood that they enjoyed before the colonial government reserved the forests in the 1960s. International efforts to conserve biodiversity have classified Zanzibar as a "biodiversity hotspot" associated with the Eastern Arc and Coastal Forest Centre of Endemism in East Africa (Conservation International 2003), spurring government plans to generate foreign exchange through a rapid expansion of tourism and the creation of national parks to diversify the islands' attractions.

The three areas of forested land discussed here are all classified as coral rag forest, important to international conservation interests as the habitat of threatened and endangered species, such as the Zanzibar red colobus (*Procolobus kirkii*), Ader's duiker (*Cephalophus adersi*), the Pemba flying fox (*Pteropus voeltzkowi*), two species of sea turtle, and several endemic birds. A privately owned sawmill had used Jozani forest since the 1930s as a source of timber, and the colonial authorities had replanted land on the edges of the forest to mahogany, some of which still stands. In the 1960s the Department of Forestry closed the sawmill; then in the 1970s it licensed pit sawyers in the forest, only to rescind the licenses some ten years later (Asseid Bakari, personal communication). At Jozani and Ngezi, government management of the forest reserves excluded local people, criminalizing practices that had been a part of daily life and exacting fines or other sanctions on those it now called offenders. In the 1980s the objectives of forest management shifted to conservation and the protection of endangered fauna. The most visible and charismatic species was the red colobus, found in and around Jozani forest. The red colobus is not, in fact, confined to the forest, with some populations roaming across the boundary into surrounding farmland and some permanently resident in the forest gardens that are such an important component of the landscape. It is not surprising that for farmers the red colobus became emblematic of government control over access to the forest, and tension grew in the form of complaints over crop raiding.[5] Tensions increased further during the 1990s when the Department of Forestry began to charge visitors a fee to enter Jozani forest—the red colobus having quickly become a major attraction for tourists from the new beach resorts not far from Jozani. With the forest now a visible source of income, the Department of Forestry faced demands for some form of revenue sharing as well as growing demands for compensation for damage to crops by the growing population of red colobus.

On the island of Pemba, Ngezi forest had been the site of perfunctory measures to reserve and protect the forest since the colonial period. A forestry program under a Finnish aid program in the 1980s had demarcated the boundaries and set up barriers to control traffic in and out of the forest. While the forest is rich in wildlife and endemic species, there are no animals such as the Jozani colobus that would be the cause of conflicts between surrounding villages and the Department of Forestry, and with the development of tourism centered on Unguja, not Pemba, Ngezi was not a priority for implementation of the new community forestry policy. Moves toward community-based management of Ngezi forest began only in late 1999 and were quickly interrupted by the violence surrounding the elections of 2000, picking up momentum again in 2002.

Misali Island had never been declared reserved forest, but public apprehension over the impacts of the growth of tourism acted as a catalyst for community action there at almost the same time as it did at Jozani. An Italian investor had received government approval in 1993 to turn the island into a resort, leading to strong protests from the fishing groups using the island, who were aware that a similar development on Mnemba Island off the north coast of Unguja had led to the exclusion of fishers, who were no longer allowed even to shelter on the island during storms.[6] On Misali, the island's cultural significance accentuated the fishers' fear of exclusion from the island they used as an overnight camp. According to legend, a visiting Islamic religious leader had no prayer mat on which to pray on the island. He told the fishers that since the island is shaped like a prayer mat and points to Mecca, it was itself a prayer mat (*Methali ya msala*), hence the name Misali, a Kiswahili rendering of Methali (Anon. 2002a). At a time of public disquiet about the impacts of tourism and associated corruption over land deals, the president of Zanzibar responded to the protests of the Misali fishing community, rescinding the proposal for tourism development and stating that the island would remain government property, managed by the community (Ali et al. 2000:2).

Three Forests and Their Communities

During the early 1990s the Finnish and Dutch governments provided funding to the Zanzibar Commission for Lands and Environment for the preparation of an integrated land and environment project, which recommended more emphasis on conservation but stopped at calls for "awareness raising" on the issue (Bensted-Smith 1990). A two-year project on integrated coastal management (ICM) implemented under the auspices of the United Nations Environmental Program (UNEP) Regional Seas Program had worked with village committees, showing the potential for participatory approaches to planning, although the short time frame and subsequent withdrawal of bilateral assistance following the disputed 1995 elections limited its impact.[7] In the light of the commitment to CBFM in the proposed National Forest Policy of 1995 and public concerns about the social impacts of tourism, the Department of Forestry accepted a proposal from an international NGO, CARE International, to assist in developing an experimental project for a community-based approach to the management of Jozani forest centered on developing ecotourism. The Department of Forestry and CARE International reached agreement on the project in 1995, initiating what has come to be known as the Jozani–Chwaka Bay Conservation Project (JCBCP), initially in collaboration with seven *shehias*, with one more *shehia* joining the project a little later.[8]

JCBCP has been described as an "Integrated Conservation and Development Project (ICDP) aiming at conserving Zanzibar's biological diversity . . . and the surrounding environment while improving the living conditions of the people surrounding the protected area" (Masoud 2003). The project in fact covers an area larger than the zone immediately surrounding Jozani forest, with the inclusion of a number of villages surrounding nearby Chwaka Bay, where there is little tourist revenue, where the main resources are fisheries and mangrove forest, and where the communities have been less ready to embrace the proposition that conservation represents a viable pathway to improved livelihoods.

On Misali Island, in the aftermath of the decision not to lease the island for development, the fishing groups from some thirty-six villages using the island and an international consultant working on the proposed land and environment project petitioned the government in 1995 to permit the creation of a Nature Conservation Trust through which the users would manage the island and its fisheries. The government rejected the request, at the same time as the European Union withdrew expected financial support for the proposed trust as part of the suspension of bilateral development aid after the 1995 election. With minimal financial support from private donors, CARE International responded to a request from the nascent Misali Island Conservation Project to assist in the formation of a community-based conservation area. The Misali Island Marine Conservation Area was established on 22 May 1998 under both forestry and fisheries legislation, and the Misali Island Conservation Association (MICA) was registered as an NGO on 15 December 1998 with a mandate "to safeguard the interests of the fishing communities around Pemba Island in response to increased development and tourism experienced in Zanzibar in the 1990s" (Anon. 2002a).

At both Jozani and Misali (and later, after 2000, at Ngezi) the programs followed similar steps. Each village formed a village conservation committee within the existing village administration. The village conservation committee was initially the designated interlocutor for both the Department of Forestry (later DCCFF) and staff from CARE International. Drawing on considerable experience in community development, CARE International staff suggested that committees within local government were not the most appropriate institutional instrument to undertake activities such as training for forest guides and rangers, advocacy on behalf of communities, and managing a proposed community credit facility that was expected to be the mechanism to mobilize the communities' share of income from the forest to build community assets for longer-term development activities. They recommended establishing independent associations in each place to represent the interests of their respective communities and assisted in establishing the Jozani Environmental Conservation Association (JECA) and the Misali Island Conservation Association (MICA), which have now taken on that role.[9]

Under Zanzibar's Forest Resources Management and Conservation Act No. 10 of 1996,[10] village conservation committees are the official signatories with the director of forestry in DCCFF to a community forest management agreement setting out the rules, management goals, and commitments to which the village has agreed. The process began slowly. The first community reached an understanding with DCCFF in 1997 on the terms of the agreement to which the forest administrator, the local representative of the Department of Agriculture, the village representative of JECA, two members of the village conservation committee, and the district commissioner were all signatories. It was only in 2000 that the agreement received government approval after wending its way for several years through different levels of government, caught in the restructuring of ministries associated with the process of reform and complicated by questions about which government department would be responsible for future national parks as well as the unprecedented nature of the proposed partnerships with communities. In the aftermath of the civil unrest surrounding the disputed election of 2000, the agreement then languished in the attorney general's office for more than a year, waiting for confirmation by the attorney general himself as a witness to the agreement and its publication in the official gazette. Only after publication in the gazette could the agreement come into force. The process then began to move more rapidly, and seven more agreements had been approved within two years. Despite the slow pace, there was general agreement that the procedure had been a necessary step since it gave the agreements legal standing, with the force of a title deed legitimizing village management of the forest resources. With a community forest management agreement in place, the village conservation committees are then responsible for integrating it into local administrative regulations, often in the form of village bylaws that the Tanzanian constitution recognizes as legitimate legal instruments (Alden Wily 1997a).

JECA and MICA, by contrast, operate more as local, development-oriented NGOs with responsibilities for many activities, ranging from training village accountants to managing credit schemes to running the visitor centers at Jozani and Misali. With the inevitable end of the donor-funded projects at both places, JECA and MICA are the institutions that will, it is hoped, continue to play the role of independent mediator that CARE International has played until now. In principle, the village conservation committees and the two associations have different roles and functions, but even people actively involved in one or the other of these institutions are not always able to distinguish between them—in part because there is a lot of overlap between members of the village conservation committees and the JECA or MICA committees. Key leaders appear to be playing the role of intermediary with the many outside agencies initiating and supporting development activities in the communities. At Jozani, the same man was introduced on different occasions as a member of the village conservation committee, of JECA, of a community-based primary education project supported by the Aga Khan Foundation, and of a microenterprise scheme sponsored by Zanzibar's First Lady. Members of the different committees were confident that they would in due course find and take on distinct roles to make community involvement in managing the forest function effectively. In the words of one JECA member: "It should be like organizing a funeral or a wedding where there are committees which take on different jobs, but it all comes together at the end" (author's field notes, Jozani, November 2002).

Committees, Associations, Agreements, and Communities

Nobody involved in Zanzibar's efforts to bring communities into resources management denies that the roles and responsibilities of the different players are still being determined and have yet to be internalized either by the government agencies involved or by the communities as embodying both positive and negative elements of what is happening. On the positive side of the ledger, committee members point out that the community forest management agreements are, for the first time, the outcome of negotiations over the management of natural resources rather than unilateral action on the part of the government. A member of the village conservation committee in one of the villages near Ngezi forest explained that their past experience had been of restrictions on their use of the forest, at the same time as the government expropriated land on the fringes of the forest for experiments such as rubber plantations, which either failed to produce or were not competitive in national and international markets. Negotiations leading to a community forest management agreement were not yet over, but his village had already been able to regain access to the forest for building poles (with the condition that permission would be granted only for reconstruction after a fire or other disaster), fuelwood, fruit, and medicines (author's field notes, Ngezi, December 2002).

Community forest management agreements also seem to be offering some assurance to communities that they may, in the future, exercise some control over who is allowed to benefit from their resources, in contrast to the preceding decades of state-imposed planning. In several villages, people said that they had watched outsiders damaging the forests but they had not kept them out since they would not benefit in any way from taking action to protect the forest. In one village on Unguja that has signed a community forest management agreement with DCCFF, the committee has received authorization from the district commissioner (representing the government) to issue permits for fuelwood cutting. Village residents may take fuelwood for their own use, but the village conservation committee negotiates sales to outsiders. In a "double control" system of monitoring, products transported out of the forest area must receive a transportation permit from DCCFF—which is issued only if the transporter has a letter from the village conservation committee confirming that the community has authorized the sale.[11] Shortly after the system came into force, the village conservation committee had negotiated a sale of poles with the army. The army would be allowed to harvest poles under the supervision of the committee, which planned to use the income for activities such as maintaining the primary school (author's field notes, Jozani, December 2002).

Community forest management agreements have given communities the power to control more closely who uses the resources and how. At another level, alignment with DCCFF's new mandate for community forest management has reconfigured the relations between villages and the many other actors advancing their sectoral interests in Zanzibar's process of reform and economic restructuring.

At Ngezi, even before any formal community forest management agreements had been signed, one village made effective use of its nascent partnership with DCCFF to fend off what it perceived to be a threat from the tourist industry and its backers in other branches of government. While the possibility of some form of tourist access had been a part of the discussions between the village and DCCFF, villagers heard during 2001 that the Department of Tourism was negotiating a contract with an international company for a major development on the nearby beach, which the village uses for fishing and for soaking coconut fiber to soften and make into rope. Alarmed at the possibility of losing access to the beach and also at negative reports of the impacts of tourism developments on the east coast of Unguja, villagers appealed to DCCFF for support in asserting their ownership of the beach. Since the beach was part of the area scheduled to come under the Ngezi Forest Community Forestry Initiative, DCCFF staff took the issue to the highest level of government, arranging for the vice president to visit the village and hear from members of the community and DCCFF staff. The unprecedented coalition of villagers and forestry staff succeeded in terminating negotiations for the tourist development. There is still disagreement between different factions in the village, DCCFF, and the *shehia* authorities as to whether there should be any tourist development in the area at all and, if so, how and where it should take place, but all those involved believe that collaboration with DCCFF succeeded in moving the decision from a ministry on Unguja back to Pemba and into the village arena.

Community forest management agreements represent an improvement on past practice where government agencies made decisions about the exploitation of forest resources without any consultation with local people. In their present form, however, they are unlikely to be a sufficient instrument to resolve the long-standing tensions and conflicts over natural resources. Agreements are legally binding written documents—but villagers point out that the documents are in English rather than in Kiswahili. Since few people in the villages speak English, few are aware of just what is in the agreements. Representatives of JECA also worry that the agreements list the responsibilities assigned to villages in ways that are subject to dispute: "The agreement says that we must patrol the forest but it does not say what that means. When the committee says we have patrolled the forest, DCCFF says that we have not. It is not clear what 'patrolling' means in the agreement" (author's field notes, Jozani, November 2002). While some disputes should be resolved through the process of dialogue that is now in place, some potentially divisive issues such as sources of funding for management activities are not addressed in the agreements and may well strain relations between DCCFF and the communities in the future.

The name *community forest management agreement* begs the question of who is the community? The answer to this question is of immediate practical relevance since it determines who is bound by the agreement and who benefits from it. The legal notices published by the government spell out in administrative terms who are the parties to the agreement. Formally, the agreement is between the community management group of any *shehia* and the DCCFF director. The agreement specifies that the community management group refers to the village conservation committee and lists the names of serving members as signatories, noting that the secretary of the committee is responsible for informing the *shehia* and DCCFF of any changes in membership. In administrative terms, therefore, it is clear who is and who is not a member of the community.[12]

A legal, administrative definition of community is not, of course, sufficient to resolve contending claims to resources. Many villagers see the management agreement as a means to enforce their claims—a way to keep others out of the forest or the fishery. They therefore consider that the agreements should solidify the rights of those they consider to be legitimate users and that the regulations governing utilization should not prevent them from deriving a livelihood from the resource. A frequent complaint is that negotiations leading to the agreement did not include the real users of the resource. The elected members of the village conservation committees do not include livestock grazers, charcoal burners, and woodcutters, on the grounds that DCCFF considers them traditionally to have been "destroyers" of the forest.

Excluding the users most directly involved in resource extraction has not only led to tensions but has also led to regulations that users believe are inappropriate or unenforceable. Some of the community forest management agreements around Jozani forest, for example, follow DCCFF practice in specifying that only dead and downed wood may be gathered for fuelwood—a rule that villagers point out is counterproductive since it acts only as an incentive to kill trees by "accidentally" damaging them or ring-barking them (author's field notes, Jozani, November 2002).[13] At Misali, fishers interviewed on the island claimed that members of the village conservation committees were not fishers themselves and had mistakenly agreed to a conservation plan that included the demarcation of a core protection zone of 1.4 square kilometers with unnecessarily stringent restrictions on use and that the fishers believed was in the wrong location to conserve breeding stocks of fish and octopus anyway (author's field notes, Misali Island, December 2002). Different interests converge on the resource, but not all interests within the community have been represented in the processes of making rules. The exclusion of the main consumptive users from the process will at the very least weaken voluntary compliance with the regulatory regime and could herald further conflicts in the future if their concerns are not addressed.

Achievements

It has been less than ten years since the Zanzibar Commission for Natural Resources announced its intention to move from exclusionary management strategies to community-based resource management. Unlike the self-initiated actions at Naidu, government has been one of the main actors in all three places in Zanzibar, initiating the programs at Jozani and Ngezi and backing the communities' demands at Misali.

There is evidence that populations of protected species have increased since the launch of the Jozani and Misali projects. Zanzibar red colobus remains on the list of endangered species, but ongoing studies suggest that the population decline has been halted; while the Ader's duiker also continues to be endangered, there appears to be a reduction in hunting pressure in and around the Jozani–Chwaka Bay area (Kombo 2000). On Misali, there were forty turtle nesting sites in 2002 when only nine had been reported in 1998. At both locations, international conservation organizations continue to monitor and to conduct surveys of wildlife and fisheries in collaboration with JECA and MICA.

As Zanzibar began to emerge from its revolutionary isolation, it counted on growth in the tourist sector as an important source of foreign exchange and investment. Unlike its neighbors on the African mainland, Zanzibar had no designated conservation areas and national parks to attract or to retain visitors. Visitors came to enjoy beaches and diving off the coast and to soak up the atmosphere of Stone Town, the old quarter of the capital city. Conservation scientists, considering the value of Jozani's ecosystems to be of national and global significance, have had little compunction in arguing for a conventional, coercive approach to conservation, questioning why local interests should hinder the interests of "the majority" in designating the area as a national park—although the protracted negotiations within government cast doubt on whether proponents of the park were in fact in the majority:

> Finally, in making decisions about land-use management and resolving human-wildlife conflicts from a national perspective, compromises must be made between different interest groups and different levels of society. In most democratic states, national interests usually prevail, at least in principle, reasoning that the interests of the majority should rule.
>
> —SIEX AND STRUHSAKER 1999:1018

By contrast, a visiting researcher in the social sciences reported that "in Chwaka, the idea of JCBCA [Jozani–Chwaka Bay Conservation Area] as a potential national park isn't even taken seriously" (Myers 2002:153). During my visits to communities in Jozani and Chwaka Bay over a period of five years from 1997 to 2002, the issue was taken very seriously and was being hotly debated by local people, NGO staff, and DCCFF—with the most important point of contention being the way in which park revenues would be shared between communities, government agencies, and other interests. An early agreement on revenue sharing stalled in the House of Representatives for several years, during which time communities received a portion of the tourist receipts according to an informal formula agreed on with the assistance of CARE International. It is not possible to isolate a program such as JCBCA from the political divisions and tensions in which any community action is embedded, and the failure to approve the revenue-sharing agreement was undoubtedly related to the conflict between the ruling party and the opposition following the 1995 election. It was only in 2002 that an allocation of income was finally approved as a first step in securing community acceptance of the proposed national park: the community receives 38 percent of income for development activities through JECA; 27 percent is allocated to park management (a part of which is also channeled through the community); DCCFF receives 24 percent; and the treasury receives 11 percent.[14]

On 27 February 2004 Zanzibar gazetted its first national park, at Jozani. Negotiations concerning the boundaries of the park, compensation to farmers, permitted activities within the park, and the revenue-sharing scheme came to a conclusion. A new Protected Areas System Board had been established to manage the islands' protected areas; the minister had issued a formal statement of intent and had held a public enquiry before final approval of the plans. As a result of the public enquiry, there had been a delay in gazetting the park in response to the demand from one village that their Member of Parliament should witness the demarcation of the park boundary to ensure that it did not incorporate any village land. The process had taken six years since negotiations began in 1997 in the context of the JCBCA.

The global history of demarcation of national parks and protected areas is marked by expropriation of land and exclusion of traditional users of the resources (Carruthers 1997; Doornbos, Saith, and White 2000; Spence 1999). Zanzibar's own history of authoritarian government, political confrontation, and heavy-handed regulation of resource use was not conducive to a participatory and community-based approach to conservation. Under these circumstances, the Jozani communities can point to some successes in defending their claims to be partners in the creation and management of the park rather than recipients of compensation determined by distant national or international agencies. Communities will receive a significant portion of park revenue. Communities have been involved in determining the park's boundaries and in modifying the zoning system of land and resource use within the park. In one seventeen-hectare area on the edge of the park, communities rejected an offer of one-time financial compensation for land, insisting instead that they should continue to use the land for what they considered to be environmentally sound activities such as gathering firewood. This land is now gazetted as a "special forest management area" within the park, to be managed under forestry legislation (which permits community management). It is inevitable that the park will not enjoy unanimous support among the surrounding communities, but this does not negate the importance of the unprecedented level of dialogue and negotiation that preceded its creation.

State management of forests has tended to entrench poverty in surrounding communities by restricting access or excluding users (Becker 2001; Peluso 1992; Ribot 2001; Westoby 1987). Community-based resource management has been promoted as a strategy that can foster economic development by restoring or securing access to resources without compromising environmental values. In practice, it is often the case that programs provide funding to diversify local economies away from resource extraction and use, and it could be argued that any observed improvements in livelihoods and security are less an outcome of CBFM than what is, in effect, targeted development assistance. Villages surrounding Jozani now earn some income from the controlled sale of fuelwood and poles harvested from the forest, as described above. Tourist revenue is now flowing to JECA and, to a lesser extent, to MICA on Misali (where boats bringing tourists to dive off the island are charged a daily fee of $20 for the boat and $5 for each visitor) for reinvestment in a wide range of activities, including vegetable production, beekeeping, and handicrafts. It is not yet clear, though, how viable these activities would be without the financial assistance that the villages received to start them up and without continued support from CARE International in marketing them.

Integrated conservation and development programs commonly encounter two issues that can be addressed through village savings and credit schemes. Men tend to dominate in negotiations with the authorities about resource management. This is especially problematic on Misali, where fishing from boats is traditionally a male activity, while women usually harvest shellfish and other species from beaches and reefs near the villages on the mainland of Pemba. Women, however, are very active in trading and in running the small enterprises that are often most able to take advantage of the small loans offered in savings and credit schemes. A second issue is the possibility of tensions between those who are involved in a community management program and those who are not. Again, this is particularly significant in the case of Misali, where there is no resident community on the island and where users of the resource are the fishers from thirty-six villages on Pemba, who may represent only a small percentage of the inhabitants of each village. A successful village credit and savings facility is strengthened by expanding its client base, making it an effective instrument for extending some of the benefits of the conservation program to the wider rural population.

As early as 1996 people in Jozani said that they wanted easier access to credit to start their own small businesses. Building on experience in other countries, CARE International assisted JECA and then MICA to launch village credit schemes modeled on a shareholding and group lending methodology (sometimes also referred to as a village bank) that has proved to be successful in West Africa (Painter 2000; Fruman 1998). By mid-2003 forty-six savings and credit groups were associated with JECA on Unguja, and nine groups were associated with MICA on Pemba. Women outnumber men in the groups, which thus act as a mechanism to redistribute at least some of the benefits from men to women. The village savings and credit schemes are open to all residents in the village, and on Unguja JECA has assisted in organizing and supporting a number of credit groups in villages beyond the immediate boundaries of the forest. The groups are reporting good rates of repayment on loans and are hoping to receive some of the income from tourism in the future as an infusion of capital in order to be able to expand and to offer more substantial loans. While the intent is to diversify local economies and to link conservation with local development, it is not clear, however, that participants consciously associate the program with conservation or whether they consider that their gains from the scheme outweigh what they have given up in the interests of conservation.

A final, though difficult to measure, achievement of community-based resource management at Jozani, Misali, and Ngezi has been the evidence that members of the communities involved in the programs have begun to feel that they have some control over their future. A decade ago, it would have been hard to imagine that a community would have been in a position to negotiate a contract with the army for the sale of poles from a reserved forest. While funds for community activities are still limited and dependent on the volatile tourist sector, the villages involved in the Jozani–Chwaka Bay program and the Misali Island program have been able to set their own priorities and invest in community assets, such as schools, mosques, or housing for a village doctor. Even before any community forest management agreements have been signed at Ngezi, at least one village has been able to ensure that it, not the tourist department, will decide on the future direction of tourist development. The word *empowerment* is much abused in the discourse of development, but there is evidence in Zanzibar that community-based resource management

PLATE 3. A Pemba Island village bank associated with the Misali Island Conservation Association.   PHOTO: AUTHOR

can contribute to more accountable governance and a shift of some powers from government to citizens.

Present and Future Challenges

Community-based resources management has reconfigured the relations between the different actors and interests centered on forests and fisheries. The new dispensation is, however, still subject to the larger political and economic forces shaping Zanzibar, and it cannot be expected to eliminate all conflicts and generate a new economic landscape on its own. Some old and deeply rooted problems continue to confront the communities, other latent tensions have come to the surface, while new challenges now face community managers as they take on tasks that had formerly been the domain of experts, technicians, and government staff.

As noted above, deciding who is the community remains a fundamental issue. Administrative decisions may determine the boundaries of which villages participate in a program and which do not, but management of a resource involves many layers of decision-making, different levels of participation, and equitable distribution of responsibilities, benefits, and compensation within a community. The JCBCP began in seven *shehias* and quickly incorporated an eighth, whose residents claimed that they had an equal interest in access to the forest—and in receiving compensation for crop-raiding by the red colobus monkeys. At the same time, many villages in all three locations saw participation in the programs as a way to exclude users from other communities from the forests or the fisheries. Ironically, community participation for some has meant exclusion for others, a conundrum for which there is unlikely ever to be a completely satisfactory solution since the very act of defining a community of user-managers also creates another group whose access to the resource they will control (Peluso and Ribot 2003). Considerations of equity demand that a balance be found between the interests of those most directly dependent on the resource and those who may have other though still legitimate claims on the resource. This is, and will continue to be, a critical issue in community-based resources management and is the subject of a later chapter in this book.

Jozani forest is one of Zanzibar's leading tourist attractions and generates sufficient revenue for all the parties to see value in the partnership. Misali Island receives some visitors, but there have been disputes with boat owners, particularly those arriving from Kenya's coastal resorts, who have refused to pay the fee to anchor off the island and to dive in the reef area. In 2002 tourist income at Misali came to a total of just fifteen million Tanzanian shillings (equivalent at the time to $15,000) (author's field notes, Misali Island, December 2002). At Ngezi, there is as yet no source of income directly associated with the planned community forest management agreements, although most of those involved are hoping for an increase in visitors to Pemba, with Ngezi forest becoming an attraction to rival Jozani forest on Unguja. In all three places, people are acutely conscious that even where there is a real possibility of attracting tourism, the sector itself is precarious and that visitors will travel to alternative destinations at times of political instability or following acts of violence over which local people have no control—as happened in nearby Kenya following terrorist bomb attacks in 1998 and 2002.

Activities to diversify local economies therefore are important as an element of community resource management programs offering a more stable, if slower, pathway to improving people's lives. All those involved welcome the opportunities offered by the Jozani and Misali credit and savings schemes. Many participants do admit, however, that their expectations of new sources of income have yet to be fulfilled. The schemes are limited to small loans partly by design and partly because of constraints on the amount of capital available from donors and from income due to JECA and MICA from resource management. On Pemba in particular, where the island's economy is less vibrant than on Unguja, there are fewer openings for new small businesses and almost no institutions that could help in identifying alternative opportunities and marketing strategies. In both credit and savings schemes, a few entrepreneurial borrowers have invested in vegetable or mushroom production for nearby hotels and tourist lodges, but most businesses are in the service sector involving food and snack stalls, small retail trade at roadside kiosks, and transporting commodities such as cloves or potatoes. In fact, many members of the groups say that they are more interested in the savings services the group provides as a way to provide for "lumpy" and irregular expenses such as school fees and uniforms (author's field notes, Jozani and Misali, November and December 2002). Alternative income-generation programs and credit and savings schemes can complement community resource management activities, but it is important to be realistic about the degree to which new business and commercial activities can replace resource extraction in places that are often at the peripheries of regional and national economies.

Finally, managing and monitoring a resource makes demands on all those involved. From the technical skills deployed in deciding when and where to harvest what quantities of building poles, thatching grass, or octopus, to the organizational skills needed to mediate between different interest groups, to the financial and accounting skills needed to manage a credit and savings scheme, communities and their partners need support to build their capacity to manage. "Capacity-building" has entered the vocabulary of development, but it is rarely broken into its component parts to give guidance in deciding just what capacities are called for in managing a community forest.

I will consider the skills and capacities important to community management of forest resources in a later chapter, but the Zanzibar story already gives some content to the concept. At the level of national policy, no community has the capacity to manage and monitor use of a resource without legal authority to sanction offenders. Members of JECA felt that they needed training in administration in order for the organization to undertake the different tasks they had been assigned. Members of village conservation committees felt the lack of technical training in their negotiations over community forest-conservation agreements. In Zanzibar, CARE International took on the task of capacity-building. It remains to be seen whether JECA, CARE International's successor NGO, will have the resources and comparable ability to draw on international expertise for support when community management at Jozani forest and Chwaka Bay makes the transition at the end of 2003 from being a project to being the normal mode of partnership between government and forest-dependent communities (Hartley and Rijali 2003). CARE International staff work full time on this assignment. JECA's members are villagers who take time from their daily activities to make community management of the forest a reality. One member of JECA explained that the communities' acceptance of the partnership with DCCFF is contingent on their perception of the benefits they will gain from participation:

> It is maybe asking too much of people. Different projects come along every day. There is Jozani and there are others. WWF also has a project. No wonder people end up asking for payments to attend meetings. People will choose with their feet and end up only going to some of the meetings.
>
> —AUTHOR'S FIELD NOTES, JOZANI, NOVEMBER 2002

In Conclusion: Timing Is of the Essence

Asseid Bakari, director of DCCFF, considers that implementation of community forest management in Zanzibar has benefited from a convergence of interests at three different levels: internationally, declarations issued at recent summit conferences on environment and development have supported community participation in conservation and resource management; nationally, Zanzibar's new forest policy of 1995 explicitly called for community management of forests; and locally, a tradition of stewardship and cultural practices favor conservation. With the government committed to political and economic reform and with support from the international community, the time was right to engage with communities and NGOs in search of an alternative to the confrontation that had defined forest management in the past (Asseid Bakari, personal communication).

If community-based resource management is to make the transition from an experimental project to normal practice, its institutions and regulatory frameworks must have legitimacy in law and with the people who implement it. In Zanzibar, the community forest management agreements are legal documents with the force of a title deed under the Forest Resource Management and Conservation Act. Village conservation committees, constituted as organs of local government, have incorporated forest and fisheries management regulations into local bylaws. It has proved to be a time-consuming process, but it is likely that the time spent to embed community management in the existing system of governance will give it a security that some other community-based experiments do not enjoy—as will be seen in the story of forest management cooperatives in the Kangra valley of India's Himachal Pradesh State (chapter 5).

It has taken more than eight years to piece together a new management regime for Jozani forest and for Misali Island, and work has just begun at Ngezi.

Members of the communities will have to devote time to implementing and monitoring the management agreements, and they have had to agree to some restrictions on their uses of the forests and fisheries in order to gain security of access to the resources. Compliance with the agreements will depend on whether people in the communities consider that they are gaining more than they have sacrificed. Long drawn-out bargaining over the allocation of benefits from entry fees paid by tourists has given the community more than many such arrangements have done in other countries, but the instability of the tourist sector will make the associated savings and credit programs an important complement to revenue derived directly from the forests and fisheries. Without appreciable income from the resource, it is questionable whether the community would see any value in investing in its management, but without added support to stimulate local economic activity, it is also questionable whether community management alone would bring significant improvements in people's lives.

It would be premature to point to three small patches of forest off the coast of East Africa as a conclusive demonstration of the effectiveness and the sustainability of community-based forest management. Participants in Zanzibar's experiment in community-based resource management are testing the ground and stepping carefully forward to bring the elusive goal of conservation-based development a little closer to realization. The new joint-management institutions have yet to be subjected to the tests of a change in leadership and shifting economic and political priorities and time. The measured pace and intense negotiations at all levels that led to the genesis and implementation of community management in Zanzibar give cause for optimism that this form of partnership has the potential to take root and to benefit both local people and conservation.

4

The Várzea Forests of Mazagão, Amapá State, Brazil

People who don't know caboclos think they are lazy. But caboclos diversify
because that way you don't have to work so hard. You put the right thing in the
right place so you always have what you need and you have time to sleep.

—TEACHER AT AN AGRICULTURAL FAMILY SCHOOL,
NEAR MAZAGÃO, BRAZIL, APRIL 2003

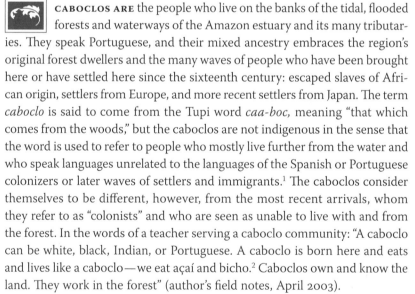 CABOCLOS ARE the people who live on the banks of the tidal, flooded
forests and waterways of the Amazon estuary and its many tributaries. They speak Portuguese, and their mixed ancestry embraces the region's
original forest dwellers and the many waves of people who have been brought
here or have settled here since the sixteenth century: escaped slaves of African origin, settlers from Europe, and more recent settlers from Japan. The term
caboclo is said to come from the Tupi word *caa-boc,* meaning "that which
comes from the woods," but the caboclos are not indigenous in the sense that
the word is used to refer to people who mostly live further from the water and
who speak languages unrelated to the languages of the Spanish or Portuguese
colonizers or later waves of settlers and immigrants.[1] The caboclos consider
themselves to be different, however, from the most recent arrivals, whom
they refer to as "colonists" and who are seen as unable to live with and from
the forest. In the words of a teacher serving a caboclo community: "A caboclo
can be white, black, Indian, or Portuguese. A caboclo is born here and eats
and lives like a caboclo—we eat açaí and bicho.[2] Caboclos own and know the
land. They work in the forest" (author's field notes, April 2003).

This chapter is about the caboclos of the Amazon estuary and the land,
forests, and water they know and work on. It is a story of people whose way of
life makes full use of the unique ecosystem they call the várzea and has proved

to be remarkably resilient in the constantly changing political and economic environment of the Amazon. The story tells of people who hunt and gather and fish, who plant trees and agricultural crops, who raise livestock on land and shrimp in the water. Some of these activities are done by individuals and families, while others are monitored and managed by community groups. Far from being remote and isolated, these managers of the forest have learned to draw on the strength of Brazil's organized labor unions to defend their interests in the wider arenas of state and federal politics. Nevertheless, forest management by caboclo communities remains almost invisible in national and international debates on the future of the Amazon, where interest centers on a small number of projects engaging communities and government in designing management systems reconciling the goals of improved livelihoods and conservation. This chapter traces the decisions that people have made about their actions in the landscape as well as their decisions about when to act individually, when to cooperate with their neighbors, and when to delegate responsibilities to a community organization. It is a reminder that communities can manage forests independently of internationally funded projects.

The Várzea and the Changing Amazon

Since the time of European contact, the Amazon has fired the imaginations of colonists and magnates, missionaries and evangelists, visionaries of all kinds, scientists, conservationists, and social activists inside and outside the region. Images of the "untouched rain forest" and references to "the lungs of the world" have constructed a view of the region as an icon of a pristine natural world threatened with exploitation and destruction by outside forces driven by greed and contempt for the primitive.

The image of the pristine green wilderness is tenacious, despite a rich and growing body of evidence that is shaping alternative histories of the Amazon (Roosevelt 1999:375–83; Slater 2002). Ash deposits in the soils tell of land being cleared millennia ago for agriculture (Soubies 1979–80). Archeologists are piecing together a history of diverse cultures, with trade networks stretching from the Andes to the Atlantic, and of populations possibly close in numbers to the present population, decimated by the diseases and plagues that penetrated far deeper into the forested hinterlands than the Spanish and Portuguese colonizers who introduced them (Cleary 2001; Denevan 1992). We are learning that even the courses of the region's waterways may often be anthropogenic, with evidence of canal-digging, dredging, and manipulation of the riverbanks to facilitate transport and access to lakes or to change and improve habitat for livestock or fishing (Raffles 2002). From the mix of species in the forest, to the soil itself, and to the water channels that dissect and knit together the different parts of the region, people are an integral part of the so-called pristine Amazonian landscape.

The várzea floodplains stretch from the estuary of the Amazon into some of its major inland tributaries. Annual flooding fed by rainfall on the eastern slopes of the Andes covers the land for several months between May and August, depositing a rich layer of silt, constantly reshaping the landscape as the waters build new shoals and islands at the same time as they erode and wash away old formations (Prance 1979; Junk 1997). Only 2–3 percent of the Brazilian Amazon and a similar percentage of the Peruvian Amazon are classified as várzea forests, but they represent important areas for settlement, with high levels of biological productivity and easy water transport to the markets of the growing cities along the rivers (Padoch et al. 1999:ix).

The ecology of the várzea as a whole is governed by the annual flooding regime, but in estuarine areas, the twice-daily tidal movement of water is a more potent force in shaping the ecosystem. With regular tidal flooding (*lancantes*) sometimes as high as two meters, the landscape is flooded for up to three hours at a time. The people, flora, and fauna of the várzea have all had to adapt to waterlogged soils, where the tidal flushes prevent the accumulation of organic matter on the ground (Hiraoka 1999:171–73). Fish and other aquatic resources represent an important component of the caboclos' livelihoods, both as readily available food and as a source of income. Any crops or livestock raised in the area must either be able to survive the daily flooding or must have access to dry areas—most caboclo families raise chickens, ducks, and pigs around their homesteads, and the animals learn to take refuge in canoes tied up to the house at high tide.

Under these conditions, the várzea forests are less diverse than the more elevated, drier areas of the Amazon basin, with a higher density of individual species. Species of value to human populations are therefore more accessible and more easily exploited. Extraction of forest products is more viable economically than it might be elsewhere, and the várzea has witnessed many of the boom-and-bust cycles that have punctuated the economic and social history of the Amazon (Bunker 1985). Cacao, rubber, timber, gold, murumuru nuts (used as "vegetable ivory" for buttons in the 1940s), and hearts of palm are only some of the products that have briefly promised great wealth, only to become exhausted through overexploitation or to be replaced by lower-priced alternatives from other sources. While archeology suggests a long history of trade between the Amazon basin and the highlands at its margins, the direction of trade and exchange shifted with European contact to a flow outward from the region to the coastal cities and European and later North American markets, leaving Amazonians to fend for themselves each time a boom collapsed (Slater 2002:13).

Difficult as the conditions of the várzea may be, the land itself has attracted commercial interests. During the colonial period, slaves from Africa worked plantations of rice, sugarcane, and cotton carved out of the forest. Over the last fifty years, growing domestic demand for meat has driven pressure to convert land to pasture, and most recently, governments have sought to relieve popular pressure from the landless in other regions by encouraging agricultural development schemes and colonization. Historically, the exploitation of labor and the tensions between Amazonians, landowners, and more recent settlers have led to outbursts of resistance, as in the rebellions of the mid-nineteenth century (Hecht and Cockburn 1989) or the intimidation of local movements by acts of violence, such as the 1999 murder of Chico Mendes, the head of the Rubber Tappers' Union. In the várzea of the Amazon estuary today, there is tension between the *caboclos* practicing mixed strategies of extraction, farming, and fishing on their smallholdings; *fazendeiros* (owners of cattle ranches on várzea islands converted to cattle pasture in the 1970s); and more recently arrived *colonos* (settlers, usually landless, from other parts of Brazil). International concern at the loss of biodiversity in the Amazon has become intertwined with concerns for social justice, although the popular dichotomies of good and evil are barely tenable in a world where occupations move between extraction, conservation, and exploitation and where identities shift from indigenous to local to rural poor, intersecting and diverging with constant economic and political change.

Escaping Boom-and-Bust with Sustainable Forest Utilization?

An international workshop held in Belém in April 2003 discussed the potential for community management of natural resources in the Amazon to bridge the gap between the goals of conservation and improved local livelihoods.[3] Workshop attendees contrasted the participatory vision of community management to the exclusionary orientation of national parks and conservation areas and challenged a proposed Brazilian government plan to establish national forests reserved for commercial timber production, with remaining forested land under different forms of protected status. During the two-day program, speakers made many presentations about experimental projects in the Brazilian and Peruvian Amazon—there were said to be thirteen projects in Brazil, all of which involved an outside institution such as a research institute or an NGO working with the community and with other actors such as labor unions or government agencies.

As an observer at the workshop, I found it interesting that no reference was made to the land management systems of the caboclo communities I had just visited in the state of Amapá, which are technically and institutionally the same as those practiced all over the tidal várzea lands of the Amazon estuary. These communities produce most if not all of the açaí consumed in urban centers such as Macapá (the state capital of Amapá) and Bélem itself, as well as up to 60 percent of the timber sold in Macapá. While the members of individual households plant and harvest the many products derived from their smallholdings, they have formed community associations that establish, monitor, and enforce rules to prevent overexploitation of the resources and that organize processing and marketing of some products, including timber. The following section tells the story of Mazagão and caboclo land management to set the scene for a consideration of the factors that have made it a viable solution to the environmental, political, and economic challenges that the caboclo communities face.

Mazagão is a small municipality southwest of Macapá with a population in 2000 of some 12,000 people. The town of Mazagão Velho is said to have been founded in 1771 by a group of white Portuguese settlers and their black slaves, who had come from a Portuguese colony in what is now Morocco. The present municipality was established in 1890 and again in 1915, when the governor of Pará moved the seat of government from Mazagão Velho to a new town of Mazagão with easier access to Macapá, the nearest port, located on the Amazon estuary (Rodrigues 2003). Mazagão Velho stands on the bank of one of the many channels known as Igarapés, which lead to larger tributaries and then to the Amazon itself. Despite its historical importance, the town is now literally a backwater, as the ease of water transport has drawn commercial activity from the settlements along the channels to the markets of Macapá. For more than three centuries this region has seen people of many different backgrounds coming and going, settling, then moving on again; yet it retains a sense of identity and community embodied in the annual festival of São Tiago, which reenacts the wars between Christian Portuguese—ancestors of today's citizens of Mazagão—and Muslim "Moors" of medieval north Africa.

Families along the Igarapés in this area live on land that is nearly all legally classified as "marine land" (*terreno da marinha*) and comes under the authority of the federal government.[4] Although few people have title to the land, they treat their smallholdings as private property, with de facto rules of inheritance and transfer. The average size of a smallholding is about twenty-seven hectares (Pinedo-Vazquez et al. 2001:230), usually divided into four categories: forest (*moradia do bicho*, "residence of animals"), fallow (*capoeira*), agricultural fields (*roça*), and home garden (*quintal*) (author's field notes, April 2003). The home garden is a small area immediately surrounding the homestead that is intensively managed for fruit, medicinal herbs, and domestic livestock and that serves as a place to look after seedlings and plants that need special care before planting them in the forest or fallow plots. Agricultural fields are clearings in the forest on higher land that is never or rarely flooded, where farmers cultivate annual crops such as maize or rice for two to three years before allowing the forest to regenerate. Fallow fields, the next stage in succession after cultivation, are enriched with perennial crops such as bananas, citrus, and trees selected for their commercial value in the medium term (five to eight years). Forestland is where mature trees dominate, and it is used mostly for gathering edible fruits, harvesting timber, and controlled hunting. With the exception of the home garden, caboclo land use takes advantage of the terrain, using patterns of flooding and drainage as well as natural and anthropogenic openings in the canopy, with the result that the vegetation cover on a smallholding is patchy and represents many different stages of clearance and forest regeneration.[5]

The forest areas share some characteristics with a so-called natural tropical forest ecosystem, with a high canopy, high biomass, and relatively sparse understory due to low levels of light. The long and continuing history of human use, however, means that the distribution of species shows the effects of exploitation or deliberate encouragement of species that have had a commercial value at different times. Around Mazagão this means that there is a marked scarcity of valuable species such as ucuúba/wild nutmeg (*Virola surinamensis*), mahogany (*Swietenia macrophylla*), and tropical cedar (*Cedrela odorata*), which were heavily logged during earlier timber booms. At the same time, there is a higher abundance of species producing non-timber products in demand during other commodity booms, such as rubber (*Hevea brasiliensis*). Açaí (*Euterpe oleraceae*) is fast becoming the most common species through the use of management practices such as deliberate seed dispersal in fallow plots, thinning or removing competitors, and pruning (Anderson and Ioris 1992:346). Most recently, smallholders have responded to an expansion of small-scale timber processing, mostly for local and regional markets, by selecting and encouraging seedlings of newly marketable timber species such as the fast-growing pau mulato (*Calycophyllum spruceanum*), which regenerate easily in fallow plots. While the earlier commercial timber species are now less abundant in the forest, smallholders are actively collecting seedlings in the wild, raising them in their home gardens, and experimenting with enrichment plantings in the forest areas with a view to using them as seed sources or to harvesting them as a source of cash in times of emergency (author's field notes, April 2003; Pinedo-Vazquez et al. 2001:234).[6]

The combination of extraction and cultivation constitutes a diverse household economy with different sources of revenue at different seasons, allowing for intensification of production or the introduction of new species and products in response to changing markets. In April 2003 caboclo households in the Mazagão area reported that they sold a total of fifty-six different products from their land, of which three (Brazil nut, açaí, and cupuaçu—a fruit related to cacao) are considered for tax purposes as "extracted" (author's field notes, April 2003).[7] Estimates of household income indicate that this diverse land use system achieves a modest level of prosperity that compares well with the income of other rural people in the Amazon and appears to be resilient in the face of the financial and economic crises that have marked the last two to three decades in Brazil (Anderson and Ioris 1992:349; Pinedo-Vazquez et al. 2001:235).[8]

The extended families of individual households care for all the land in their smallholding. Processing of some products, such as açaí, is also done by family members. Processing of timber, however, is organized and supervised by community associations, as is marketing of timber and other products such as processed açaí. It is at this point that the otherwise individual family farming system of the caboclos finds its place in a wider network of community institutions and social movements that provide services and support where individuals and families may be unable to provide the resources, capital, or political influence that are needed to maintain their way of life.

The most immediate community-level institution is the producers' association (Associação do Produtor da Region de Mazagão), of which there are about fifty-two in the Mazagão area.[9] The association is geographically based, serving all the residents on one stretch of a stream or Igarapé, with an average of fifty households in each association. The association, in practice, defines the community, since all residents of the Igarapé must belong to the association and new residents can buy land and move into the area only after securing its approval.[10] The associations have three elected leadership positions, each with a two-year term of tenure: president (*Presidente*), secretary for social welfare (*Secretario de bem-estar Social*), and union delegate (*Delegado Sindical*), who represents the Amapá Rural Workers' Union (Sindicato dos Trabalhadores Rurais do Amapá [SINTRA]).[11] In the Mazagão area, men and women serve as presidents in different associations, and every member of an association must also be a member of SINTRA.

The associations hold monthly plenary meetings of all members at which they discuss matters of common concern to the community. The member of one association explained that it deals with "everything from what to do with shrimps to what to do about drug problems." One association, for example, has selected two families as the only members authorized to market açaí. The families retain this privilege on the understanding that they will find the best prices for the fruit and that they will invest the profits from their business in buying and running boats to provide transport services for other association members traveling to the cities (Miguel Pinedo-Vazquez, personal communication). On another Igarapé, some members had been clearing land on the river banks for water buffalo pasture. Water buffalo feeding on the river banks destroyed vegetation that is vital shrimp habitat. As shrimp harvests began to fall, the association decided to ban buffalo grazing on the river banks. When one buffalo owner refused to get rid of his buffalo, the association took action, and "his buffalo began to die mysteriously."

Members do not pay any subscription fees to the association. It is, instead, funded by a percentage of the income from small sawmills operated by families who receive permission from the association to operate the mill. There are one or two mills on each Igarapé, built to a caboclo design using equipment left over from the larger commercial sawmills from the most recent timber boom of the 1970s.[12] Members of the association take timber to the sawmill as and when they harvest it, with 80 percent of the income from the sale of the timber staying with the household and the remaining 20 percent going to the sawmill. The sawmill, in turn, pays a percentage (set by the association) of its share to the association's community fund.

In some places, the association also receives a small percentage of individuals' earnings from the sales of shrimp or timber. This income is placed in a community fund used for emergencies and community priorities as determined by the monthly membership meetings. In one association, for example, the community fund has been used to top up the prices for products sold when market prices are low. In one place, the fund has even been used to pay for a sterilization operation for a member who had numerous unwanted pregnancies, affecting her ability to work.

The associations have no specific mandate to manage forest, but they do set rules about how to harvest timber, and they monitor production to avoid damage to the forest. In the Mazagão area, the associations have ruled that each household must retain an area of mature forest, the *moradia do bicho* ("residence of animals"). The associations are the intermediary in moves to develop forest management plans that are acceptable to the national forestry establishment and that meet international standards for sustainable timber production set by organizations such as the Forest Stewardship Council (FSC). Government approval would give the associations and their members access to national funds for reforestation and forest management activities, while FSC certification would expand the markets for their timber. Fundacão Floresta Tropical (FFT, the Tropical Forest Foundation), the international NGO responsible for developing FSC certification in the region, has indicated that the associations in the Mazagão area make it possible to produce timber at a scale suitable for marketing while retaining the capacity to monitor its members' activities and enforce rules for environmental protection and sustainability. As of mid-2003 progress in securing government approval for management plans was slower, with the forestry profession arguing that current smallholder practices are no more than ad hoc activities and that a plan must be based on inventories and estimates of standing volumes of timber and harvest schedules. The associations, with support from SINTRA, are now forging links with research networks to document and to present their case that the várzea forests regenerate from small openings in the canopy and that várzea forest management should be based on the caboclo system of fallows and enrichment plantings.[13]

Each association and all its members belong to the Amapá Rural Workers' Union (SINTRA). Established in 1959, SINTRA has its roots in the liberation theology of the Catholic church at that time. SINTRA was banned during the period in which Brazil was under military dictatorship, but the civilian administration of President Cardoso legalized SINTRA again in 1994. SINTRA is known for its activism on issues of land rights and the rights of peasants and represents the interests of the associations and their members with government and commercial interests. Recently, SINTRA successfully lobbied to open timber markets in Macapá to smallholder producers, and it is now trying to have more forest products classified as "extracted" in a bid to reduce the taxes levied on forest smallholders.[14] In a move that has created a direct linkage between caboclo forest management and conservation, SINTRA succeeded in having the *moradia do bicho* recognized as legally designated environmental conservation areas (Área de Proteção Ambiental [APA]), giving the associations access to national conservation funds for reforestation. While SINTRA was able to have existing forestry legislation modified to accommodate smallholders' practices, associations are still required to develop family forest management plans (Plano de Manejo Florestal Familiar [PMFF]), which has led to some of the technical issues mentioned earlier.

Considerable international attention has focused on the role of the Brazilian Rubber Tappers' Union (Conselho Nacional dos Seringueiros [CNS]) in securing access for its members to extractive reserves in the Amazon, but there is some tension in the estuarine areas between SINTRA and CNS. In Ipixuna, a várzea area near the state capital, there have been conflicts between the caboclo community and a *fazendeiro* (livestock rancher) over the impacts of grazing on the floodplains and wildlife. The community had planned to establish a community reserve to protect the wildlife, and it approached the *fazendeiro* to buy his land (hoping to leverage conservation funding from the state government with the assistance of SINTRA). The plans were disrupted when the CNS put forward an alternative plan to the state government for an extractive reserve against the objections of SINTRA and the local association, who felt that CNS was pursuing the agenda of international and urban conservation organizations rather than acting in the interests of the rural poor. SINTRA was confident that it would convince the authorities to back the plan for a community reserve, but SINTRA officials in Macapá tell the story as an example of what they see as the intervention of a new actor with international visibility but little local experience (author's field notes, April 2003). In view of the important role played by the labor movement in support of the forest communities of the Amazon, the emergence of tensions between two major unions could act against the interests of their members in the future, although differences in strategy are still not irreconcilable. The delicate role of intermediaries and their relations with forest communities is an issue that recurs with such frequency in the story of community forestry that I will consider it at length in chapter 9.

Amália's Story

The people who live and work in the constantly changing landscape of the tidal várzea floodplains identify themselves in terms of their knowledge of and stewardship of their forest resources, not in terms of how long they have been there or their racial heritage. They have devised a way of life that has the flexibility to adapt to the changing political and economic environment of Brazil and Latin America as a whole, and they have organized themselves in a way that maintains their individual interests while calling on the strength of their own organizations and a regional labor movement to represent them in state and federal arenas. In the words of one observer, the várzea landscape "reflects practical decisions of the inhabitants . . . who perceive the forest as a foundation, rather than an impediment, to economic production" (Anderson and Ioris 1992:364). It is time now to tell the story of one woman and her family as a reminder that the caboclos of Mazagão are people with a history, who make decisions every day based on their experience and what they have learned as they deal with changes and forces whose origins are often remote from them and beyond their control.[15]

Amália describes her parents as being "from the várzea. A pure caboclo family." Her grandmother was Portuguese and her father was from northeastern Brazil. Her mother, Maria, was born on the island of Ilha Cametá at the mouth of the Amazon. The island was one of the earliest industrial centers of the Amazon, producing fish and fish skins for export to Europe. Ilha Cametá had once been wealthy, with a timber industry that collapsed with the exhaustion of the valuable, easily exploited species. Maria worked there when she was young, sorting murumuru nuts and andiroba nuts that were being exported to Europe to substitute for copra after the Second World War. She met her husband, a caboclo from Breves, while she was working at Ilha Cametá. After they married, they moved to nearby Mixana Island, two days' travel from Macapá. The timber industry had moved there, and they worked for a company that had a concession. Shortly after arriving, however, they moved again because "somebody came and took the land."

Maria and her husband then moved to Ilha dos Porcos, across a channel from Macapá, where they worked throughout the 1950s and 1960s for BRUMASA, a large timber company. Amália was born at Ilha dos Porcos. BRUMASA hired workers like Amália's family to plant trees in areas that the company had harvested. BRUMASA wanted them to plant only virola, but they planted all kinds of trees, including açaí. "Caboclos have always planted açaí," Amália explains. BRUMASA was a victim of the collapse of the timber boom at the end of the 1970s, and the BRUMASA field manager claimed ownership of the land, although BRUMASA had in fact received only a concession from the government to log the land. He began to cut down the açaí the family had planted. When they complained, he told them that they had the right to use açaí only in a plot measuring one hundred meters around the house. Instead, the family continued planting trees and reforested an area of some two thousand hectares. The former field manager summoned IBAMA (the federal environmental agency) and the police, forcing them to agree that Amália's family could occupy only a small piece of land—as a favor, not with any legal title. With hindsight, Amália and her mother remember the BRUMASA as having treated them very well, but are bitter at the bad treatment meted out to them by the field manager and IBAMA.

The plot of land they received was only a *quintal* (home garden), and they were not allowed any fields to plant crops, leading to tensions in the family. They did plant timber trees such as cedar and virola, but the field manager cut them down, saying that they had the right to own the garden but not the trees. Despite this treatment, Amália's father stayed on the land, but she and her brother João began to look for somewhere to move, eventually going to live with relatives on another island, Ilha Pará, who welcomed them because they believed that Amália and her family knew how to care for the land.

Amália and João had the use of the land, but in time, relations between them and their relatives became tense, so they decided to move somewhere else. They felt that they knew how to look after the land and forest, but needed to have their own land. "We were getting tired of building and looking after home gardens and forests for someone else." João had met someone from an Igarapé near Mazagão, and in the late 1970s they both went to live there. When João's friend asked if they would like to buy the land, he and his sister decided to buy it. Unfortunately, shortly after "buying" the land they found that it actu-

PLATE 4. Amália's family in Mazagão.   PHOTO: AUTHOR

ally belonged to someone else, and a woman from Mazagão Novo claimed it. SINTRA was active in the region, and Amália approached the union to arbitrate. She went together with a SINTRA representative to negotiate with the woman, offering to pay not for the land but for the trees on the land. Amália describes the land as being "in bad shape. There were only four lemon trees and four cupuaçu trees." She did not find it too hard to pay for the property, because it did not have much value. Nevertheless, she had to pay two people in the end because she still had to pay the original "seller," who demanded payment for the house as well. Once they had bought the house, Amália and João convinced their parents to come and live there, bringing some of their plants with them from Ilha dos Porcos, including seedlings of açaí, cedar, and virola. Her father, who has since passed away, moved there in 1986 or 1987. The household now consists of Amália, her mother, her brother João, and a changing number of relatives and adopted children.

Amália remembers that when they moved to the Igarapé it was "a place that had been violated [*violada*] and no one had taken care of it." Even açaí palms were scarce, because they had been cut by *Palmiteiros*—individuals contracted by companies with concessions from IBAMA to cut heart of palm. Her solution was to adopt the four different management zones of land that other caboclos use and to begin re-creating the landscape, treating the land, she says, with "Amor." Some sixteen years later, she and her family are active members of the association, and she is frequently asked by NGOs working in the area to work with other farmers in the region as an "expert" demonstrating techniques for land restoration and regenerating forestland. Telling her story, she concludes that "a terra da várzea dá de comer á gente mas não de graça" ("in the várzea the land gives you food but it is not free").

Amália's Story and the Community in Forest Management

Amália tells of her family moving frequently to different places and learning different skills to recover from setbacks or to take advantage of new opportunities. Beyond its intrinsic interest, the story gives many insights as to how and why the people of Mazagão, their families, and their community institutions have all played a part in fashioning and maintaining the tidal várzea forests in a way that supports them and their families and provides some security at times of economic and political uncertainty. The story not only puts a human face to the boom-and-bust narrative that frames so many accounts of the Amazon, it also demonstrates the value in an uncertain environment of learning and deploying skills acquired along the way. Amália and her family have been industrial laborers, rural workers, and individual entrepreneurs. They have drawn on their experience as workers to seek assistance from SINTRA in their dispute over land at Mazagão, and as farmers they have enriched their smallholding with seedlings brought from Ilha dos Porcos and with some of the reforestation techniques learned when they worked for BRUMASA. Their ability to move from one place to another and from one activity to another has not sheltered them from the "bust" periods of the economic cycles, but it has given them access to options in terms of support networks and economic activities to help cope with the unexpected.

Individual stories, statements by local leaders such as teachers and union activists, and the activities of the associations all point to an acute awareness of changing markets and their power to transform livelihoods for better or for worse. In Mazagão, caboclo smallholders have successfully taken advantage of the strengths of both individual and collective action in production and marketing by nesting their individual production systems within the larger collective structures of the Igarapé associations and SINTRA for processing, marketing, and political action. Individuals may change the mix of crops and products from their smallholdings to meet changing market demand, but it is only with the strength of numbers afforded by the associations and SINTRA that individuals can improve conditions of market access and reduce transaction costs such as processing, transport, or taxation. Caboclos are profoundly aware of the value of forests as the source of their livelihoods, making it all the more surprising to hear from the organizers of formal community management projects that the first step and the major challenge in moving toward sustainable utilization of the Amazon must be "to introduce the mentality of forest producers to rural Amazonian populations."[16]

Individual histories and experiences are important in shaping the decisions they have made about their land use and production. The larger history of the region is at least as important in establishing the political landscape in which the Igarapé associations and the labor movement have come to be the institutional expression of collective interests.

Since the time of European contact, extraction of resources through domination and exploitation of subaltern people—indigenous Amazonians, African slaves, and landless laborers—has been the norm. The conventional narrative of environmental degradation blames a thoughtless peasantry for clearing and burning the forest to cultivate plots in an endless destructive cycle, moving on as the cleared land is quickly exhausted. An alternative narrative, however, shows the subalterns surviving the successive collapses of exploitative production and going on to create land use systems utilizing rather than exploiting the forested ecosystems. As conservation of biodiversity becomes a priority, the international community has incorporated some groups, such as the indigenous Amazonian peoples, into a vision of a protected rain forest. Other groups such as the Quilombolas (escaped slaves of African descent)[17] and the caboclos, however, still find that either they and their land use practices are invisible when it comes to demarcating the boundaries of protected areas or they are considered to be the agents of destruction. They are cast as intruders and are forced to seek allies in a struggle to have their way of life recognized as sustainable and compatible with the objectives formulated by others of national parks, extractive reserves, certified timber production, or community-based resources management.

From the rebellions of the nineteenth century to the struggles of the Rubber Tappers' Union in the final decades of the twentieth century, the people of the Amazon are heirs to a long history of social activism and resistance. Syndicalism has deep roots in rural society, with SINTRA playing a prominent role in support of rural people facing dispossession or loss of access to critical resources (Diegues 1991, 1997; Lima 1999). The role of the Catholic Church has been more equivocal in view of its close links with the political establishment, but at times the church has sheltered labor activism in the face of suppression. It may be tempting to envision a social movement led by organized labor supporting the political and economic empowerment of Amazonian communities through community-based resources management, but it is necessary to recognize that the tensions already visible between SINTRA and CNS in the state of Amapá are indicative of diverse and not always compatible interests in the land and its resources. SINTRA articulates its mission in terms of representing a social class—rural workers. CNS represents workers within a sector—rubber tappers (expanding more recently to include other extractive activities). The interests of the class of rural workers and the sectoral interests of the rubber tappers may not always coincide, as the case of the community reserve at Ipixuna has shown. At the same time, both SINTRA and CNS have difficulty in responding to the demands of the landless poor from other parts of Brazil for land in what they see as the unexploited vastness of the Amazon.[18] A single social movement is unlikely to be able to serve the diversity of interests in the region, and it is more likely that there will be a greater differentiation of labor-based organizations representing and negotiating on behalf of labor-based and sectoral constituencies.

Experience with different forms of activist organization is no doubt a factor in the readiness of individual caboclo households to delegate some control over their livelihoods to the Igarapé associations. The division of responsibilities between households, associations, and the union reflects a practiced understanding of where effort is best deployed individually and where collective action is more effective. The household is best placed to make decisions about allocating its labor to different productive activities, even if some of the resources they exploit such as fish or wildlife might not be privately owned. The community—whose membership is defined by the association—is best placed to formulate rules to avoid overexploitation of resources, to monitor utilization, and to sanction violations of the rules. The boundaries of the territory over which the association has authority are defined by the Igarapé and the islands that its waters cover at high tide, which neatly maps human communities onto the ecosystem they use. Finally, experience has shown that even the remotest parts of the region feel the effects of markets and political decisions taken in distant centers of power. On their own, the associations could offer little more than a regulatory mechanism to conserve resources and a channel for more effective marketing of their products. Through their memberships in the unions, the associations can become actors in the negotiations and struggles over the future of their region, rather than powerless bystanders.

The tiered hierarchy of responsibilities that characterizes the smallholder forest management systems of the tidal várzeas stands in marked contrast to the models of CBFM being tested in the world of conservation and development projects. Nearly all projects work on the premise that some form of community-based institution should take responsibility for all aspects of management, from production to harvesting to marketing. At the same time, it is common for management to be reduced to regulatory procedures for implementing an allowable cut based on an inventory of timber volume and growth rates. Institutionally, the prevailing model is a management committee representing the interests of the community. Recognizing that communities are heterogeneous and encompass diverse interests based on ethnicity, gender, age, class, education, and other factors, project managers take great care to design complex mechanisms to ensure representation of different interests. Yet with the constraints on decision-making imposed at the outset by a restricted definition of management, these carefully crafted community institutions may ultimately find their role limited to implementing regulations and imposing sanctions on offenders.

The Mazagão associations may be invisible in studies and analyses of CBFM because individual ownership and production are integrated into a system in which community institutions play only a part. Yet the constructed community institutions in many internationally funded projects are left with little more than an implementing function with very little say in the critical domains of decision-making about how they wish to manage the forest resource. The Mazagão associations are a reminder that forest management is an undertaking incorporating many activities, some of which may best be carried out by individuals and some by one or more levels of collective institutions. CBFM need not imply that the community is responsible for every aspect of management—but at the same time, it is an empty concept if members of the community are left with no real power to make decisions.

Looking Ahead: Challenges for the Mazagão Associations

There is little reason to believe that Amazonia will no longer be subjected to the boom-and-bust economic cycles that have marked the last three or four centuries. The region is perhaps less marginal to national economies than it has been in the past, but despite efforts to build industrial bases in the rapidly growing cities, much of the planned future economic growth is still based on the extraction of resources, with oil and gas being the latest commodities to attract attention. The caboclos of the Igarapé associations of Mazagão manage their smallholdings for a diversity of products. Diversification buffers them in the case of dramatic fluctuations in prices for specific products, but they are not isolated from the wider social impacts of changing markets, especially urbanization. To cultivate smallholdings along the Igarapé demands an intimate knowledge of the soils, topography, hydrology, fauna, and plants of the tidal várzea forestland. Many people worry that their children will lose this local knowledge as they attend an urban-based education system and move more often between their rural homes and new opportunities for employment in the cities. Some communities have invested in establishing their own schools, the *Escola Familiar Agroextrativista* (Agricultural-Extractivist Family Schools). As part of a curriculum approved by the Ministry of Education, students in the family schools are expected to engage in projects using data they gather from the family farm, and parents are invited into the school to lecture about their farming and forest management activities. The schools receive support from SINTRA, through which they have become part of the Solidarité Internationale des Maisons Familiales Rurales,[19] an international network based in France that offers assistance in fundraising, curriculum development, and planning. It remains to be seen whether this approach to education will succeed in stemming the loss of skills and people to the cities, but the ability to take advantage of an international institution for support once again demonstrates the value of the associations' membership in SINTRA, with its access to national and international resources.

An appraisal of any resources management system must consider its impacts on the natural environment and the ability of the management institutions to monitor change and to take action when there is evidence of depletion of resources. The history of Mazagão with its cycles of extraction of timber, rubber, and other products makes it difficult to disentangle the many factors affecting the present forest vegetation. The distribution of species shows evidence of past logging in the scarcity of valuable species such as virola, while it also shows evidence of contemporary preferential selection and care for species such as açaí or pau mulato. The associations do, however, appear to have the ability to take appropriate measures in the face of threats to the environment. When catches of shrimp began to fall because of damage to riparian vegetation by water buffalo, the association banned grazing by the river and punished recalcitrant members who did not voluntarily remove their animals. They have also called on SINTRA to assist them in securing legal recognition of the *moradia do bicho* as conservation areas and have proposed a community reserve at Ipixuna. Detailed ethnographic and anthropological research in the area shows that personal conflicts and elite interference are no less common here than in any other community,[20] but the associations do appear to be capable of managing these tensions and mobilizing their members to act in the collective interest when necessary.

The support of organized labor in the form of SINTRA has been a vital factor in the success of the Mazagão associations. The biggest challenge they face in the future may in fact come from a possibly widening divergence of interests in the ranks of the unions' constituency as rural society in the Amazon becomes more complex. There is a sense of a latent confrontation over turf in the way that SINTRA representatives in Mazagão and Macapá talk about the recent arrival of the Rubber Tappers' Union in the region, although solidarity in the interests of organized labor still seems to prevail. Both organizations are united in their opposition to planned colonization schemes, but the demands for justice of the Landless Workers' Movement makes it less easy, at least for a class-based organization such as SINTRA, to dismiss all newly arrived settlers as intruders. In practice, the identification of the caboclo as one who "owns" and "knows" the land has allowed some settlers to become accepted in time as caboclos and therefore no longer outsiders.

Conclusion: Who Does What Best?

It is curious that a model of forest management in which community institutions play a vital role is almost invisible to the governments, researchers, activists, and communities who are designing and experimenting with community-based resource management projects to further the goals of conservation and development in the Amazon. On the whole, invisibility is probably not a disadvantage for the associations. To exist in isolation would be problematic, but links with SINTRA give the associations access to government and other sources of support when needed. Nevertheless, a higher level of national or international visibility could help in taking advantage of opportunities such as timber certification and international markets for "green," or natural products. Association leaders and their partners in SINTRA are alert to the possible benefits of tapping into global interest in the forests of the Amazon, but they are also acutely aware of the risk of losing control over their ability to determine their own priorities and to pursue their own way of life.

The Igarapé associations and their members may not lose much by remaining invisible, but a wider recognition of their experience could enrich efforts to design community-based regimes of forest management elsewhere. The history and the ecological setting that have shaped this model of smallholder forest management are unique to the tidal várzea forests of the Amazon estuary and cannot be replicated. Where the experience of the caboclos of Mazagão speaks to other people in other places, though, is in the disaggregation of forest management into its component activities and the delegation of responsibilities and benefits to those best placed to do the job. Tending the forest gardens on the banks of the Igarapés demands a level of individual enterprise and local knowledge that argues for household-level management. Households join forces to articulate and safeguard community interests through the association, while SINTRA provides a platform from which the community's voice can reach governments and international agencies. The Igarapé associations demonstrate that there may be more to be gained in identifying who can accomplish which task best and in crafting strong institutions to support them rather than in constructing one inclusive organization with a mandate to organize and supervise the implementation of all aspects of forest management.

5

Kangra Valley, Himachal Pradesh, India

There are so many Co-op functions going on. Industries Dept. does not interfere with industrial Co-op Societies, Agriculture Dept. does not interfere with Agri Co-ops and Horticultural with horticulture Co-op Societies. Then why should the Forest Department? Is it the reward of total involvement of public in bringing out a very beautiful forest in the heart of population, or the Forest Dept. is interested to show the increase of acreage of forests to their credit?

—KANGRA DISTRICT COOPERATIVE FOREST SOCIETIES UNION 1993:3

THESE HEARTFELT words are in a 1993 document prepared by several cooperative forest societies in the Himalayan district of Kangra, sent to the prime minister of India, the governor of the state of Himachal Pradesh, and other government leaders. A copy of the document is included as supporting material in a civil suit brought before the High Court of Himachal Pradesh during 2000 in which representatives of the Kangra District Cooperative Forest Societies Union ask that the Forestry Department recognize their existence and return to a policy of collaboration with the cooperatives that it had implemented from the 1940s to the 1970s. The Forestry Department, which is committed under national and state policy to joint forest management (JFM) with communities, contests the case and has taken no action to implement the recommendations of a seminar held in March 2000 under the auspices of the Himachal Pradesh Cooperatives Development Union at which it accepted that the cooperative forest societies (CFSs) had a role in managing the district's forests (Ahal 2002:56).

India's JFM program sets conservation and the needs of local communities as the objectives of forest management and declares that partnerships between state Forestry Departments and local communities are the mechanism by which these objectives will be met (RUPFOR 2002:4). Nearly fifteen years after JFM became national policy, more than 63,000 village forest protection committees are involved in the conservation and management of fourteen million hectares of forestland. The government of India reports increases in forest cover as well as improved income in JFM villages and intends to extend the policy to all villages classified as forest villages by 2007 (Ministry of Environment and Forestry 2003). Yet at the same time as the minister was announcing these statistics and plans for the future, a panel of Indian researchers summarized the findings of their investigations of JFM with the statement that "devolution policies emerge as a further extension of state control, at best a meagre palliative for mobilised forest users, rather than a real move towards greater democracy, improved livelihoods, and healthier forests" (Sarin et al. 2003:vi).

The story of the tribulations of the Kangra CFSs[1] and their determination to survive in the face of the hostility of the state Forestry Department are reminders that community partnerships with government agencies in managing forest resources are not a uniquely contemporary phenomenon and that their existence can be undermined in the face of a government decision to extend nationally a model that had evolved locally. The story highlights the difficulty of relying on administrative procedure to effect a shift in power from government agencies to local institutions, but it is also a reminder that local institutions are rarely exemplars of equity and justice and that the exclusion of groups such as women or the landless can sap the legitimacy and capacity of community-level initiatives to reclaim management of forest resources.

A History of the Kangra CFSs

States and Forests in Kangra Before 1935

The Kangra District of Himachal Pradesh State is centered on the east-west valley of the Beas River. The valley, which is 128 kilometers long and up to 58 kilometers wide, drops from an elevation of 6,975 meters above sea level on the snow-covered slopes of the Dhauladhar range of the western Himalayas to 350 meters in the foothills at the edge of the rich agricultural plains of the Punjab. With a population of over a million, Kangra has the highest population of the twelve districts of Himachal Pradesh, distributed unevenly between three different zones: a lower, dry area in the south; fertile, irrigated agricultural lands with the highest density of settlements in the middle reaches of the valley; and sparsely populated, steep, wooded slopes leading to alpine meadows at the highest elevations in the Dhauladhar range, where pastoralists bring their animals for summer grazing. The people of the Kangra valley exploit the different environments along the altitudinal gradient, with pastoral groups moving their animals at the end of the summer from high elevation pastures to lower winter pastures, grazing on the stubble in harvested fields that the herds fertilize with their dung as they pass through. The valley has also benefited from trans-Himalayan trade routes leading eastward toward Tibet and westward to the Hindu Kush and Afghanistan, generating sufficient wealth among its ruling elite in the past to support a number of important Hindu places of pilgrimage and a cultural heritage represented by a distinct Kangra school of miniature paintings well known to connoisseurs of south Asian art.

During the precolonial period, the rajas who controlled the Kangra valley presided over a system of property relations regulating access to and use of the land, water, forests, and pastures essential to the valley's well-being. While individuals did not formally own property (all land being vested in the raja), they could enjoy hereditary usufructary rights to land, water, or other resources, and those rights could be mortgaged in the same way as property (Ahal 2002:1; Baker 1994:66–68). Within this long-established system of rights enjoyed by individuals and households, the people of Kangra have pooled their resources and labor in institutions such as irrigation associations, known as kuhls (Baker 1994), or informal work groups such as women's groups, formed to share labor at harvest and other periods of intense agricultural activity (Berry 2001).

The British presence in the Kangra valley began with the annexation of the Punjab in 1846. The district was administered as a part of the Punjab until 1966, when it was incorporated into the union territory of Himachal Pradesh, which became a full state within the Indian union in 1971. In 1852 the deputy commissioner and settlement officer for Kangra declared that while all vegetation on land outside the demarcated village boundaries should be government property, the soil of these so-called wastes was the property of the revenue-paying (in other words, land-owning) members of communities and that ownership of the soil should be held in common. Following this decision, the "General Rules for Forest Conservancy in Kangra" approved in 1859 established the principle of joint ownership (of the soil and of the trees in the forest) with a rule that one quarter of the income from the sale of trees in the forest should be paid to the coproprietary body representing the land owners (*khewatdars*) of the village. The rules stated that this share, known as *haq chuharram*, was not intended as compensation for ownership of the soil of the forest, but was expected to stimulate the interest of local people in protecting the forests (Chhatre 2000:6–7). The new state of Himachal Pradesh declared state ownership over all forests in 1971 and disavowed the institution of *haq chuharram* through the Village Commonland Vesting and Utilization Act of 1974 (Dhiman and Bhatia 1990:26; Chhatre 2000:9). Nevertheless, *haq chuharram* persists in the popular memory, with a material existence in the form of official documents in Urdu, Hindi, and English still in the possession of village committees. Consequently, the refusal of the present Forestry Department to pay communities a quarter share of income from the sale of trees is an urgent matter for villagers in Kangra District.

The Forest Act of 1878 established the pattern of centralized government reservation of and control over forests in India, but its implementation was not uniform all over the country. Bengal and many parts of the Himalayas represented "zones of anomaly" where local usufructary rights were incorporated into the system of reserved and protected forests (Rangarajan 1996; Sivaramakrishnan 1999). In Kangra, a significant portion of the forested land was demarcated as protected forests, a category that did allow for the registration and exercise of customary rights, unlike the more common category of reserved forests in which no customary or informal rights were recognized. This unusual situation may have been the reason that Kangra was the site of the experiment with CFSs initiated by the colonial authorities in 1940 (Chhatre 2000:6).

During the early twentieth century, Kangra experienced a period of demographic growth, driven at least in part by its close economic and political links to the Punjab. Demand for timber grew, coupled with an expansion and intensification of agriculture encouraged by the revenue department through tax incentives for land clearance. The Forestry Department perceived a threat of deforestation and erosion and took action to implement its mandate under the 1878 Forest Act of ensuring the "orderly extraction" of timber and valuable forest products, such as resin, over which the department had established firm control by the end of the nineteenth century (Guha 1990:43–47). In successive settlements or demarcations of nonagricultural lands, the Forestry Department extended its control over forested lands and so-called wastes, justifying its actions in terms of the perceived impending disasters of erosion and desertification triggered by overgrazing and deforestation (Saberwal 1999). The inexorable constriction of rights of access to the forests provoked anger and resistance, expressed in frequent outbreaks of arson in the reserved forests and violence against forestry officials referred to in reports during the 1920s as "conflagrations" or "firings in the forest" (Springate-Baginski 2001:48). In the face of popular action against its policies, coupled with criticisms from the revenue department of the poor financial returns being recovered from the Kangra forests, officials began to contemplate the possibility of involving local populations in a less confrontational approach to forest management (Chhatre 2000:15; Ahal 2002:5).

CFSs from 1935 to the Present

In 1935 a conference of Indian forest officers held in Madras adopted a resolution proposed by the chief conservator of forests for Punjab deploring the state of undemarcated forests and proposing that "the practicability of forming village forests should be examined, and the Government may kindly be asked to appoint a committee to decide what particular steps should be taken in each district of the outer Himalayas."[2] Two years later, the Punjab government set up a commission chaired by Sir Colin Garbett to hold public hearings and to deliberate on the future of forest administration in the Himalayan districts of the Punjab. The government asked the commission to consider three questions, which bear repeating since they would still be appropriate questions to ask of any forest administration today:

- What difficulties are experienced by those who live in and near forests as a result of the existing systems of forest administration?
- How can these people be best interested in the conservation of the forests?
- How can their cooperation with the Forestry Department be encouraged and secured?

The Garbett Commission recommended that in Kangra the forests should be managed locally by an elected village level body (*panchayat*) under government supervision. The commission recommended that this village-level management should apply not only to remaining *shamilat,* or common lands, but to all forests regardless of legal classification. The Punjab government accepted the commission's recommendations and instructed the Forestry Department in 1938 to formulate a scheme to put them into practice. The scheme that emerged involved a partnership between the Forestry Department, Revenue Department, Cooperatives Department, and participating communities. The Punjab government approved the scheme in 1940 for an initial five-year period, to be renewed at five-year intervals if the experiment proved satisfactory. Work began immediately to organize the new CFSs, which were to be the village-level management body recommended by the Garbett Commission. By 1945 the Cooperatives Department had registered forty societies covering 17,500 hectares of land, and the government approved the extension of the scheme for a further five years (Ahal 2002:10).

The choice of cooperatives as the institutional model for the new forest management groups was not entirely fortuitous. As described earlier, the people of the Kangra valley have a history of inter- and intracommunal cooperation, from the interdependence between pastoralists and agriculturalists, to the management of the kuhl irrigation systems, to less formal arrangements for pooling labor. During the late nineteenth century, the cooperative societies being established in Britain and the Raffeisen cooperative savings societies in Germany attracted the interest of social activists in India, who saw them as a way to pool capital and to develop socially equitable small-scale industries capable of competing with some of the British industrial products flooding the rural Indian economy. In 1904 a group of landowners in Una (south of Kangra) pooled their forestland to form the first cooperative in what is now Himachal Pradesh. The members of the Una Chil Cooperative joined forces to tap and market resin (*chil*)[3] from the pine trees on their own, private land and were so successful that they expanded the services the cooperative provided to some basic thrift and savings schemes.[4] Other *chil* cooperatives were established in due course, and their success led the Forestry Department to establish further cooperatives—the *chor* cooperatives on village commons (*shamilat* land) to promote soil conservation and "scientific forestry." In addition to these cooperatives, some landless laborers formed grass cooperatives to bid for the rights to cut grass on land controlled by the *chil* or *chor* cooperatives. By the time the Punjab government came to designing its village forest management system, self-initiated and government-sponsored cooperatives were an established institutional presence in the region, with a government Cooperatives Department to supervise and regulate their operations. The choice of cooperatives registered with the Cooperatives Department as the institution to manage village forests in effect meant that the Forestry Department was expected only to provide technical support and to monitor implementation of management plans, leaving the Cooperatives Department to assist with day-to-day management of finances and the internal governance of the CFSs.

When more than three quarters of the landowners over eighteen years of age in a village agreed to its formation, a CFS could be formed. On registration with the Cooperatives Department, the CFS took over the responsibility for managing all forests within the village boundaries as well as any privately owned forestland a member wished to bring into the scheme. All forests in the village thus came under one working plan established "in accordance with the provisions of the Indian Forest Act 1927 and . . . according to working plans drawn up in consultations with the Societies by a forest officer authorized by the government for the purpose and approved by the government" (1941 Kangra CFS rules, quoted in Chhatre 2000:16). Members paid an admission fee of one rupee and signed a binding agreement to follow the working plans established by the society and the Forestry Department. The structure and governance of the CFSs came under regulations and bylaws common to all cooperatives under the Punjab Cooperative Societies Act of 1912 and its successors, including the Himachal Pradesh Cooperative Societies Act of 1968. Regulations stipulated procedures for meetings and rules for decision-making, dispute resolution, and financial management. It is important to note that since membership in the CFSs was open only to revenue-paying landowners, they were not representative of the whole village. The landless were excluded by definition, and few if any women or members of scheduled castes were registered as property owners.

The Forestry Department accepted that the cooperative societies would receive the income from the sale of timber and other forest products (harvested according to the working plan) after payment to individuals of the *haq chuharram* share associated with their property and after deductions to cover the costs to the Forestry Department of preparing and implementing the working plan as well as certain allocations required by law such as a reserved fund, an education fund, a forest improvement fund, and a percentage to be used for charitable purposes. Since many of the cooperative societies were established in areas of badly degraded lands with the explicit intention of regenerating and rehabilitating the forest, the government also established a fund of up to Rs. 50,000 per annum for the whole of the district for grant-in-aid payments to cover costs such as the preparation of working plans and salaries for forest guards in cases where the cooperative societies could not recover their costs due to the poor condition of the forest (Chhatre 2000:16–18; Ahal 2002:15–18). The scheme explicitly affirmed the right of the cooperatives to benefit directly from forest management, but in referring to preexisting rights such as the *haq chuharram* and by making the funding for the grant-in-aid payments subject to government renewal, it lent itself to contesting interpretations of which payments were entitlements, which payments were inherited from the past independently of the CFS program, and which payments were temporary, discretionary allocations from the government. These disputed claims continue to cast a shadow over attempts to reach an accommodation with the Forestry Department today over the status of the remaining CFSs.[5]

Government reviews of the CFSs appear to have been positive enough to secure renewal until 1973. By 1956 seventy-two CFSs had registered in Kangra District, although two later lost their registration due to allegations of mismanagement and corruption, leaving a total of seventy. From 1956, however, no further cooperatives were approved, and political support for the scheme eroded as Himachal Pradesh placed ownership and control over natural resources at the center of a struggle to establish its place in the political geography of an independent India.[6]

In 1955 the chief minister of the Punjab raised three questions about the structure and roles of the CFSs. He questioned the viability of the scheme since it had extended to only seventy villages representing less than 10 percent of the forest area in Kangra District and asked whether this was not extending unwarranted preferential treatment to a small number of villages.

He also questioned their legitimacy as village institutions since membership was limited to property owners and the cooperatives themselves had no formal relationship to local government. Finally, he noted that, as constituted, the scheme meant that income from all forestland in the village went to a restricted group of individuals rather than to all members of the community, recommending that income should instead be paid to the village assembly (*panchayat*) to be used for public works. Subsequent disputes between the cooperatives and the Forestry Department have obscured the pertinence of the chief minister's reservations about the scheme. In 1937 the Terms of Reference of the Garbett Commission asked how current bureaucratic forest management could deny villagers access to essential resources, thus imposing hardship and generating popular resistance and even violence. In 1955 the chief minister asked whether the alternative village-based regime of forest management did in fact benefit the whole village without creating new categories of exclusion and whether its impact was on a scale sufficient to warrant the level of funding and human resources invested in the scheme. The first set of questions points to the rationale for reorienting conventional forest management, the second set points to important principles by which to evaluate alternative models of forest management.

Despite the chief minister's reservations, the Punjab government renewed the scheme with increased funding for the grant-in-aid program every year until 1961. That year, the government cancelled the grant-in-aid program and issued orders to prohibit the formation of new CFSs at the same time as it renewed the scheme as a whole for a further ten years, until 1971. In 1967 India nationalized all trade in non-timber forest products (NTFPs), which deprived the CFSs of lucrative sources of income, such as resin production. The Himachal Pradesh government extended the scheme for a further two years in 1972, but has preferred since then to see the Forestry Department take control of all the forests in the state. Although the Forestry Department recognized the contribution of the Kangra CFSs to forest conservation in an integrated working plan for all of Himachal Pradesh drafted in 1968, in practice it has moved to enforce its own jurisdiction over lands that the CFSs had been managing and has ceased to make any payments to them for income from timber and other forest products since 1974 (Ahal 2002:12–13). In the village of Tripal, for example, the Forestry Department sold timber rights to commercial contractors in 1971 and 1972, disregarding the provisions of the existing working plan. The contractors clear-cut an extensive area of old growth forest that the CFSs had protected since 1949, and the Forestry Department has consistently refused to make any payment to the CFSs on the grounds that it is a "defunct" institution with no rights to the forest (author's field notes, Kangra, July 2002).

PLATE 5. The secretary of a village cooperative forest society in Kangra, with the village forest.

PHOTO: AUTHOR

Over the last thirty years, the CFSs have persisted in a state of uncertainty over their status. The Forestry Department has moved to a position of active hostility based on its contention that the original scheme was a temporary expedient to facilitate the regeneration of degraded lands, that there is therefore no further role for the CFSs, and that since membership is restricted to property owners they cannot play a role in JFM, which seeks to serve all sectors of society, including women, the landless, and scheduled castes. The CFSs reply that their legal existence under the cooperative department has never been rescinded, that rights such as *haq chuharram* predate the scheme and cannot be overridden by the Forestry Department, and that they can adjust their membership rules and procedures to ensure greater equity and representation. There have been several attempts within the Himachal Pradesh government to review the position of the CFSs, but they have so far all failed to make headway with the various committees, becoming embroiled in the wider politics of different interests within the State Assembly (Ahal 2002:12–13; Springate-Baginski 2001:50). In 1996 the thirty-six remaining active CFSs registered as the Kangra District Cooperative Forest Societies Union in order to pursue their case through political lobbying and the court system. In October 2000 the High Court of Himachal Pradesh accepted a petition from the union to hear its suit against the state of Himachal Pradesh (High

Court of Himachal Pradesh 2000), although by early 2004 no date had yet been set for the case to be heard.

The Kangra CFSs Today

The formation of the Kangra District Cooperative Forest Societies Union indicates that some people, at least, still see value in the CFSs and are determined to keep them alive. Before moving to an analysis of the implications of the Kangra story for other CBFM initiatives, it is useful to examine the residual roles of the Kangra CFSs today in the context of their forest management activities and their relations with the village community, other government agencies, and the NGOs that are now working with them.

During the 1990s the Himachal Pradesh Forestry Department implemented at least three internationally funded programs designed to involve local communities in forest management: the Indo-German Dhauladhar Farm Forestry Project, the National Social Forestry (Umbrella) Project, and the Integrated Watershed Development Project (Dhiman and Bhatia 1990:5–6). By 2001 the earlier projects had come to an end, and there were five separate projects under way in the state directed at implementing the national JFM program (Vasan 2001:37). In the Kangra valley, memories of these different projects are still fresh, but few if any of the various committees and management plans they generated are still functional. In many villages, by contrast, the CFSs continue to exist, hold meetings, and maintain records and accounts, and thirty-six of the original seventy societies are active enough to join forces to sue the state. In most cases, the only funding available to the societies comes from membership fees—which members continue to pay—and sometimes from the proceeds from the auction of grass gathered in the forest (although the Forestry Department does not recognize their right to organize such auctions).[7] It would appear that, despite efforts to question their legitimacy and to create new institutions sidetracking the CFSs, in some villages, at least, they have a resilience that suggests that they are rooted in and serve their communities in ways that the more recent projects do not.

In villages that still have an operational CFS, there continues, in fact, to be informal and unsanctioned cooperation between the society and the Forestry Department, particularly in patrolling and guarding the forest. The CFSs still pay forest guards (*rakha*) out of their own funds. The societies may themselves take action against offenders, or they may hand the case over to the Forestry Department guard responsible for the area. Both the society's *rakha* and the Forestry Department guard were present at informal meetings I attended with three separate CFSs in July 2002. Officially, the Forestry Department has explicitly warned its staff not to collaborate with the CFSs (letter from the divisional forest officer for the Dehra Range, Kangra District, quoted in Springate-Baginski 2001:50), but in practice Forestry Department staff cannot monitor all activity in the area for which they are responsible, and they continue their working relationship with CFS forest guards. Nevertheless, the uncertain status of the CFS guards does mean that it is easier for an offender to exploit the situation and to escape arrest or punishment by playing off one authority against the other—which has led to further complaints on the part of the Forestry Department that the CFSs are not capable of protecting the forests.

The CFSs play an important role in the allocation of wood and timber for household use. In the village of Tripal, each household is entitled to one tree every five years for building purposes, a family may receive permission to cut wood for cremations, and women are allowed to collect dead wood in the forest for firewood. Committee members said that they were responsible for giving permission for these longstanding use rights in the forest, but that they had to request approval from the Forestry Department for firewood to be used for weddings and other large celebrations, which is time-consuming since the request must be processed by several government offices at different administrative levels. In Tripal, only society members have rights to firewood for weddings and to timber for house building and repairs, which society officials did concede raised questions about equity and the ability of nonmembers to get access to forest products (author's field notes, July 2002). In some communities, the CFSs have broadened membership to include women and scheduled castes, but questions remain as to the degree to which these groups are actively involved in the societies' decision-making.[8]

Active CFSs continue to organize and to supervise annual auctions of grass in the village forests. In Sarah, households bid for the rights to harvest grass that they may use themselves for fodder, thatching, or rope-making, or they may sell on the rights to a third party and use the income for themselves (Springate-Baginski 2001:49). Some CFSs have restricted the right to bid for grass-cutting rights to their members (author's field notes, July 2002), while others have an open auction, using the income to cover the society's costs or to pay for public works in the community, such as building and repairing school buildings or maintaining paths and trails through the forest (Ahal 2002:20–21).

Finally, the CFSs appear to play a role as an alternative village voice representing local interests. Under rules established by the Cooperatives Department, currently serving civil servants may not be members of CFSs, and members are explicitly prohibited from overt activism on behalf of a political party. This may explain why there is resistance to proposals that the CFSs should be reconstituted as specialized committees within local government. While such a move would appear to have the advantage of shielding village forest management from the uncertainty of project time constraints and funding by embedding it firmly in local governance, many people are wary of allowing a critical resource to become an object for factional wrangling.[9] The view of the CFSs themselves, as expressed in the quotation that opens this chapter, is that registered cooperatives in other sectors are free to manage their own affairs, so CFSs too should be left to engage in the task for which they were established without being absorbed into the structures of local government. Meanwhile, the CFSs see their very existence as a source of collective strength in resisting what they perceive to be continuing attempts on the part of the Forestry Department to deny villagers access to forests and a source of income for the community. Whatever the outcome of their suit before the High Court, representatives of the Kangra District Cooperative Forest Societies Union point to their success in bringing the case to court as proof that "collective action gives us the strength to demand our rights from the government" (author's field notes, Kangra, July 2002).

Contested Narratives: What Divides the CFSs and the Forestry Department?

The application to file suit submitted to the High Court of Himachal Pradesh by the Kangra District Cooperative Forest Societies Union states "that the present suit is being filed to the effect that the individual forest cooperative societies were handed over the management of forests in return of one fourth share in the sale [of] proceeds. . . . However the societies are not being given their due share, though they are continuing to plant, protect and manage the forests."[10]

The legal dispute between the two parties is framed in terms of whether the CFSs are still authorized to manage their village forests under a government order issued by a former administration. The CFSs contend that since they continue to have a legal existence as registered cooperatives, they continue to be the village-level entity responsible for managing the forests. The Forestry Department's position is that since the order establishing the cooperative societies has not been renewed since 1973 and that since subsequent national legislation placed all of India's forestlands under the control of the state Forestry Departments, the scheme has been dissolved and the institutions it created have no further right to be involved in forest management. In narrowly legal terms, a judge may be able to rule on the current status of the cooperatives and whether they still have the right to manage forests and receive one quarter of any revenue. The contrasting narratives of the achievements or failures of the CFSs make it clear, however, that more profound issues are at stake and that a judge's decision would not bring such an acrimonious dispute to a close.

Three themes recur in the voluminous correspondence and the many reports compiled since the launch of the CFS scheme in 1940. Forestry Department officials have questioned whether the CFSs are, in fact, regenerating and managing the forests; they have challenged the legitimacy of the societies on grounds of equity and internal governance, pointing to the relatively small number of societies and their restricted membership, coupled in some cases with accusations of corruption; and they have insisted that the Forestry Department is legally and constitutionally the owner of all forests in India, conceding limited rights and privileges in those forests only as and when it sees fit. The first two issues can be, and have been, argued using quantitative and qualitative data from surveys, although evidence is rarely conclusive and the same data is used to contradictory effect by different interests. The third issue is a more profoundly political and ideological question and is at the heart of many debates about the role of communities in forest management in many countries: do state claims to forested lands extinguish all claims of citizens living in or close to forests—even where the presence of those citizens may predate the existence of the state and its resource management agencies?[11]

Reports within the Forestry Department and other government agencies were positive about the impact of CFS management on forest protection and management until the 1970s. The chief minister of Punjab raised questions about the scheme in 1955, but he did not appear to doubt their effectiveness in protecting and regenerating forests. In 1968 the integrated working plan for the whole of Himachal Pradesh recommended continuing to implement the plan in Kangra through the CFSs, stating that "the Co-operative Societies have been greatly instrumental in winning over the interest of the local people in the all important matter of forest conservancy" (quoted in Chhatre 2000:22). The Himachal Pradesh Institute for Public Administration prepared an independent review of CFSs in 1969 that stated that "plantations undertaken by societies 30–40 years back have fully been established and their stocking can be favourably compared with stocking of plantations in Government forests" (quoted in Springate-Baginski 2001:50). Nevertheless, Forestry Department reports and critiques of the CFSs after 1971 consistently pronounce the experiment to have been a failure (G. C. Chaudhary in Springate-Baginski 2001:51; Dhiman and Bhatia 1990:22), and they state flatly that they disagree with the positive appraisals of other agencies (Sharma n.d.:7 §9.3). In 2002 Ahal used the Forestry Department's own data to compare stocking rates in Forestry Department and CFS-managed forests in Kangra, concluding that there was now no significant difference between the two (2002:34), although forests allocated to the CFSs in the 1940s had been among the most severely degraded in the district.

Forestry Department claims that it is the only body with the institutional strength and technical expertise to conserve forests are not borne out by its actions in the field. It has insisted that closing forests to grazing and any human use is the only possible silvicultural prescription—in an ecosystem where an accumulation of pine needles and grass cover on the forest floor prevents regeneration of oaks and broadleaf species (widely used for fodder and fuelwood and other nonindustrial uses), thus shifting forest composition toward a monoculture of pines (useful for resin extraction and timber).[12] Throughout the lower elevations of the Kangra valley, villagers also question the Forestry Department's proclaimed commitment to the improvement of degraded land, pointing to the rapid spread of Lantana brush (*Lantana camara*) over the last decade. Lantana competes with regenerating trees and is poisonous to livestock. It is recognized as a pest throughout the region, but as far as affected communities know, there has so far been no effort on the part of the Forestry Department to control Lantana, nor is there any research under way to address the problem (author's field notes, Kangra, July 2002).

Forest ecology is of course only one element shaping agency decisions about management and priorities for research. The Forestry Department's actions in implementing its working plans in Kangra do cast further doubt, though, on its assertion that it alone is able to manage forests in the long-term interests of the nation. Villagers in Kangra have complained that the Forestry Department allows resin tappers to use excessive quantities of acid to promote faster flows of resin, a procedure that damages the trees (Ahal 2002:34). Others tell of concessions granted to commercial interests to clear-cut timber in protected areas. They concede that the CFSs could improve their protection of the forest, but worry that not only do they receive no support from the Forestry Department but that the department has placed obstacles in their way through actions such as a ban on building roads or trails in the forest, which makes it difficult for the *rakhas* (forest guards) to patrol and limits the ability of the village to fight fires (author's field notes, Kangra, July 2002).

With respect to questions of equity and internal governance, there is no denying that CFS membership excludes women, the landless, and scheduled castes. During a workshop organized in 2000 by the Himachal Pradesh cooperative department on the future of the CFSs, the societies accepted that they will have to modify their rules (Ahal 2002:55). It remains to be seen how this will be done and whether groups that have formerly been excluded will be active in the societies' deliberations and work. Leaders of NGOs working with other cooperatives in Kangra have observed that active participation represents an investment in the present in return for possible benefits in the future.

Entrepreneurial and more prosperous groups in a community are more likely to be willing to make this investment than the dispossessed, for whom there may be more pressing priorities (Ajit Kumar and Rajeev Ahal, personal communication). Some CFSs do say that they have women among their members, but there are many informal social and cultural barriers against women's participation (Agarwal 2001). Meetings held in public spaces discourage women from acting in ways that might be perceived to be inappropriate—such as speaking out to contradict an older male village leader. Women may not be able to leave household chores to attend meetings. Gender is of course only one dimension of exclusion, and class and caste divisions can be more divisive even than gender in institutions for local governance (Berry 2001).

It is ironic that the Forestry Department should be so insistent that exclusive membership and a concern for gender equity should be grounds for denying the right of CFSs to manage forests. The Indian Forestry Department itself has been criticized for decades for its hierarchical, male-dominated internal culture. For many decades, international financial support to the Forestry Department for social forestry, integrated watershed management, and JFM has included budget allocations and grants for internal structural reform to recruit more women and for staff training to become a less autocratic, more consultative, and more facilitative institution (Lele 2002; Poffenberger and McGean 1996; Poffenberger and S. Singh 1989; RUPFOR 2002:12; Singh 2002:18–19). Appraisals of progress to date are still critical of the continuing control exercised over decision-making by Forestry Department staff, of continued elite domination in JFM institutions, and of continued exclusion of women and disadvantaged groups within the community (Agarwal 2001; Hobley 1996; Kumar 2000; Sarin et al. 2003; Sarin et al. 1998; Saxena 1992). It is at the very least questionable that the outcome of Forestry Department control over the CFSs would be a more equitable, inclusive, and participatory institution serving the forest communities of Kangra.

The dispute between the Himachal Pradesh Forestry Department and the Kangra CFSs is unlikely to be resolved by scientific evidence demonstrating which institution's forests are in better ecological condition or by opening membership of village forest management institutions to underrepresented social groups. It is a dispute about who owns and controls land and resources, not about how the resources are managed (Blaikie 2001:13). The Forestry Department contends that the state of Himachal Pradesh owns all forestland and that the Forest Act of 1980 placed all forestland in India under state governments to be managed through the agency of their forest departments, extinguishing any prior rights that communities or others may have exercised (Ahal 2002:47).[13] From the perspective of the Forestry Department, it follows logically, that whatever the results of CFS stewardship of forests, they exist only at the department's discretion. Department staff can be brutally honest in articulating the position that it alone should be in control of all aspects of forest management. One report complained that "the officers of Forest Department as per present bye laws [sic], have little control on the working of CFS. In fact the control is mostly technical and advisory" (Sharma n.d.:8). Another paper bluntly insisted that "there should be complete control of Co-operative Forest Societies, including financial, technical and administrative by the Forest Department" (Dhiman and Bhatia 1990:24). The issue at stake appears to be state control over forested land rather than the state of the forests on the land.

Community Management as an Expedient Bandwagon? Learning from the Kangra CFSs and JFM

In 1992, shortly after the Indian government announced the adoption of JFM nationwide, Indian forester N. C. Saxena warned that the balance of power in JFM was heavily in favor of forest departments, which can cancel or dissolve forest protection committees without appeal, and warned that "the need for autonomy and a democratic process at the community level is currently not reflected in the state resolutions" (1992:30). Saxena's warnings still have resonance today even as the Ministry of Environment and Forests celebrates the success of the JFM program with an announcement of a plan to extend coverage of the program to 170,000 forest villages by 2007 (Ministry of Environment and Forests 2003). The 1990 government notice made conservation and meeting local needs the main objectives of forest management, but in a 1999 survey in Madhya Pradesh 76 percent of foresters answered that "forest protection" was its most important objective (Kumar 2000:46). The rhetoric of JFM is of devolution, partnership, and participation, but as of 2000, in all states except Gujarat, the Forestry Department retained direct control over forest protection committees, whose decisions are subject to veto by the Forestry Department and which are required to have a representative of the Forestry Department as ex officio secretary (Lele 2002:2). It is perhaps not surprising that there is concern that JFM is an expedient way to shift the burden of protection and regeneration to communities while retaining decision-making authority and control over benefits from management with the state forest departments.

The Himachal Pradesh Forestry Department has adopted different strategies to extend or consolidate its control over forest resources in Kangra. It has denied the effectiveness, legitimacy, and legality of existing institutions such as the CFSs, adopting the discourse of empowerment and social equity to justify its position—even though it is often itself cited as an example of an undemocratic, authoritarian, and exclusive bureaucracy. It has controlled the formation of new institutions and severely restricted their decision-making rights in the course of other CBFM projects over the last twenty years, few of which have taken root and survived the end of project funding. By declaring the existing CFSs to be extinct and ordering Forestry Department staff to cease any interaction or cooperation with them, it has also criminalized existing practices, giving itself a rationale to enforce more rigid control in the name of maintaining the rule of law. Sadly, there is little evidence that these strategies are successful even in protecting and regenerating forest cover, let alone in realizing JFM's proclaimed social objectives of improved livelihoods and empowerment.

The survival of the Kangra CFSs tells of the refusal of forest users to relinquish what they consider to be rights of access and utilization sanctioned by custom and their capacity to protect and even to enhance the condition of a resource that is central to their livelihoods. In demanding that its staff should control the CFSs, the Forestry Department is undermining the autonomy that gives the societies legitimacy in the eyes of their members and communities, without addressing the acknowledged issues of equity and representation in their membership and governance. The continuing impasse suggests that the Forestry Department seeks to hold on to or extend its power rather than to make progress toward its professed commitment to conservation and meeting local community needs.

The Kangra forest cooperatives are not the only existing village-level forest management institutions caught in the process of expanding the national policy of JFM. In Orissa (Conroy, Mishra, and Rai 2000) and in Uttar Pradesh (Sarin et al. 2003) the introduction of JFM has extended state control to forested lands that had previously not been under Forestry Department jurisdiction. It is notoriously difficult to make the transition from an experimental innovation to large-scale implementation of a new practice or policy, but success depends on sensitive adaptation to local contexts and learning from experience. Successive Indian administrations have made a commitment to a profound shift from bureaucratic authority over forests to partnership with the people who live in and close to the forests. The change is not easy, but it will not be facilitated by forcing one institutional model onto all forest communities. Partnerships demand dialog and a sharing of both responsibilities and benefits. In Kangra District, there is little dialog between potential partners, and the Forestry Department appears attached to an instrumental vision of JFM as a mechanism to regenerate trees and control poaching at less cost to itself, not as a more equitable way to build community assets through improved management of the forest resource. More than a decade after JFM became national policy, it is still questionable whether a new relationship and balance of power between state and local interests in forests will emerge or whether forest communities are simply being offered a slightly increased share of what they believe was once theirs anyway.

6

The Community Narrative of Forest Loss and Degradation

[Policy narratives] come to play a central role in policy and project-level decision-making. They do this by structuring options, defining what are to be considered relevant data, and ruling out the consideration of alternative paradigms from the outset. . . . They are hard to challenge and slow to change, even in the face of mounting evidence that does not support them.

—HOBEN 1995:1008

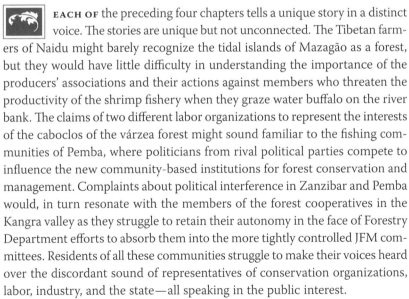 EACH OF the preceding four chapters tells a unique story in a distinct voice. The stories are unique but not unconnected. The Tibetan farmers of Naidu might barely recognize the tidal islands of Mazagão as a forest, but they would have little difficulty in understanding the importance of the producers' associations and their actions against members who threaten the productivity of the shrimp fishery when they graze water buffalo on the river bank. The claims of two different labor organizations to represent the interests of the caboclos of the várzea forest might sound familiar to the fishing communities of Pemba, where politicians from rival political parties compete to influence the new community-based institutions for forest conservation and management. Complaints about political interference in Zanzibar and Pemba would, in turn resonate with the members of the forest cooperatives in the Kangra valley as they struggle to retain their autonomy in the face of Forestry Department efforts to absorb them into the more tightly controlled JFM committees. Residents of all these communities struggle to make their voices heard over the discordant sound of representatives of conservation organizations, labor, industry, and the state—all speaking in the public interest.

The growing area of land under community ownership (White and Martin 2002) is evidence that communities have established a presence both locally and internationally in the discourse and practice of forest management. The controversy over the Kangra forest cooperatives demonstrates, though, that this presence is still precarious, while the people of Jozani are not alone in finding themselves embroiled in a continuing negotiation over the concrete meaning of terms such as "participation" or "management" and even what or who constitutes the community. Recognition that communities are important partners in forest management is only the latest episode in a history of competing claims to access and control over resources in the course of which forest communities, society, and the state seek to realize their visions of what constitutes a forest and of "the purpose of forests."[1]

The conventional narrative of human intervention in forest landscapes tells of the triumph of state intervention to halt the loss of forests in the face of Malthusian pressures from growing populations, which are assumed to be ignorant practitioners of environmentally destructive land uses. In each of the preceding stories however, the people of Naidu, Zanzibar, Mazagão, and Kangra have experienced a sequence of events that recurs again and again in a voluminous and growing literature of ethnographies, case studies, and monographs on different aspects of communities and forest resources.[2] Each of the stories is unique, but together they weave an alternative, community narrative of forest loss. This narrative tells of the loss of access to forest resources that had provided for many of the communities' material and spiritual needs. It also tells of the loss of forest cover to intensive timber harvesting, mining, and other extractive activities declared by the state to be in the public interest, from which communities have received little if any benefit themselves, while experiencing damaging environmental impacts such as silted water supplies and eroding soils.

The communities' narrative unfolds in four episodes:

- Forest communities lose access to and control over the resource, usually to a state agency or to commercial interests in a process of privatization.
- Extractive use accelerates clearance or conversion of the forest, to the detriment of local livelihoods. Communities get organized to reclaim their right to be involved in the decisions that determine what happens to the forest.
- Forest communities negotiate and agree to some form of partnership with the state agency. They sometimes receive outside assistance, and they sometimes negotiate on their own.
- Different interests have different expectations of what "community management" means, leading to contestation over the implementation of the management regime.

The communities' narrative does not have a point of final closure. The fourth episode leaves open the possibility—even the probability—of further events generating new episodes in the future. Each of the many stories from around the world that together constitute the different episodes of this narrative bears the unique signature of the time and the place where it has taken place, but the narrative as a whole presents an alternative to the more commonly told tale of inexorable forest degradation and destruction.[3]

It points to more complex interactions between an array of different actors and interests and the potential for reaching accommodation between those interests and safeguarding the livelihoods of people for whom forests represent an important material asset without endangering the ecological functions and symbolic meanings of forests.

Losing Access and Control

The four chapters that follow will examine that part of the narrative in which communities have struggled and negotiated to reclaim their rights of access and control to forests and the continuing contestation over the meanings of community management. Before moving to that analysis, though, it is important to realize that states as different as socialist China, colonial India, and postcolonial independent Tanzania, as well as states with developed market economies such as Brazil, the United States, or Canada, all arrived by different means at the same model of a bureaucratic government agency with a mandate to manage vast areas of forest in the public interest.

This model of rational, state-directed management of forest resources has a long history and has emerged as the norm over the last two or three centuries (Perlin 1991). The dominant pattern of government intervention has been one of increasing control over forest resources and the loss of access to forest resources by groups that have traditionally or historically depended on them. Forest communities have experienced the loss of access and control in different ways: as a gradual takeover through increasingly restrictive legislation, in the form of violent dispossession and punitive action after a conflict or warfare, or as the extinction of territorial and tenurial rights in a new constitutional dispensation or as a consequence of a dramatic transformation of the state itself—as in the case of the Chinese revolution.

Taking Over One Step at a Time: The Colonial and Postcolonial Experience

Discussion here centers on what Peluso and Vandergeest (2001) have called "political forests"—land that the state declares to be legally "forest" and therefore a form of state property. It should not be forgotten, though, that a comparable process took place in Europe as peasants lost their customary use rights to forests through legislation regulating utilization of and creating private property in what had formerly been common resources. In England, the Black Act of 1723 criminalized a number of activities in the forests, turning offenses such as poaching into a capital offense (Thompson 1975). A century later, peasants in the French Pyrenees disguised themselves as women and attacked forest guards sent to enforce the 1827 Forest Code, which favored commercial charcoal burners and the iron industry by creating private property rights in the forests where local people had previously exercised customary rights to gathering fuelwood and pasturing their animals (Sahlins 1994).[4] In October 1842 Karl Marx published a series of articles about legislation in the Prussian Provincial Assembly taking action against wood theft, concluding that the passage of such legislation extinguished customary rights enjoyed for centuries by ordinary citizens and thus demonstrating that the institution of property itself is a form of theft (1975).

In Europe, forest communities lost their access to forests through a process of attrition, as the extension of private property enclosed the commons and extinguished a rich array of customary rights. On the whole, the forest estate was not taken over in a single act of appropriation by the state, which chose to regulate forest management rather than to claim ownership. In the colonies being established at the same time by the same countries, however, the colonial powers moved to claim direct ownership of the land.

In the past, historians have seen passage of the Government Forest Act of 1865 in India as a defining moment in the takeover of forested land by a colonial state (Guha 1990; Grove, Damodaran, and Sangwan 1998; Poffenberger and C. Singh 1996:56–62; Stebbing 1922). More recently, scholars have concluded that a closer reading of India's forest history shows that the alienation of forestland was not complete and uniform over the whole of the subcontinent. It was only after a later Forest Act in 1878 that the Indian forest service received its mandate to exercise almost complete control over designated forestland and that private property was limited to continuously cultivated land, rejecting all traditional uses of forestland such as grazing, gathering, or swidden cultivation as grounds for claims to ownership. Furthermore, both during the colonial period and after independence, state governments have had the authority to shape the forestry legislation in force on their territory (Barton 2002; Sivaramakrishnan 1999). As a result, the level of control over forest use has varied, with certain states conceding some level of access and control to forest communities, sometimes in response to local tenurial conditions and historic practice, as in Kangra, or in the face of popular resistance at other times, as in Kumaon (Guha 1990). Nevertheless, until the implementation of JFM in 1990, most forest communities lost their access to essential resources and found themselves excluded from extensive areas of the landscape by virtue of the official demarcation of those spaces as "forest."

The story of the creation of political forests and communities' loss of access to the resource recurs all over the world. In francophone West Africa, the colonial forest code of 1900 created the instruments of control over forests, establishing a bureaucratic system of permits, concessions, and reserved areas (Ribot 2001:2). Inland, in what is now known as Mali, the forestry code of 1904 nationalized forests and limited local rights of access to a small number of noncommercial uses—and the forest service had the authority to limit or abolish even those rights if it believed that they might compromise the integrity of the forest estate (Becker 2001:507). Successive decrees and a more elaborate forest code for French West Africa ratified in 1935 entrenched state ownership of forestland and reinforced state control over forest management and utilization (Ribot 2001:4). For some thirty years after independence, the newly independent states of the region incorporated the codes of their colonial predecessors into their own legislation and continued the regulatory and coercive forms of implementation of the past (Bertrand 1985; Elbow and Rochegude 1991; Leach and Fairhead 2000; Ribot 1999).[5]

The deliberate, step-by-step extension of state control over forestland is most often associated with colonial domination. It has not, however, been confined to territories under a colonial power. In Thailand (Siam at the time), forest reservation laws were applied in 1938, followed in 1941 by legislation that defined forest not by vegetation cover but as "all land that does not belong to any individual based on the land law" (quoted in Sato 2000:156). Later demarcation placed the control and protection of forests firmly in the hands of the Royal Forestry Department (Peluso and Vandergeest 2001; Sato 2000; Thongchai 1994; Vandergeest 1996; Vandergeest and Peluso 1995).[6]

Many postcolonial states have continued to extend their jurisdiction over land through the practice of demarcating forests (Lynch and Talbott 1995: chap. 3). In the Dutch East Indies (later Indonesia), an edict issued in 1808 initiated direct government control over the production of teak and management of teak forests in Java. Further regulations, edicts, and reformulations of the forest laws introduced in 1865 reinforced government control over specific commercially valuable species (especially teak) and over land, extending the reach of the forestry laws to the other islands of the archipelago (Peluso 1992:44–78). The process did not end with Indonesia's independence, as the new state consolidated its authority over forestland with the establishment of a forest ministry. In 1984, the first year of the country's fourth five-year development plan, the ministry classified up to 90 percent of the territory of the outer islands of Kalimantan and West Papua (formerly Irian Jaya) as forestland, extinguishing the customary rights of as many as sixty-five million people living in those areas and "making thousands of communities . . . squatters on their ancestral lands" (Fay, Sirait, and Kusworo 2000).

Violence, Warfare, and Dispossession

The colonial and postcolonial scenario of creeping legal encroachment and disenfranchisement may be the most common and richly commented scenario of the alienation of forests, but forcible and violent dispossession have also played a role, particularly in the Americas and in the British settler colonies of southern and eastern Africa and Australia (Castro 1995; Dargavel 1995; Griffiths and Robin 1997; Moyo 1995:262–68). During the nineteenth century white settlement in South Africa was backed by military action, followed during the period of apartheid by forced removals from lands assigned to the white population (Carruthers 1995; Jacobs 2003; Poonan 2002). In the case of Australia, the doctrine of "Terra Nullius" declared that the land had been empty at the time of first British colonization and therefore open for appropriation and settlement, in effect rendering the original Aboriginal inhabitants invisible and denying their humanity (Lines 1991:21–53). Legal decisions during the 1990s have voided "Terra Nullius" and accepted Aboriginal rights to customary territory, but the process of restitution is proving to be protracted, contested, and divisive even within Aboriginal communities (Borch 2001; Turnbull 1991).

In the former Spanish and Portuguese possessions of Latin America, the outcome of dispossession was not long-term state ownership of extensive areas of forest, because the state's claim to the land was the expedient by which it was to be granted to private and commercial interests as a reward for services to the crown or to encourage settlement, bringing new territories more directly under the control of the state. In postcolonial times, the states of the Amazon basin deliberately used concessions—often including the indigenous inhabitants on the land as a labor force—as a means of consolidating border areas (Bunker 1985; Hecht and Cockburn 1989:55–75). The strategy was inclusion for purposes of nation-building, rather than exclusion for purposes of conservation, a model common to much of Latin America (Richards 1997), prompting resistance on the part of the indigenous inhabitants as well as other dispossessed groups, such as escaped slaves of African origin in Brazil and Colombia (Acevedo and Castro 1998), caboclos, rubber tappers, and others (Hecht and Cockburn 1989:161–91; Melone 1993).

Even where national policies favored settlement over the transfer of land to state resource management agencies, some of the supposedly unoccupied lands became a part of the public domain in the form of protected areas such as national parks or forest reserves from which the former inhabitants have been excluded. The legacy of forced removals still hangs over many national parks, where displaced communities are unwilling to accept that customary activities such as hunting and gathering should have become offenses on what they still consider to be their land.

In the United States, most of the forested land under the jurisdiction of government agencies, such as the U.S. Forest Service, the Bureau of Indian Affairs (BIA), or the National Parks Service, has been reserved in the name of protection and multiple use in the public interest.[7] Extensive tracts of the land under federal or state management, however, entered the public domain through processes of alienation, which are remarkably similar to what occurred in other parts of the world under regimes with far less aspiration to democracy and legal process than the United States.

Many forested areas entered the public domain as "unoccupied" land only after the forcible removal of Native American populations during the wars of the nineteenth century (Burnham 2000; Churchill 2002; Huntsinger and McCaffrey 1995; Spence 1999). Within the reservations to which the Native American nations were confined, the treaties they entered into with the federal government placed them in a position of tutelage, with the BIA (a federal agency) given the mandate to manage their natural resources. From the outset, the BIA (or its predecessor, the Indian Office) was accused of mismanagement of the forests under its authority. Even Gifford Pinchot, the first chief of the U.S. Forest Service and an ardent advocate of "scientific forestry," was so offended by the corruption and dubious deals between the agency and commercial interests that he personally formulated forest management plans designed to generate a sustainable stream of revenue first for the Cherokee Nation in North Carolina and later for Chippewa-owned timber land in Minnesota (C. Miller 2000:17–19). His plans do not appear to have been implemented. In 1910 the BIA established its own division of forestry, which has continued to be the target of criticism for its mismanagement of Native American resources. In 1996 the Native American Rights Fund (NARF), representing a coalition of Native American groups, filed a class-action suit in the U.S. courts, alleging mismanagement of revenue from natural resources amounting to at least $2.4 billion. By September 2003 the courts had ruled in favor of NARF, ordering the BIA to account for all funds for which it had been responsible since 1887. While the U.S. Department of the Interior has appealed the decision, the case has highlighted the abuse of the so-called trusteeship under which Native American forests and other resources have been managed for well over a century (Harper, Guest, and Echohawk 2004; National Association of Social Workers 2003).

In the southwestern state of New Mexico, Native American (Pueblo Indian) and Hispano communities witnessed a century of erosion of their ownership and access rights to the critical natural assets of water, forest, and grazing land following the U.S.–Mexican war of 1846–1848. In a process that Coward has characterized as "making and remaking property" (2004), the layered patterns of ownership and access to water, grazing land, and forests that had taken shape from the earliest Pueblo settlements of the fourteenth century, through the Spanish and Mexican administrations, were reinterpreted in the light of U.S. concepts of property, which favored individual over community ownership. Government land adjudications often refused to recognize community ownership of common land, while speculators exploited legal decisions, thus allowing the partition of communal lands to purchase prime plots of land and water rights (Carlson 1990; Coward 2004; DeBuys 1985; Rodriguez 1987). The outcome of successive disputes over usufruct and ownership was that within a century large tracts of Pueblo and Hispano communal land were alienated, considered legally to be in the public domain and incorporated first into the newly declared Carson National Forest in 1906 and subsequently in 1915 into the Santa Fe National Forest.

The loss of access to the resources that sustained Native American and Hispano communities in the past has led to entrenched poverty, with New Mexico ranking as the poorest state in the United States, and the rural counties that are home to the Pueblo and Hispano communities are the poorest in the state (Coward 2004:2). A potent mix of grievance at a history of injustice and loss of control to outsiders has erupted at times into violence, with strong overtones of racism against Hispanos and Native Americans, often centered on environmental conflicts over the use of forests, grazing, and water (Pulido 1996: esp. 125–91; Kosek 2004b). As might be predicted by the narrative that this chapter proposes, since the early 1990s these communities have been organizing to negotiate new agreements with the U.S. Forest Service under which they are now carrying out forest restoration activities, setting up small-scale timber enterprises, and developing protocols to monitor the impacts of the partnership (Atencio 2002; Moote 2001; Poffenberger and Selin 1998:85–89).

Revolution and New Dispensations

For millennia, rural movements of resistance against injustice throughout the world have demanded land reform and redistribution as the most fundamental step in creating a new society (Bercé 1986; Tuma 1965; Migdal 1977). Where discontent and resistance have led to rebellion and where rebellion has succeeded in overturning the old order, land reform is often a priority for the new revolutionary regime. Following the Mexican Revolution, the 1917 constitution allowed for the allocation of land expropriated from large landholders as well as of former state land—including forestland—to *ejidos*, rural communities with legal standing and tenurial rights to their land. In practice, the government controlled the use of *ejido* forests and allocated concessions for logging to commercial interests without consulting the elected *ejido* bodies. As described in the case of the UZACHI association of Oaxaca (chapter 1), it was only during the 1980s, after determined action on the part of *ejido* residents, including physical blockades of roads leading into their forests, that the federal government finally conceded full management rights to communities (Bray et al. 2002; Klooster 1999). The Mexican experience is significant as an example of a transfer of ownership to communities, not just of agricultural land but also of forests, following a revolutionary change of government.

The Mexican case is also important because of its rarity. During the twentieth century, where popular revolutions have taken place, the new postrevolutionary dispensation has tended, in fact, to alienate communities from resources rather than to grant them secure access. Revolutionary regimes in the USSR, China, Vietnam, and Laos all moved quickly to lay claim to state ownership of land, consigning rural people, at the stroke of a pen, to a position in which their rights to use land and natural resources were held in sufferance to the party-state.

In 1949 land reform was one of the highest priorities of the newly established People's Republic of China. Constitutionally, all land came under the ownership of the state. There were separate dispensations, however, for agricultural land and other lands described variously as hill land (*shan di*), grassland (*cao di*), forestland (*lin di*), and wasteland (*huang di*) (Richardson 1966:54–60). Policies toward agricultural land have moved between redistribution as private landholdings, cooperativization, collectivization in communes, and household smallholdings. Nevertheless, despite the changing institutional forms, agricultural land has always been subject to some form of direct decision-making by local village or party leaders and the peasants working the land. More remote national or provincial government agencies have, however, always exerted tight control over access to and use of hill lands, forestlands, and wastelands (Huang 1993; Liu Dachang 2001; Liu Shouying 1993; Menzies and Peluso 1992). In some cases, the state has directly controlled and exploited large areas of natural forest—as in the state forest surrounding Naidu. In other cases, the state has allocated these wildlands to households for management, but has restricted harvesting and marketing, has often imposed targets for planting and for species planted, and has even regulated details such as spacing and layout of forest plots.[8] The rationale for such close supervision has always been that only the state is capable of the scientific management needed to produce sufficient forest products for the nation and to ensure an adequate level of environmental protection for the greater good of society—despite abundant evidence that state management has at best failed to ensure adequate environmental protection and has at worst been the principal agent of environmental degradation and forest loss (Ross 1988; Shapiro 2001; Smil 1993). The struggles of the people of Naidu since the state began logging in the 1950s are an eloquent example of the way in which forest communities have resorted to passive and active resistance to retain access and to prevent the destruction of the forest resource.

The legacy of state control continues to cast a shadow on land and resource use, even in reforming socialist and postsocialist economies. Talking about agricultural land in Romania, Verdery has described the tortuous path to new property relations in a context where even the contours of the land and the trees in the landscape are the site of contested memories of the past, of personal and political conflicts, and of unrealized expectations for the future (1996:133–67). In Vietnam, moves to reallocate what had been collectivized and state-owned land to households and villages have continued to draw a sharp line separating cultivated land and forests (Boissau, Castella, and Nguyen 2001; Zingerli 2003). During the land reform of 1994 in Laos, which ended a brief experiment with collectivized rural production, households received long-term rights to agricultural land, defined as permanently cultivated flat land. In an echo of Peluso and Vandergeest's political forests (2001), though, the state has continued to control and restrict access to and utilization of forestland—defined simply as all land not designated as agricultural land regardless of whether it has any trees on it (Ducourtieux, Laffort, and Sacklokham 2002:6). Even as the twentieth century drew to an end, the process continued of excluding people from forestland to which they have enjoyed access in the past.

With few exceptions, then, even states with an ideological commitment to equity in land distribution have continued to exclude forest communities from the forests or to allow them only limited access on terms determined by the state. Nevertheless, all over the world, whatever the specific mechanisms and pathways that led to exclusion, the formerly invisible people and the dispossessed are returning to reclaim their rights. Through legal appeals, political action, and even on occasion threats of violence, communities and their representatives are organizing themselves and building coalitions with other groups with an interest in the forests to enter into negotiations to gain access to forest resources and to be counted as partners in decision-making about the future of their forests. The following chapters will examine how this change has been taking place and will discuss some of the issues that are emerging as communities enter into a variety of different arrangements with different partners in a venture that all agree to call forest management, even if they do not always agree on what management means when translated into a plan of action in the forest.

Reading the Communities' Narrative

The well-worn conventional narrative of deforestation and environmental degradation has served to justify the various histories of dispossession and alienation described above. The assumption of culpability on the part of ig-norant forest dwellers has justified demarcation of the political forest and the exclusion or eviction of forest dwellers. In the conventional narrative, state management is the resolution or the dénouement of the plot. In the United States, "nondeclining even-flow" and "multiple use sustained yield" came to project a vision of a state of equilibrium in which managerial expertise succeeds in satisfying competing interests in the forest. These phrases, which articulated the goals of U.S. Forest Service management for a long time, represented an end point in the narrative after which stability and rational use were expected to take over for the foreseeable future.[9]

In practice, excluding forest communities in favor of management by the state and its agencies has brought neither ecological sustainability nor social stability. Management in the public interest has instead generated intense pub-lic debate over the economic and ecological impacts of forestry, over questions of equity and justice with regard to the distribution of the costs and benefits of management, and over concerns about the inability of resources agencies to meet the demands of their mandate to manage forest resources. Far from being the end of the story, demarcation of the political forests has set the stage for the communities' narrative proposed at the beginning of this chapter, in which the different actors meet, engage in dialog, and journey through the episodes and events that follow.

In proposing an alternative communities' narrative, I am aware of the danger of the abuse of narrative. There is a rich body of critical scholarship demonstrating the power of a hegemonic narrative to reduce complexity to an appealing and predictable paradigm, offering a simple description of both the problem and prescriptions for its solution, often in the face of mounting evidence contradicting the narrative (Blaikie 1985; Cronon 1992; Doornbos, Saith, and White 2000; Hoben 1995; Homewood and Rodgers 1987; Moore 1993; Peet and Watts 1996; Roe 1991, 1995; Sheil and Wunder 2002).[10] Hoben's analysis of how the Malthusian narrative of degradation drove the disastrous government and international donor responses to the Ethiopian droughts of the 1970s and 1980s is a powerful reminder that lives are at stake, that the construction of a narrative is more than just a literary and analytic device (1995). Roe observes in a survey of development narratives that have served to concentrate power in centralizing states:

> Crisis narratives are the primary means whereby development experts and the institutions for which they work claim rights to stewardship over lands and resources they do not own. By generating and appealing to crisis narratives, technical experts and managers assert rights as "stakeholders" in the land and resources they say are under crisis. —ROE 1995:1066

Recent logging bans in countries such as Thailand and China, which extend to small-scale harvesting by individuals and households as well as large-scale timber operations, demonstrate the persistence of the narrative of forest degradation. The communities' narrative proposes an alternative approach to sustainable and equitable management of forest resources. To follow Roe's line of reasoning, again, "our efforts should shift to creating and engaging counternarratives to the more objectionable narrative or modifying that narrative to make it less objectionable" (1991:288).

In creating a counternarrative, it is necessary to take to heart Haripriya Rangan's warning against the danger of detaching people and places from the land in which they live and the political realities they experience (2000). The purpose of the communities' narrative is not to replace one (objectionable) paradigm with another—possibly also objectionable—paradigm. It is to construct a framework to facilitate ordering events and finding connections between the experiences, decisions, and actions of people and agencies in diverse forested landscapes around the world. It can "create meaning and validate action, . . . mobilize action, and . . . define alternatives" (Fortmann 1995:1054). The events or points of inflection that punctuate the communities' narrative—organization, negotiation, contestation—are moments at which it receives new impetus, direction, or change of pace. They can also serve as points of interrogation or themes for an exploration of the dynamics driving the stories. Exploring those themes can, in turn, point to factors that could enable communities to represent their interests more forcefully in negotiations about forest resources or suggest the conditions that privilege community over private or state actors as the locus for making decisions about forests.

The four chapters that follow touch on themes suggested by the communities' narrative. "Invoking the Community" (chapter 7) makes the transition from alienation and dispossession to the contemporary interest and experimentation with CBFM. It traces how "community" has entered the lexicon of forest management and raises questions about "who is the community" and why it matters how the boundaries are drawn between who is in and who is out. Chapter 8, "The Capacity to Manage," asks what is expected of communities in forest management and whether they have access to the support and assistance that could empower them to manage effectively. The chapter questions whether communities are becoming partners in forest management or whether their exclusion from the forest is being made final with offers of alternative and not always viable land uses and sources of livelihoods. Moving to the negotiations episode of the narrative, chapter 9, "Negotiating Partnerships," contrasts the ideal of partnership with the evidence of frequent misunderstandings, tensions, and unequal relations between communities, government agencies, and intermediaries such as NGOs. While carefully designed partnerships can provide a forum in which to search for common ground in negotiations, a poorly negotiated partnership can set the scene for misunderstanding, tension, and continued or renewed loss of forest. In the final episode of the communities' narrative, different expectations of the outcomes of community-based management lead to further contestation and negotiation. Chapter 10, "Governance and Empowerment," considers how a commitment to empowering communities to manage natural resources is a commitment to give authority for making important decisions about the future to those who will live that future. It involves a political realignment of power and decision-making authority, bringing discussions about the enabling environment for CBFM into the arena of larger debates about devolution, empowerment, and governance.

CBFM involves building frameworks and fora for negotiating different interests in forest resources. It calls for strengthening institutional and technical capacities to ensure that the outcomes benefit communities without compromising the ecological health of forested landscapes. Drawing together the lessons from the stories of Naidu, Zanzibar, Mazagão, and Kangra, then using them, supplemented at times by references to other places around the world, to explore the themes highlighted by the communities' narrative of forest management, this study challenges the different actors in forest landscapes to learn from these experiences and to proceed at a pace that gives time to test and monitor the outcomes of any actions. In concluding, chapter 11 calls for the affirmation of basic principles of justice, equity, and wise stewardship of resources and guards against the imposition of prescriptive guidelines that limit options for forest communities rather than opening new opportunities for the future.

7

Invoking the Community

Unless policy on tenure and natural resource management seriously considers the . . . option of communally-based resource management regimes, there is little reason, either from the historical record or from an analysis of the factors and dynamics involved, to be optimistic about the future of the environment.

—MURPHREE 1993:5

COMMUNITY IS a concept whose meaning and salience differ according to the observer's point of view. This chapter traces the history of communities' exclusion from forests and describes how different actors in CBFM have more recently invoked community as much as an instrumental pathway to more effective management as an ethical imperative. It tells how communities have reentered the arena of forest policy and management and explores the diversity of interests within communities. It considers how communities set boundaries to distinguish between who is and who is not included as well as to differentiate themselves from the other social, economic, and political entities in which they are embedded. Despite the challenge of embracing diverse interests, community emerges from a sense of shared experience of a place, from common values, and in the capacity to cooperate and take collective action.

The appeal of community is a surprisingly recent phenomenon. Nineteenth-century political philosophies tended to visualize history as a linear advance toward a higher, more advanced model of society. The norms and values that distinguish community were considered a hindrance to social change, regardless of whether progress was toward a more egalitarian future—the vision of Marx and the Communists—or toward a model of market-driven economic prosperity. A determination to dissolve the bonds of community and to replace them with rational, usually centralized, planning drove the social engineering of the "high modernist" schemes of states as different as the Soviet Union, India, or Tanzania (Scott 1998), as well as international development programs of the 1950s and 1960s, in which modernity was expected to be the outcome of transforming, rather than strengthening, communities (Holdcroft 1984; Korten 1980:2–3).

By the 1970s and 1980s, even as some countries such as Indonesia were still extending the claims of central government to ownership of large new tracts of forestland, others were questioning the effectiveness of government agencies in realizing long-term goals for forest production, conservation, and social and economic development. While agency decision-making took place in political centers remote from the forests, their field staff encountered constant challenges to the policies they were charged with implementing and daily acts of resistance on the part of local people excluded from the forest. Confidence in rational, bureaucratic government agencies was giving way to a new rhetoric invoking the community and privileging the local.

Community Rediscovered

A rich body of scholarly work has documented and analyzed forested lands as contested spaces that have become emblematic of the struggles of subaltern groups—the poor and landless, women, ethnic minorities—to secure their livelihoods and cultural heritage against powerful forces such as a centralized state or commercial timber or mining interests (Castro 1995; Guha 1990; Hecht and Cockburn 1989; Peluso 1992; Laungaramsri 2001; Sahlins 1994). Academic interest in struggles over the control of forestland resonates strongly with the concerns of politicians, activists, and the general public over issues such as deforestation, human rights, government accountability, or globalization and its local consequences. Interest in community as the possible site of an alternative model of responsible stewardship of forested land has grown in step with disenchantment at the performance of both public management of forests through state agencies and of private management epitomized in the public perception (if not necessarily in practice) by rapacious logging of pristine forests for the benefit of multinational corporations.

Early invocations of community were a direct challenge to state agencies' claim to be managing forests in the public interest. Critics charged that there was little evidence that the "public interest" extended to or included communities in and around forests under agency management. In North America, timber sales to large corporations appeared to have left a legacy of logging communities buffeted by boom-and-bust cycles as harvesting and processing moved from one forest or region to another, following the most easily accessible sources of timber (Danks 2000; Flader 1983; Lee, Field, and Burch 1990; Marchak 1983). In many other areas, forest communities have also lost access to forest resources from which they have been excluded in the name of conservation and the preservation of endangered species. Whatever the reasons for the economic and social fragility of these communities, it is evident that they have not, until very recently, been consulted about or been parties to the decisions about forest management that have shaped their futures.

In developing countries, a similar critique of forest management agencies' distortion of the public interest concluded that in restricting or prohibiting local use of forests, state control over forest management had entrenched poverty in forest communities (Bertrand 1985; Bigombe 1998; Friedmann and Rangan 1993b; Guha 1990; Moench and Bandyopadhyay 1986; Peluso 1992; Poffenberger, McGean, and Khare 1996; Romm 1981). Not only was state control judged detrimental to rural livelihoods,[1] but critics also charged that coercive enforcement of forest boundaries and regulations was a source of conflict and violence, locally in the form of sporadic attacks on forest staff (Sundar and Jeffrey 1999:38) and sometimes on a wider scale in the form of more organized, internationally known social movements such as the Rubber Tappers' Union (Conselho Nacional dos Seringueiros) in Brazil (Hecht and Cockburn 1989:166–87; Melone 1993) or the Chipko movement in India (Guha 1990:153–57; Rangan 2000; Shiva and Bandyopadhyay 1986). Poverty, violence, and state control over forests combined to fuel calls for the inclusion of communities in forest planning and management (Bromley and Chapagain 1984; Buckles 1999).

In India, the social-forestry program launched in the mid-1970s sought to alleviate shortages of fuelwood and other forest products by encouraging tree-planting on wastelands and degraded forest areas. The program demonstrated that rural communities had the capacity to manage trees, although it was criticized for inappropriate selection of species and inequitable allocation of benefits. More importantly, perhaps, social forestry was said to have avoided the issue of making state forestland accessible to the poor by deflecting the focus to communal lands, which were often a vital source of fodder, fuelwood, and other resources for women and the landless (Arnold 1990; Shiva, Sharatchandra, and Bandyopadhyay 1987). In the 1970s the successful transfer of responsibility for smallholder irrigation systems in the Philippines from the National Irrigation Agency to community associations was influential in demonstrating that resource management bureaucracies were capable of making the transition from direct management to support for community management. Despite the many differences between management of irrigation systems and other natural resources, the Philippine experience inspired further experiments, including community management of forest resources, in the Philippines and other countries (Korten 1987).

The movement toward CBFM has also gained momentum from international struggles for human rights and social justice. Popular demands for land rights and, by extension, rights over forestlands have highlighted the injustice of excluding forest communities from forests and from decision-making about their management. By the 1980s a sense of crisis accentuated by a need to find more cost-effective approaches to the exercise of their mandates seems to have made state forest management agencies around the world more willing to consider that breaking the monopoly of official and commercial interests over forest resources could be an opportunity, not a threat. The agencies rediscovered communities, recasting them now as potential stewards and caretakers, no longer as destroyers of the forest.

Mixed Motives for Invoking Community

The consensus that emerged in the 1980s bringing communities into the spotlight, if not to center stage, of forest management obscures differences in the motives of different actors and interests for invoking the community. With national governments, international donors, and a spectrum of NGOs all supporting activities described as community-based management, it is not surprising to find almost as many definitions of CBFM as there are programs and projects around the world. A sampling of recent publications from different countries and regions—in which, revealingly, the voices of communities are rarely heard—shows two main rationales for involving communities in resource management: an instrumental, utilitarian argument and an argument based on social justice and human rights.[2]

Government resource management agencies struggle to stretch their budgets to meet their responsibilities. Revenue from logging concessions or the sale of permits has been the main source of funds to pay staff, to patrol boundaries, to carry out planning, and to monitor operations. At a time of static or reduced funding for government agencies and calls to limit timber harvesting in favor of conservation, agencies have been looking for more cost-effective approaches to carrying out their mandates. Some CBFM programs can be quite explicit in stating that a major objective is to reduce the government's financial burden, as in this evaluation of a Swedish-funded CBFM project in Vietnam:

In the long run, the Government cannot pay for forest protection (50,000VND/ ha/year) for all forest areas regulated as protection forest, especially in critical protection areas.

The subsidy in forest protection also increases the dependency and passivity of local people. So it should put into trial another way of paying for forest protection with a view to promoting up [*sic*] the production and economic value of the forest.   —VU 2001:6

Not all utilitarian arguments for CBFM are so narrowly focused on reducing the costs of forest management. It is more common for governments, resource management agencies, international donors, and NGOs to situate CBFM in the discourse of international development, with its proclaimed goals of poverty eradication and improved governance. While this has shaped a favorable political environment for CBNRM, it also raises questions about the ways in which international trends have molded policies and programs that seek to empower the local.

Forest conservation as a strategy for rural development links rights of access and the condition of forest resources to sustainable rural development and the reduction of poverty in forest communities. The expectation is that the shared interests and values in a community will facilitate supervision, monitoring, and enforcement of rules, while simultaneously reducing conflict by aligning the interests of the management agency and the community. The Indian Ministry of Environment, for example, presents JFM as a way to improve rural livelihoods through more effective forest conservation, using the mechanism of a contractual agreement to share responsibilities and benefits:

JFM is a forest management strategy under which the government (represented by the Forest Department) and the village community enter into an agreement to jointly protect and manage forestland adjoining villages and to share responsibilities and benefits. . . . Under JFM, an FPC (Forest Protection Committee) takes the responsibility of protecting a forest patch from fire, grazing and illegal harvesting. In return, it gets a greater access to forest produce and a share of income earned from that forest patch.   —RUPFOR 2002

In many places, advocates of CBFM have made the association with struggles for human rights and land, highlighting the continuing legacy of the history of exclusion and dispossession of communities from forests. In the Philippines, the fight for indigenous people's land rights has been integral to the call for a shift in control of forestland from the Department of Environment and Natural Resources (DENR) to forest communities. Mexican *ejidos* fought a sometimes violent struggle in the 1970s and 1980s to gain control over harvesting and processing of timber from government parastatal corporations. In Brazil, peasant and indigenous people were at the forefront of the land-rights movement opposing the military dictatorship of 1965–1988. More recently, indigenous peoples around the world have placed demands for secure rights to forested lands at the center of their quest for social justice and equity (Indigenous People's Forest Forum 2003; Martinez-Alier 2003).

A recent evaluation of the role of international networks supporting community forestry assessed their effectiveness in promoting the goals of CBFM, nearly all of which address aspects of social justice and equity:

- empowerment—inclusive decision-making, including marginal voices
- equitable income generation and livelihood strategies in communities
- access to and control of forests by the local communities
- ecological sustainability and conservation
- two-way flows of information in appropriate forms and languages

—COLCHESTER ET AL. 2003:2

Advocates of community forestry in the United States focus less on land rights, but call for an activist movement centered on communities and forest workers:

Community forestry represents nothing less than a radical realignment of relations between people and forest ecosystems. Community forestry is driven by a vision of forestry in which the sustainability of the communities and workers that depend on and steward forests is part and parcel of the long-term ecological sustainability of the forest ecosystem itself. . . . Community forestry challenges the inequity and social injustice that have historically accompanied forest resource extraction, and it makes the claim that achieving ecological sustainability is not possible without also achieving social sustainability.

—BAKER AND KUSEL 2003:190

Whatever the outcome on the ground, both communities and their partners are likely to be disappointed in the face of such high expectations tied to such widely differing rationales and arguments for CBFM. Without a cautious analysis of community, there is a danger that community-based management could become just another short-lived development fashion, not a serious option in realizing sustainable, equitable utilization of forest resources. As Tania Li has observed, however, despite the possible dangers of such mixed signals, the very breadth of concerns that constitute the fabric of CBNRM gives salience to efforts to secure the place of communities in decision-making about forests and natural resources utilization: "Arguments for CBNRM combine environmental sustainability, social justice, and development efficiency with assertions about practicality and 'good sense'—there is value in clear resolute axioms in making headway in the policy arena" (2002:265).

Rehabilitating the Community

In a study of rural communities in the United States, Walter Firey observed in 1960 that a viable resource is the material basis for secure livelihoods and the confidence in the future on which communities can build the shared interests, values, and norms that make for a healthy community. A healthy community, in turn, would be expected to act to maintain the viability of the resource on which it depends. Elaborating on Firey, others have pointed to the depth of local knowledge of an ecosystem as a resource in itself (Baker and Kusel 2003:154–60; Ballard 2004; Berkes 1999; Bliss et al. 2001; Chambers 1997: esp. chap. 8; Colfer and Byron 2001:9–10; Korten 1987:1–6). Communities, being closest to the resource, are expected to be best placed to judge what is happening to it and to draw on internal social mechanisms to monitor and take action if necessary.

A powerful force in revising earlier negative judgments of community has been the growing body of evidence documenting the capacity of community institutions to manage natural resources, sometimes over long periods of time. Ethnographic and historical research coupled with insights from the fields of institutional and organizational theory in the political and social sciences have built a convincing case that community institutions and values can be a source of strength and resilience rather than an obstacle to change. Government regulations reinforced community action to make Japan self-sufficient in timber and forest products while increasing forest cover during the period of self-imposed isolation and autarky from the seventeenth to late nineteenth centuries (McKean 1992; Totman 1989). A pathbreaking study of irrigation systems in Andhra Pradesh in south India showed how village-based institutions regulate a complex agricultural landscape involving different land users and livestock owners (Wade 1988). Accumulating evidence of communities' capacity to manage natural resources constituted the empirical foundation on which to build theoretical frameworks to explain what it is about community that creates capacity to engage in collective action to care for and regulate natural resources, including forests.

Community management requires collective action, decision-making, and conflict resolution with respect to a commonly held resource or services provided by the resource. In distinguishing between common property resources and open-access resources, scholars such as Ostrom have shown that under certain social, political, and environmental conditions, communities have the will and the capacity to craft institutions for effective management of resources held in common. Ostrom and others propose that the conditions under which institutions for common-pool resource management can exert effective control and governance over the resource include a clear understanding of who is and who is not a member of the community with access to the resource; the authority to set and enforce the community's own rules and penalties for utilization or abuse of the resource; and a belief that management of the resource can yield net tangible benefits in terms of income, products, and services (Ostrom 1992). The rules governing matsutake harvesting in Naidu village in Yunnan (chapter 2 above), for example, conform to these predictions of common property theory, although it remains to be seen whether the community-based management regime that is evolving will have the resilience to adapt to changing markets and to further possible changes in government policies regarding rights and access to forested land.

If earlier theories of social change saw the norms and values of community as hindering progress, a more recent recasting of these bonds as "social capital" has opened the way for a more nuanced understanding of the mechanisms facilitating and mediating relationships within a community and between people and the environment. The premise is that where people experience a "shared present, past and future" (McCay 2001:185) they will interact and communicate their observations and responses to shared experience. Over time, norms and values emerge that build trust, permit expectations of reciprocity, and facilitate the exchange of information. It is these emergent qualities that constitute social capital and facilitate collective action (Castle 2002:332–37; B. Miller 1992:29–31).[3] Social capital may be a resource fostering collective action, while at the same time it may also operate as a mechanism deployed in the form of social sanctions to enforce adherence to community norms and decisions (Etzioni 1996). In studying the response of a forest community in northern California to a halt in commercial logging, Danks has documented the importance of social capital in forging a consensus between different interest groups in the search for creative solutions, but she has also pointed out that social capital alone has a limited effect without physical capital such as communications equipment and office space or financial capital such as the funding needed to organize and engage in lobbying activities (2000:41).

In its evolution into a positive force as a source of social capital, community has become an "enchanting concept" (Agrawal 1999) charged with the hopes of international development practitioners as well as governmental and nongovernmental institutions for a new strategy to realize their various visions of a better future. As an antonym to earlier top-down models of development, community has often been placed, implicitly at least, in opposition to wider institutional forces such as the state and market. Closer examination shows, however, that communities are situated within webs of exchanges and interaction with other communities and are nested in hierarchical layers of unequal relationships with powerful individuals, governments, and markets. Community is the site of relations and connections, not separations (Li 2001:158). Agrawal's statement that "the consequent entrenchment of community took place, it should be obvious, in interactions with the state" (1997:24)[4] concisely captures the irony, for example, that the Kangra forest management cooperatives (chapter 5) were originally a creation of the colonial authorities of the Punjab.

Community has spatial and social dimensions, both of which are implicit in the invocation of community for improved forest and resource management, but both of which are easily distorted if treated simplistically without regard to the specific geography and history of any community. The appeal of community in the search for a realignment of relations between humans and the environment remains rooted, however, in the belief that a convergence of local knowledge, common values, and bonds of trust and reciprocity grows from the shared experience of a particular place.

Problematizing the Community

Community has many, sometimes conflicting, dimensions, which can unsettle the assumption that it is the place where interactions between natural capital (the forest resource) and social capital might be most effectively negotiated. Ecological, social, and administrative boundaries rarely coincide to define a community spatially. Communities are not socially homogenous entities and may in fact be highly inequitable. Many traditional communities are strongly patriarchal, marked by severe imbalances of power. Traditional leaders may be tainted by collaboration with a discredited, unjust regime, as is the case in some communities in South Africa (Kepe 1998). Occupation, gender, and ethnicity can all be markers of identity in the same individual at different times. Assumptions that resource-dependent communities are uniformly impoverished and are therefore suitable targets for community-based resource management programs are condescending or misguided, forcing people into futures envisioned by outside agents, not by members of the communities themselves (Li 2002:279). A critical appreciation of the multifaceted nature of community should contribute to crafting more robust institutions for community-based resource management.

Communities of Place: Questions of Boundaries and Scale

The simplest description of community might be "people who live within certain spatial or geographic boundaries"—who have a shared experience of a common place. Living and working together in the same environmental conditions, a group of people can envision a common future or "common environmental imaginaries" (Peet and Watts 1996:30), which is the essential first step in building the social bonds and trust needed to move toward that future (B. Miller 1992:29–30). Each producers' association near Mazagão in Brazil (chapter 4) serves all the residents living along the banks of one Igarapé (stream). The boundaries of an association define a clear geographical space, and in representing all the residents along the Igarapé, the association is recognized as the institutional manifestation of the community. The association, at the same time, is accepted as the legitimate arbiter of who is in the community and who is not, since all residents must belong to it and since new residents can move into the area only with its approval.

Such clarity is not the norm, however. In Botswana, communities (for the purposes of the CBNRM policy) are defined as people living in or around a wildlife management area (WMA) or a controlled hunting area (CHA). WMAs and CHAs are clearly defined, mapped geographical spaces, based on an ecological appraisal of appropriate land use. There is no doubt about who is and who is not a resident of the communities in these areas. It is not unusual, though, to find very different sets of resource users incorporated within the physical boundaries of a community. A community-based organization can apply for and receive government approval to manage its natural resources, but it may be difficult to reconcile the different interests of resource users, who may include pastoralists and hunter-gatherers in the same community (Rozmeijer and van der Jagt 2000; Rozmeijer 2003). Sharing a bounded space and the same environmental conditions may facilitate building community, but they are not a sufficient condition for cooperative or collective action (Agrawal 1997:18).

In practice, the boundary defining a community in most CBFM programs and projects is an administrative unit of local government rather than any ecological unit (a watershed, a mountain, or a forest). The case of Botswana—and of many failed watershed management programs—demonstrates the difficulty of mapping human communities directly onto ecosystems, but caution is also needed in assuming that administrative boundaries map neatly onto the shared space and environmental imaginaries of a community. China is sometimes credited with one of the world's most extensive areas of community-managed forestland (White and Martin 2002:6–7) but community refers to the lowest unit of government administration, the municipality (*zhen*), which often incorporates several village committees (*cunwei*). Decisions about allocation and utilization of forested land are made by the government organs of the municipality in accordance with production or planting targets, policies, and regulations established by the local forestry bureau of the state forestry administration. In some places, resource users have been able to create village-based institutions controlling access to and utilization of some NTFPs, such as matsutake in Naidu (chapter 2), but barring these exceptions, management of community forests usually remains firmly under some form of state direction and control (Xu and Zuo 2003).

Many of the tasks in forest management are well suited to the capacities of a community-based institution where people are in direct contact with each other and the resource. Adjudicating claims of crop damage by red colobus monkeys around Jozani forest (chapter 3) requires experience of local cropping patterns, familiarity with the movements of families of colobus monkeys, and the trust and respect of affected farmers. The members of the Jozani Environmental Conservation Association (JECA) are residents of the villages immediately surrounding the forest and have the shared experience and personal relations to make the association's decisions legitimate and enforceable. It is more common, though, for a forest or the territory of large wildlife species such as the elephant to cover a geographical area larger than the area under the control of one community. Several communities may be responsible for one ecological unit (forest), making it necessary to have institutional mechanisms to mediate, adjudicate, and resolve boundary disputes and conflicts between different communities using the same resource (Agrawal 1997:31). In Zanzibar, JECA and the Misali Island Conservation Association (MICA) are expected to perform this function in the future, although during the formative years of the community conservation programs in both locations, CARE International has mediated between the affected communities and the Department of Commercial Crops, Fruit, and Fisheries (DCCFF).

Not all management tasks, however, are suited to the scale of day-to-day experience and personal interactions. A single community in a remote, peripheral area is in a weak position to take advantage of market opportunities for products and services derived from forest management. The small scale of a community may also compromise its capacity to face threats from outside or to negotiate with larger, more powerful entities such as private corporate interests or changing national policies. Joining forces with others facing similar challenges is one strategy that can amplify the otherwise weak voices of individual communities. As members of the Amapá Rural Workers' Union (SINTRA), the Mazagão producers' associations have access to a powerful and respected organization well placed to represent their interests in Brasília. In the Kangra valley, the Himachal Pradesh Cooperatives Development Union has acted on behalf of the CFSs to put pressure on the Forestry Department to accept the cooperative societies as legitimate partners in the JFM program.[5] Whether these larger institutions are third-party intermediaries such as CARE International or are national organizations acting on behalf of communities, it takes careful work and negotiation to build partnerships that do not overwhelm or force their own agenda on the community-based institutions.[6]

Social Dimensions: Communities of Occupation, Identity, and More

In the four stories that form the first half of this book, residents of each community share a common experience of place, but they also share a diversity of occupations, social status, age group, gender, and cultural markers such as diet, language, or religion with other groups and individuals in the same location or in a wider sphere of activities and exchange. Place is only one of many dimensions of community with which the same individual might identify.

In Naidu, place maps neatly onto community. All residents in the village are entitled to harvest matsutake, and the elected village government enforces rules during the harvesting season to ensure that there are no free-riders in the community (table 2.1). The rules for matsutake harvesting and marketing, however, do not cover other activities in day-to-day village life, and the community in this case could be described as an occupational community formed around sustainable harvesting and marketing of one product, matsutake mushrooms. The experience of defending Naidu's claim to the surrounding forest during decades of often tense relations with the forestry department has forged a common "environmental imaginary" in the village, but the community has so far chosen to take collective action only in relation to its main economic occupation, matsutake harvesting and marketing.

Culture is a powerful marker, which is a source of the shared norms and values of community. Ethnographers and anthropologists may struggle to capture the essence of the caboclo identity, but the people who live along the waterways of the Brazilian Amazon have no doubt that they are caboclos, the people who live and work in the forest, who eat açaí and bicho (chapter 4, p. 50). Caboclo identity is closely tied to the landscape of the tidal flats, forests, and waterways of the várzea, but each of the communities near Mazagão is also defined by the Igarapé on which it lives. Being a caboclo involves knowing and working the forest, so it is not surprising that the more formal community institution—the producers' association—does not play a part in the household's production in the forest, but is called on to represent the community in its interactions with the markets beyond the Igarapé and to monitor compliance with rules and practices agreed by association members. Both place and a sense of cultural identification shape the community, although neither is sufficient to constitute community on its own.

Multiple Interests and Overlapping Identities

The legislation that established the Kangra CFSs specified that a cooperative society could be formed when three quarters of the landowners over eighteen years of age in a village agreed to its formation (chapter 5, p. oo). Administrative space (the village as demarcated by the revenue authorities) marked the physical boundaries of the cooperatives, but age, class, and gender[7] marked their social boundaries. Registered cooperatives, whose members were a subset of all the residents in the geographical community, became managers of all state forested land and any private forested lands that members brought into the scheme. The construction of community in this case entrenched differentiation along several social and economic axes—a historical legacy of inequity that the contemporary Forestry Department is turning to its advantage in its efforts to replace the cooperatives with JFM committees.

Another example from Yunnan Province in China illustrates how community disaggregates into multiple overlapping interests and identities operating simultaneously in synergy and in contention.[8] The story tells of women in a village taking action when they felt that outside interests in collusion with local officials threatened to destroy the forests surrounding their village, but it has an uncertain outcome due to constant realignments of different interest groups within the village.

The residents of the village identify themselves as a distinct ethnic group that is not recognized by the government. The village is officially designated a Naxi village, although residents speak a language unintelligible to Naxi people and they claim separate customs and a separate history. They are proud of the many associations (*Hua*)[9] that help to organize village life and promote cooperation between different groups. Older people belong to the *Himmo Hua*. Men between the ages of sixteen and sixty belong to an archery group called the *Yimei Hua*. Women belong to the *Mohe Hua*. One of the customary roles of the *Mohe Hua* has been to provide food and drink at funerals as well as fuelwood for cremation pyres. During the late 1970s and early 1980s women in the *Mohe Hua* worried that in the shift from collective to individual production they had lost some of the positive aspects of the collective, such as preventing livestock from damaging crops. The group arranged for one member each day to keep watch and to fine the owners of any offending animals, using the income to purchase a small gift (a blanket, a thermos) every year on International Women's Day for each household in the village.

PLATE 6. Members of the women's group collect firewood and pine needles in the village-owned collective forest in Yunnan Province.   PHOTO: AUTHOR

In 1995 a company owned by the township government received a concession to log the forested hills surrounding the village. Legally, the company had the right to log only state-owned forest, but villagers suspected collusion and profiteering on the part of the village government when the company also began to log village-owned collective forest and even the freehold forest allocated to households.[10] Despite villagers' demands for payment of a fee and some controls on logging, harvesting continued, leading to a free-for-all in which men in the village also took to logging and selling timber. Fearing landslides and damage to their fields, the women's group decided to extend their livestock-watching activities to monitoring the forest. In 1998 the village government (under pressure from the central government to reduce forest degradation) approved a set of rules the women had drawn up, limiting harvesting and grazing, requiring payment of a logging fee, controlling harvesting of matsutake, and imposing fines on offenders. The group now patrols the forest and is convinced that they are more effective than men would be: "Women have to go into the hills to collect firewood and pine needles,[11] so we see what is going on. If men saw something happening, they would just fight.

Women try to solve problems. Also, it is not acceptable here to hit a woman, so no-one would dare to try to fight with a woman forest guard."

Little more than a year after approving the rules, the village party secretary announced that the document approving the forest management rules—which he had signed a year earlier—was not valid. He accused the women's group of undermining the unity of the village with unnecessarily strict rules, causing conflicts with neighboring communities (of different ethnicities). He claimed that the forest no longer needed their protection since "state forests are under the care of the production brigade." According to the women's group, the village and township governments now harvest timber whenever they want, justifying their action as "taking care" of the forest. The women's group continues to patrol and to enforce their rules in the village-owned collective forests and in the freehold forests allocated to households, which are visibly in better condition than the state-owned forest.

The story shows that the unique life experience of each individual sets her or him at the center of a network of relationships built on shared—or conflicting—interests and values with others living in the same place. The overlapping facets of community have in some respects empowered the community to act, and in other respects they are a continuing source of tension. Village government is elected (though candidates must be approved by the local Communist Party) but responds to demands from higher levels of government as well as from its village constituency. The villagers share norms and values derived from their construction of a separate ethnic identity, which reinforces their determination to defend their resources from the perceived incursions of outsiders from other communities and the township logging company. Women have also acted in the context of their gendered roles within the household (concerned at the loss of fuelwood and pine needles and the threat to their fields) and as members of the *Mohe Hua*—a traditional village institution.

The recognition of a plurality of interests is inseparable from a recognition of converging interests within a community. There is rich ethnographic evidence that individuals or even whole communities may consciously draw on different determinants of identity at different times in order to take advantage of new opportunities. In Kenya, Bettine Ng'weno has shown how the coastal Digo people have negotiated and renegotiated land ownership and inheritance, appealing at times to their historical heritage as a matrilineal clan-based society and claiming at others times a contemporary religious identity embodied in Islamic law that explicitly transcends community and customary law (2001). In the Philippines, communities in Palawan have strategically identified themselves as "indigenous," despite a history of migration and intermarriage with others, in order to take advantage of government provisions allowing exclusive access and stewardship rights to forested land for indigenous peoples (McDermott 2001).

These examples do not exhaust the possibilities for parsing the social dimensions of community. Occupation, cultural identity, religion, age, class, and gender are among the most public expressions of different interests within a community, and others could be added to the list, such as level of education or seasonal residence (nomadic pastoralists, seasonal forest workers). What is more significant, however, than the observation that communities are not homogenous is the evidence that individuals identify with multiple interests: the women's group in Yunnan took action as women, as farmers concerned about landslides, and as ordinary villagers confronting official corruption; a resident of Naidu might see himself as a Tibetan, a village elder, a high school graduate, and the owner of several yaks. The challenge for community-based resource management institutions is to embrace and respect plurality while searching for the common ground of shared interests and values.

Shifting Boundaries and Changing Interests

The bounded community is neither static nor uncontested. Boundaries, however constituted, mark the physical contours and the configuration of interests in a community at one moment in time. In a study of a northern Californian community faced with the closure of a timber mill after severe reductions in harvesting on the neighboring national forest, Danks notes:

> Designating what community is and who are its members is not only an analytical issue but a political one as well. If special benefits accrue to members of a group, such as a community, then the definition of who is included in that group becomes very important—and therefore often contested. . . . The question is not only "what group is the legitimate local representative, but also . . . what set of interests do these people or groups represent?"
>
> —DANKS 2000:60–61

Politically imposed boundaries change in response to political imperatives, as demonstrated by repeated disputes over the redrawing of district boundaries or parliamentary constituencies in the United States and other electoral democracies. Political boundaries exist only as long as the state has the power and legitimacy to enforce them, with alternative territorial or communal entities emerging at other times, as has been seen in the case of failed states such as Somalia. International environmental organizations have also redrawn boundaries as they map the distribution of vegetation and fauna to identify ecoregions to be set aside for the purpose of conservation—a practice charged with assumptions about the composition of "original natural communities," the impossibility of coexistence between humans and endangered species, and priorities in land use (Brosius 2004).

Even where the physical location of a boundary is constant, its meaning may change with time, depending on who is observing it. Fortmann (1995) describes the different stories about the 1966 fencing of grazing land in Zimbabwe, as told first by older men in a communal area on one side of the fence and then by the white settler who formerly owned the neighboring farm and erected the fence. Examining the narratives against the backdrop of the present, Fortmann demonstrates that the story of the fence as told in the communal area tells of more than a grievance, but also serves to underline contemporary demands for renewed or continued access to resources on commercial farmland now being taken over by black commercial farmers with the support of the state. When built, the fence had represented the injustice of the racial division of society, while thirty years later it had become the physical manifestation of the unfulfilled promises of a new postindependence order.

On a larger scale, the process of land restitution in South Africa has brought the meaning of boundaries into stark relief as groups dispossessed under the apartheid regime struggle to regain rights to their lands and as other disenfranchised groups seek to retain their identity and sources of livelihood without resurrecting the constructed racial categories of the past. The outcome of negotiations between national parks and communities forcibly relocated in the past has often left the boundaries of the protected areas intact, returning ownership to the community while restricting land use within the boundaries to activities agreed to be compatible with conservation objectives.[12]

For some South African communities, the past and present meanings of boundary-making are particularly painful to confront. In Northern Cape Province, the descendants of the precolonial people of Namaqualand had been classified under apartheid as "coloured" and assigned land in "Coloured Rural Areas" held in trust by the state. Although they were not of mixed race (the normal definition of "coloured" under apartheid), many of them had lost their original Nama language and used Afrikaans, the language of the dominant white population, as their lingua franca. Under the Transformation of Certain Rural Areas Act of 1998 the trust lands were to be transferred "to the people or representative structures," following a referendum on the new form of ownership and representation.

In the course of extended public consultations, it became clear that while the racial classifications of the past had confined the residents of the former trust lands to the least productive grazing lands, people had, over time, come to perceive the land as theirs. Their communal ownership of land had become a source of an identity that they feared losing under a new dispensation. Fear and mistrust led at times to resistance to the mapping and marking of boundaries that were a part of the consultation. In one homestead more than two hours' drive from the nearest town, Om Piet, the eighty-year-old head of the household, refused for many months to allow surveyors onto his land. Referring to a compilation of all references to land that he could find in the Bible, he told representatives of the NGO working with the community that "the land belongs only to God and it is not for us to mark it and divide it" (author's field notes, November 2002). The outcome of the January 2003 referendum in five areas that voted was that one area chose to transfer its land to the municipality, the vote was too close to be decisive in a second, and three others voted to keep land ownership in the hands of newly created communal property areas.[13]

The multiple and changing layers of meaning attached to politically constructed identities such as "coloured" and "Nama" are reminders that with the passage of time the social categories and configurations of interests that characterize a community are no less fluid than the physical boundaries that mark who is in and who is out. Ethnicity, occupation, gender, or caste, for example, have all been marks at different times either of subordination and inferiority or as shared identities around which to mobilize in pursuit of justice and a voice in community decision-making. The support of international advocacy groups for indigenous people's land rights has encouraged many groups such as the Nama to claim or reclaim an identity that would formerly have had little resonance with their aspirations or their daily lives.[14]

If perceptions of community identity change over time, assumptions about the interests of different groups within a community may also have to be revised with changing circumstances. There are reports, for example, that young people in Indian communities today are less willing to commit time and energy to JFM committees than people of the same age had been ten to fifteen years ago. For some, at least, new opportunities for employment in urban areas offer better prospects for an improved life, eclipsing their interest in the modest increases in income that can be derived from the community's forest activities. At the same time, as described in chapter 5, the Indian forest service has questioned the legitimacy of the Kangra CFSs on the grounds that their membership does not include women and the landless—two interest groups within forest communities that have historically been excluded from decision-making about land use and are now invoked as key user-groups by an agency that is widely perceived as consistently ignoring them and failing to serve their interests in both the past and present.[15]

Finally, the composition of communities is constantly in a state of transition. Migration into and out of an area changes the age and gender structure of communities and may bring an entirely new group of residents who do not necessarily share the values of longer-term residents. In Brazil, the caboclo identity embraces movement into and out of the community while retaining a distinct sense of difference from the so-called colonists, people the caboclos see as not knowing the land or working in the forest. In upland Indonesia and the Philippines, by contrast, migration into the uplands has had the effect of blurring distinctions between indigenous and migrant land use practices and dependence on forest resources (Li 2002:268). Forest communities in the western United States are adjusting to a changing labor force as reduced levels of timber harvest are accompanied by a surge in commercial harvesting of NTFPs such as mushrooms and floral greens by a new generation of forest workers, many of whom are of Central American or southeast Asian origin.

A particularly dramatic demographic transformation is taking place in resource-dependent communities in eastern and southern Africa due to AIDS. Statistics document the exceptionally high mortality rates among men between the ages of twenty and forty-five. Anecdotal evidence suggests that during the mid-1990s in Uganda the impact of AIDS extended to changing practices in the management of trees. The costs of caring for a sick relative drove women to harvest forest trees illegally for sale as a short-term strategy to raise money for treatment. At the same time, surviving widows and families were planting more trees around their homesteads and in their fields as a longer-term strategy to generate a regular flow of additional income from the sale of lopped branches for fuelwood or charcoal. The disease has not only shifted decision-making in affected communities from men to women, but has also changed the preferences and priorities of village women with respect to forests and trees (William Gombya-Ssembajjwe, personal communication).

To recognize that communities may have porous or shifting boundaries and that their members may have different yet overlapping interests is not to question their capacity to act as managers of forests and natural resources. It does mean though, that there may be times when they look to partners outside the community for support and assistance in building more resilient community-based institutions accommodating different interests or capable of adjusting to changing circumstances.[16] To ignore the question of "who is the community?" however, is to invite disputes and conflict over who bears the costs and who benefits from community action, undermining decision-making and compromising the ability to monitor utilization of the resource.

The Heterogeneous Community as Resource Manager

The utilitarian rationale for invoking community in forest and resource management argues that social capital builds social fencing, which protects the resource and facilitates more effective monitoring and enforcement of rules regulating resource utilization. The ethical argument focuses instead on communities' rights of access and on their right to derive benefits from the resources on which they depend. From either perspective, it is necessary to know who is in the community and who represents it. Diverse and changing interests within and between communities weaken both the utilitarian and the ethical arguments for community involvement in resources management. Without deliberate efforts to negotiate consensus and to respect boundaries between communities and between different interests within communities, even the most carefully crafted visions of the future may not be realized.

In 1996 the Kenya Pastoralists' Forum—an NGO representing the interests of pastoralists—organized an information workshop in the northern town of Isiolo for representatives of local pastoral communities, to debate the implications of subdividing group ranches, a legally recognized form of communal land. One of the workshop facilitators appealed to his audience to reject subdivision so that the pastoralist community in this semiarid area could continue to enjoy the benefits of extensive tracts of grazing land. Workshop participants were mostly male, representing groups as diverse as the cattle-herding Samburu, Somali camel traders, and the nomadic Rendille, prompting one man to ask, "In this group, just who is the community?" Focused on the complexity of balancing collective ownership of land against privatization, the representative of the Pastoralists' Forum brushed the question aside, saying, "That is a theoretical and academic question that need not take up our time here."

In the years following the workshop, his optimism has unfortunately been shown to have been misplaced. Far from being academic and theoretical, the question of "who is the community?" has been a source of tensions and conflicts between different groups, blocking attempts to develop sustainable, community-based income-generating activities such as the sale of gum arabic collected from acacia trees, ecotourism, or the use of a large area of grassland as a holding area for livestock to be sold to meat companies.

Local elites easily exploit divisions within communities to dominate local institutions, but they risk isolation and a lack of support when those institutions are threatened. The Kangra CFSs have almost certainly suffered from their neglect of the diversity of interests within the community. A more inclusive institution could maybe have launched a popular movement in defense of local interests against the Forestry Department's actions. The 1940 decision to define only landowners as the community of forest managers in Kangra jeopardized the long-term future of an institution that might, despite its flaws, have offered a framework for community-based management of forest resources in the valley.

Change and diversity are especially difficult to confront in reconstituting shattered communities that have experienced forcible dispossession, dispersal, and loss of identity. Native American communities, South African communities evicted from their homes during apartheid, and Aboriginal Australians—all have lost their lands, have seen their institutions of governance deliberately dismantled, and have been subjected to attempts to eradicate their cultures and even their languages. They are not alone, but are perhaps among the best known shattered communities. Even if some form of restitution takes place, it is followed by a slow process of reconstruction and recovery of identity, accompanied by a difficult search for legitimate institutions to reach consensus and make decisions on behalf of the community. Mediation and facilitation from outside can sometimes assist in brokering an agreement that allows the community to move forward.

Shattered, splintered communities are faced with a painful search for legitimate decision-making institutions and the task of reconstructing a shared environmental imaginary. Other communities with a less traumatic history still face the challenge of addressing pluralism and diversity of interests, but they can build on existing institutions and the overlapping of interests that attends diversity. Individuals in a community experience their lives through the many facets of their identity. A fisher on Misali Island, for example, shares some values with one group—octopus fishers on Misali perhaps—and others with another group—woodcutters in the mangrove forest surrounding their village on the island of Pemba perhaps. Plurality of interests in the community makes it likely that there will in fact be areas or domains of converging mutual interest. Institutions that open space for the expression of diverse interests and offer a forum for reaching accommodation or understanding are likely to have the legitimacy to make and implement decisions in the name of the community.

However inclusive the management institution, it is necessary to recognize that it will not eliminate existing power relations within the community. In the Middle Hills of Nepal, there have been cases where merchants from nearby villages who are not forest users have become members of registered forest associations, leading to a breakdown in the associations' functions and renewed degradation of the forest (Varughese 1999:214–16). In the mountain areas, the failure to include nomadic pastoralists who are seasonal forest users has compromised communities' ability to manage forests, as the pastoralists have resorted to illegal use of forests or have turned to subsistence farming on ecologically fragile hillsides (Winrock International 2002:17–18).

The entrenched power relations embodied in gender are usually inadequately addressed, if at all. JFM regulations in India require women's representatives on village committees. Long-standing gender roles within communities, however, make it difficult for women to translate representation into substantive bargaining power and the ability to influence or shape the committees' decisions (Agarwal 2001).

Active participation in a community institution is not free of cost. Participants need to be able to devote time and energy to attend meetings and to take part in implementing decisions. With the proliferation of development projects, there is a risk that participation may become an inequitable burden, excluding the very people the projects are supposed to benefit (Vasavada, Mishra, and Bates 1999). A member of the Kazingo forest management committee near Rwenzori National Park in Uganda told an East African forum of community groups managing natural resources: "People see us spending time going up the mountain [to monitor resource harvesting by the community], attending community meetings now and then, all without pay, and they say ... look at them, they have time to waste" (quoted in Watkin 2001:25). If institutions are to be local and provide benefits equitably to the community as a whole, they must be inserted carefully into existing patterns of social obligations and work schedules, otherwise only elite members of the community will be able to take part.

Conclusion: The Intangible but Indispensable Community

Community is an appealing but vexed concept invoked at least as often by way of contrast to an alternative—the state, the region, the bureaucracy—as it is for tangible or functional attributes of its own. Almost any attempted definition of what community is rather than what it is not is open to criticism as being too restrictive—if it is not too broad. It can be shown to be ahistorical or apolitical, and it can be analyzed as a hindrance to change or as a vehicle to empower local interests. It is not necessary, however, to appeal to an idealized vision of homogenous and harmonious communities to recognize that where groups of people live in proximity to a natural resource on which they have some level of dependence, they are likely to share an interest in its future, with experience of reaching consensus when needed to achieve common objectives.

Rather than seeking to define community, it may be more useful to identify some characteristics that foster the kinds of trust, shared values, and expectations of reciprocity that build the capacity to take action in pursuit of a collective interest. Shared space with defined environmental endowments and conditions shapes the common environmental imaginaries through which the community articulates its beliefs, values, and goals with respect to natural resources. Physical boundaries do not in themselves define community, but clear rules of inclusion and exclusion establish a context for expectations of shared values and reciprocity. It is important for there to be direct relations and communications between members of the community. Finally, communication is the medium of social exchange that forges bonds between individuals, facilitates the sharing of knowledge and experience, and allows negotiations between different interests.

Under these conditions, community is likely to be the level of decision-making and action where interactions between natural capital (the forest resource) and social capital are most effectively negotiated to realize a shared vision of sustainability, equity, and empowerment. Nevertheless, not all decisions about resource use require collective action and consensus. Nor is resource management the only domain of decision-making faced by an individual or a household. In Mazagão, individual households are responsible for managing and harvesting the trees on their plots. The producers' association processes and markets the timber. The mandate of the community-based institution includes only those areas of community life where collective action secures more reliable stewardship of the resource and more equitable distribution of benefits.

Community emerges where people recognize a shared interest in a shared space. Communities gain the strength to negotiate with others and to take action in defense of their interests where they recognize diversity and work with the multiplicity of skills and experience that comes from difference. Ideally, they combine principles of justice and equity with a capacity for collective action in a cohesive community-based institution, whose local knowledge equips it to care for the resource more effectively than the state or other administrative agencies. In practice, inequalities within communities, a multiplicity of identities and interests, and changing demographics make justice, cohesion, and local knowledge elusive qualities. Community-based institutions are, more realistically, the fora in which diverse actors negotiate and renegotiate to identify a domain of overlapping interests and concerns. The challenge is to build resilient community-based institutions that balance plurality of interests and the cohesion of shared interests, norms, and values.

8

The Capacity to Manage

When we allocated freehold mountain land there were no trees and nobody really cared what went on. Now that trees are coming back, we are seeing all kinds of conflicts. There are conflicts inside families, between families and user groups, between villages, and between counties. Some places have set up local organizations to deal with this, but we need to know more about how to put together and work with local organizations.

—YUNNAN PROVINCE FORESTRY DEPARTMENT OFFICIAL
(AUTHOR'S FIELD NOTES, KUNMING, AUGUST 1993)

IN THE early 1990s China moved from complete state control over forest resources toward conceding a degree of management authority to communities or households. It was not long before the complexity of the endeavor began to awe forestry staff. Over the previous decade, the de-collectivization of agriculture had proceeded remarkably smoothly, with an almost immediate response on the part of farmers, reflected in increased grain production and rising household incomes. Involving communities in forest management proved to be a very different task. Degraded land in many places did regenerate rapidly, but new areas of contestation emerged. Farmers chafed against restrictions on harvesting and selling timber. Government planning targets requiring large-scale plantings of a limited number of species led to glutted markets and low prices. Conflicts proliferated over boundaries, illegal harvesting, and violations of rules of access and forest use. Forest management, it transpired, consisted of many activities and skills unfamiliar to forestry officials, from negotiating and securing consensus about the goals of management to communicating technical skills to understanding markets.

This chapter turns from the complexities of defining community to ask what skills and capacities are involved in management—the other half of community management. The chapter first asks whether communities are in fact becoming partners in forest management—or are they being kept out of the forest with offers of alternative, though not always viable, land uses and sources of livelihoods? The chapter then asks what skills and capacities does it take to engage in forest management, and do communities have access to the support and assistance that would empower them to manage effectively for the long-term benefit of the whole community?

What Constitutes Management in the Forest?

Forest-dependent people have always manipulated vegetation to produce a preferred mix of species and products. Practices such as controlled burning, planting seedlings in fallow fields, propagation by root suckers, pruning, and coppicing all witness to a common human ability to learn from observation and to apply what is learned to achieve desired outcomes (Donovan 2001:8–10). There is little evidence, however, that the practitioners of these techniques conceive of them in terms of a discrete category of "management" distinct from daily activities such as gathering and production of food, fibers, medicines, or materials for shelter. Forest management as an organized undertaking following codified procedures and principles has its roots in European estate forests in the seventeenth century and in the government resource management agencies of the more recent past.[1]

Theoretical analyses of the meaning of resource management describe a process of determining goals, in the form of a desired mix of material, ecological, and spiritual services, and the application of technical skills to a resource to achieve those goals. In this analysis, resource management is a process of appropriation and redistribution of natural assets disaggregated into five components that together constitute a management system: access and control over the resource,[2] utilization of the resource, systems for acting on the resource, mechanisms for allocation and distribution, and mechanisms for transfer of the resource (Wéber 1996). Management involves decisions about relations between people and ecosystems, how to take action to implement decisions, and how to distribute the benefits of those actions.

Forest management as a professionalized activity has evolved over time. It has moved from an almost exclusive interest in wood and timber to encompass a range of other products and services. The international discourse of conservation and sustainable development has introduced explicit goals of sustaining biodiversity and promoting intergenerational equity. Recognition of the rights of marginalized groups resident in or near forest areas has drawn attention to aspects of forest resources that have not previously had a place in the profession, such as respect for the cultural values of indigenous people or opportunities for employment. In describing his people's goals for forest management, the coordinator of forest and wildlife activities for the Huron-Wendat Nation in Québec placed the need for winter employment for Huron-Wendat youth as his first priority, followed by the need to improve moose habitat—the symbol of his nation (Louis Lesage, personal communication). In a country where forest management has emphasized economies of scale in timber production and reduction of labor costs through mechanization, the Huron-Wendat Nation has had to take the initiative to enter into an agreement with the faculty of forestry at Québec's Laval University to devise and test new forest management technologies to meet these demands.[3]

The products and services derived from different forested ecosystems offer an almost inexhaustible range of management objectives—and opportunities for contestation and negotiation about them. In savannah woodlands, wildlife management and tourism might conflict with grazing, charcoal burning, or the gathering of wild foods. In cleared fallow fields in the montane forests of southeast Asia, food, medicinal herbs, and fuelwood may be of most value to some members of a community, while logs from commercial species may be the main source of income for others. In the Amazon basin, rubber tapping might be compatible with hunting and gathering but not with timber harvesting. Even a commitment to leave a forested landscape untouched to conserve biodiversity represents a management decision not to intervene rather than to utilize the resource directly. Where options are not mutually exclusive or where there is sufficient forested land for users to have access to separate areas in order to avoid incompatible uses, management may be more concerned with optimizing production and less with processes of decision-making and setting priorities. In practice, however, there are few such places, and they are getting fewer. At its heart, forest management is the art of coming to a decision about who will have access to forests, for what and how, in a context of changing patterns of demand, use, and dependence on the resource.

Managing Forests or Keeping the Community out of the Forest?

It is still unusual to find governments "letting go" (Alden Wily 1997b) and empowering communities to make fundamental decisions about their use of forests. State agencies commonly offer management rights to communities only over degraded land or land of low productivity,[4] retaining full control over the most productive forests or allocating concessions to large industrial operations. Agreements between resource management agencies and communities tend to be framed within the agencies' existing conservation or reforestation agendas, offering a share of revenue or the right to collect and market some forest products with little scope for local decisions about goals and objectives (Larson and Ribot 2004; Ribot 2002; Vasan 2001; Xu and Zuo 2003). The phenomenon is so pronounced in some states in India that the joint forest management (JFM) program has been accused of treating community involvement as a form of cheap or even unpaid labor on land that the Forestry Department itself is unable to restore. Describing planning for JFM in Uttarakhand, Madhu Sarin observes: "The plans were actually written by Forest Department staff and subsequently implemented with the involvement of only the *sarpanch* and/or some of the elected panchayat members or by the *Pradhan* of the Gram Panchayat. Villagers provided only wage labor" (Sarin et al. 2003:56).

Where communities have succeeded in restoring and rehabilitating degraded land, the newly valuable resource once again attracts the attention of forest agencies. In Nepal, for example, community forest user groups have been so successful that the authorities are now demanding that they pay a higher percentage of their income to the government and have introduced more stringent technical requirements in the preparation of forest management plans as a strategy to oblige the groups to depend more closely on the state's own forestry technicians (Gautam, Shivakoti, and Webb 2004:139).

It is common that communities are not only constrained in the basic decisions they can make about management goals, but are also prevented from deriving substantial revenue from forest resources (Dove 1993). Agreements between communities and government resource management agencies often give rights to gather non-timber forest products (NTFPs) while restricting their sale and retaining timber harvesting rights or the rights to grant concessions to commercial companies. In Kangra, it is the state Forestry Department, not the forest management cooperatives, that auctions the rights to tap resin, one of the most valuable commercial products from the pine forests of the valley. Elsewhere in India, Saxena reports that until 2000 even the processing of brooms from grass collected by tribal village women in Orissa could legally be undertaken only by a government parastatal, which had been known to act against informal groups of gatherers trying to make and sell brooms in local markets (Saxena 2003:172).[5] Ironically, the parastatal that took action against the women's groups was the very government agency that had a mandate to advocate for the interests of tribal communities in the state.

Many internationally funded CBFM programs promote the harvesting and marketing of NTFPs as a source of income for forest communities. The products include herbal medicines, locally consumed foods (such as açaí in Mazagão), and materials (such as rattan) whose spatial distribution throughout the forest makes them difficult to harvest commercially by outsiders who do not know the forest environment well. While some NTFPs such as matsutake in Naidu do represent an important source of income, others may represent only a small and even insignificant element in household livelihoods. It is possible too that a focus on NTFPs and "new" sources of income from forests serves to deflect utilization from the most easily marketed forest products—timber, fuelwood, or charcoal. Where a NTFP does become valuable, governments again lose little time in imposing new controls on its harvest and sale. As the global demand for rattan soared in the 1980s, the Indonesian government first banned the export of raw rattan in 1986 and then extended the ban to exports of semiprocessed rattan in 1988. The intent was to stimulate value-added processing in Indonesia itself—albeit in industries associated with large industrial corporations or government parastatals, not in small enterprises in forest communities. The outcome was a shortage of processing capacity and a glut of unprocessed rattan on the market, substantially depressing the prices paid to forest-dwelling rattan harvesters (Fried 2000:231).

The apparently contradictory strategy of empowering communities to manage forests while restricting their activities to so-called minor forest products gives credence to Dove's contention that poverty, powerlessness, and exclusion from valuable resources are related and that the "search for 'new' sources of income for 'poor forest dwellers'" is often, in reality, a "search for opportunities that have no other claimants—a search for unsuccessful development alternatives" (1993:18). The devolution of management authority is accompanied by fears of continued or increased loss of forest cover, justifying the retention of agency control over timber production and management plans as a precautionary measure to ensure that forest cover is maintained or improved. The plausibility of such a justification is barely defensible, however, in the light of the alternative narrative of forest history that draws attention to the unsustainable levels of harvesting and exploitation of forest resources under state control.

There are many reminders around the world that community management does not necessarily ensure improved protection for biodiversity and forest resources.[6] Farmers and gold miners encroach on the forests of the Eastern Arc Mountains of East Africa (Newmark, Mariki, and Bayona 2004). In Papua New Guinea, community leaders have offered logging concessions to international timber corporations (Filer and Sekhran 1998; Marshall 1990). Nevertheless, there is evidence too that management by communities does not inevitably lead to degradation and that the outcome can be long-term maintenance or improvements in forest cover. Over the last four hundred years in China, the most sustainable forest management systems were those that were managed by smallholders and communities. Some of these systems continue to be practiced today, a testimony to their ecological viability and their resilience in the face of dramatic political upheavals and social change (Menzies 1994).

There is contemporary evidence, too, that improved stewardship is related to the degree of decision-making authority enjoyed by community managers. In the initial phase of a program to return control of the Duru-Haitemba forest in Tanzania to surrounding communities, suspicious villagers insisted that the majority of the products they were extracting from the government forest reserve were indispensable to their livelihoods and should not be subject to restrictions. When it became clear that full control over the forest really was being transferred to the village, they quickly enacted their own regulations controlling or prohibiting the extraction of many of the products they had previously identified as indispensable (Alden Wily 1997b:3). Management by communities is not inevitably a signal for uncontrolled and destructive exploitation, although it becomes problematic if the promises made to communities turn out, in practice, to be little more than efforts to limit utilization and to buy people's acquiescence to continued exclusion from the resource.

Capacity-Building for Effective Forest Management

Institutional and technical capacity-building for communities have become obligatory components of project documents in international development. Ironically, communities themselves have fewer opportunities than donors or NGOs to articulate their needs for skills and support. When forest communities or their representatives have had the opportunity, they have spoken of the need for access to legal and political mechanisms to secure their rights (Parsons and Prest 2003), technical support and facilitation in conflict mediation (Danks 2000), assistance in locating sources of funding (Watkin 2001), and the need for expertise in marketing (Bisong 1999). The capacities that would equip communities to manage forests can be described under five headings:

- the capacity to build community-level institutions to set priorities and to resolve or mediate conflicts
- the capacity to represent communities' interests in the wider social and political arena
- the technical capacity to manage the resource
- the capacity to participate as informed actors in markets
- the capacity to build community assets with benefits generated from managing the resource

The Capacity to Build Community-Level Institutions to
Set Priorities and to Resolve or Mediate Conflicts

Legitimacy, Representation, Conflict, and Mediation
A member of a community conservation committee near a national park in
northern Tanzania described the qualities of a good committee as one where
"people understand their jobs and responsibilities and attend meetings. If
you don't attend you should be out. It must follow up on agreed tasks. A committee is not doing its job if violations of the law are not being reported" (author's
field notes, Tarangire, August 2000). In his view, the committee must take
on the responsibilities of office and must carry out its tasks in a transparent
and accountable way. If these basic conditions are not met, the institution is
of no value to the community.

The committee member's statement summarizes the fundamental importance of an institution's legitimacy. If community management is to be an
alternative to the authoritarian model of management by a government agency,
then consensual community-based institutions for management must have
the legitimacy for their actions to be recognized as binding and for sanctions
against offenders to be enforced (Weber 1978:50–51). Fair representation and
accountability are fundamental in establishing an institution's legitimacy in
the eyes of the community. Without them, it will have to resort to coercion
to make and enforce decisions (Mascarenhas and Scarce 2004).

Institutions for community management face the challenge of demonstrating that all interests have an opportunity to be heard. Deeply entrenched
differences and hierarchies of power can undermine the capacity of a community institution to manage the resource. To create an institution where
representation is based on a defined set of stakeholders at one point in time
is likely to be problematic. It crystallizes a transient configuration of interests
and relationships. Individuals and their relationships to, their interests in, and
their expectations from the resource are constantly changing, however, and
institutions must be able to adjust and adapt, acting as a forum for continuing
negotiations in response to change rather than seeking to reach an agreement
shaped by the moment, which sets a rigid framework for the future.

Rules to ensure broad representation in community institutions can be
elaborate, with requirements for minimum participation by women, the landless, indigenous people, or other groups whose voices are rarely heard in local
governance. A study of women's representation in JFM committees in India
makes it clear, though, that traditional social norms and the way in which the
institution conducts its business can effectively silence women's representatives on the committees (Agarwal 2001). Many community institutions have
shown great skill in devising arrangements to deal with conflicting demands

on forest resources. A study of community forest associations in Nepal found that some villages had created a number of subcommittees representing different interest groups—making it easier for women, for example, to discuss their concerns without the presence of men in their meetings. Others had created different categories of membership. In one place, teahouse owners, who consume more firewood than other villagers, were allowed to contribute less labor but to pay for membership and to purchase firewood rather than to receive a free allocation (Varughese 1999 cited in Gibson, Ostrom, and McKean 2000:239).

Representation is a matter not only of physical presence but also of procedures, which make it possible to express a point of view and to have it heard. Many activist NGOs see CBFM as a transforming social movement. In reaction to the authoritarian style of state resource management agencies, they have promoted a model of informal, loosely structured fora as a more democratic kind of institution in which all views have a chance to be heard with equal respect. The idea is appealing but misleading. Informality does not necessarily foster participatory governance. In the absence of rules of engagement and agreed procedures, informality and an unstructured style of organization can lead instead to dominance of the most powerful and articulate over the small, weak, and less articulate (Colchester et al. 2003:19–21).

Management involves agreeing on tasks, following up on them, and taking sanctions when necessary. Since communities are not homogenous, all these tasks are likely to be open to contention and disagreement. Management therefore demands the capacity to resolve or mediate conflict by airing differences and managing pluralism rather than by insisting on reaching consensus (Leach and Fairhead 2001:238). Where internal mechanisms and entrenched interests block even the possibility of an understanding, outside mediation may reinforce the community's capacity to manage conflict.[7] The independence of an outside facilitator can help to expand the domain of possibilities beyond conventional oppositional understandings of forestry and conservation to find the ground over which negotiation is possible.

Monitoring and Enforcement

State forest management agencies often see patrolling and monitoring as among the costliest and most difficult tasks of their mandate. It is hardly surprising, then, that they are particularly responsive to the utilitarian argument that management by communities means communities themselves taking responsibility for the monitoring and enforcement of rules. In some places, villages have, in fact, taken over monitoring entirely from government forest guards. In the Duru-Haitemba forest in Tanzania, referred to earlier, the eight communities managing the forest jointly field some one hundred village forest guards, where previously there had been just two government forest guards (Alden Wily 1997b:7).

Both physical accessibility and clear rules are essential for effective monitoring and enforcement. In Naidu, the forest stands just a short walk or bicycle ride away from the village, making it easy to send regular patrols both during matsutake harvesting days and during the days when the mountain is closed. Village rules make it clear when people are allowed to harvest and what tools they are allowed to use, and checks are in place to ensure that no one goes unsupervised—there must be at least three people in each group of mushroom pickers. The forest under village management at Naidu is visibly more productive and in better condition than the neighboring state-owned forest, where forestry department staff have to issue permits from their offices in another village, travel to the forest to supervise the pickers, and then have to take offenders back to process any fines or punishment. Proximity to the resource and restricting access to a pool of users who know each other well—residents of the village—reinforce the community's capacity to monitor and to enforce management rules.

Effective monitoring and enforcement are of little value, though, if it is not possible to take action against offenders. Government agencies expect that communities will patrol the forest, but rarely give them the powers they need to take action against infringements of the rules. During negotiations over the transfer to five communities of a section of the forest surrounding Mount Kenya, the district forest officer complained to a group of community representatives that villagers never punished people who had been caught illegally cutting wood in the forest. The villagers argued that they had given up trying because they had to hand poachers to the forest department, which rarely, if ever, took action. One participant said that the last time his village had handed over a poacher, they had had to take him at their own expense to the nearest court (forty-five miles from the village), where the magistrate simply released the poacher with a mild warning (author's field notes, Meru, August 2000).[8]

Almost identical stories have been reported from Mexico (Tucker 2004:582) and many other parts of the world. Tanzania is one of the few countries to have a formal legal mechanism allowing communities to translate the rules and regulations they have devised into bylaws with full legal standing in the courts (Alden Wily and Mbaya 2001:182–84)—a procedure that the communities surrounding Jozani and Ngezi forests in Zanzibar were pursuing to give themselves the capacity to implement the rules that had been so carefully developed to manage their resources. In most countries, though, national governments are wary of granting communities the legal authority they need to sanction offenders.

Mobilizing the Capacities of Existing Institutions
or Building Capacity in New Institutions?

The ideal local institution to manage a productive forest resource would be a legally empowered and accountable body, rooted in the cultural norms and the history of the community, with procedural rules to ensure that all voices and interests are represented and heard. Its members would have access to the information and technical support needed to negotiate on behalf of the community, and they would have the authority and capacity to take decisions and act quickly when necessary.

Inevitably, few if any institutions fulfill all the conditions of the ideal type. It is not surprising, then, to find some communities establishing new institutions to take on the task of forest management, while others seek instead to mobilize the capacities of existing institutions. Where outside agencies have initiated moves toward community management, they too must decide whether to create new institutions or whether to build on older, existing institutions. New institutions risk being perceived as artifacts of a project with little local accountability and a limited life span, while older institutions may perpetuate or intensify existing inequities and power relations.

The residents' associations along the Igarapés of Mazagão have evolved in synergy with the local model of forest management. Households make the day-to-day decisions about allocation of land, harvesting, and regeneration following principles and rules to protect the resource, which they have formulated as members of an association. Membership is inclusive—all residents along the Igarapé are members—and confers both rights and obligations. The associations have the capacity and legitimacy to monitor compliance and to enforce sanctions within the community as well as the capacity to represent the interests of the community in wider markets and in the state and federal policy arenas through their partnership with the Rural Workers' Union.

Representative local institutions might be expected to have the strength and legitimacy to survive and to serve a community well, but an institution's continued survival does not ensure its accountability and legitimacy. Local institutions in the successor states to the former Soviet Union still exist, but they have not been able to make the transition from their former role of implementing state plans to acting as a forum representing diverse interests centered on forest resources. It has proved exceptionally challenging to reconstruct new institutions on disintegrating structures poorly adapted to a changed social and economic context.[9]

Well-meaning attempts to revive remembered "customary institutions" must also contend with the distortions of an imagined past and the changed conditions of the present. In Mali, the Samori Participatory Forest Management Program supported during the 1990s by an international NGO chose to reconstitute a precolonial form of forest management remembered in oral histories collected during the preparatory phase of the project. Implementation of the system has been problematic. Shifts in settlement patterns have undermined the ritual authority on which the traditional system was based. A century of political changes has put in place administrative structures that do not map neatly onto precolonial structures. Democratization has introduced new elements of governance, including contested elections for chiefs who are no longer ritual figures but act as local agents of government or political parties. Legally, the reconstituted customary management system is a not-for-profit association, with no authority to approve rules and bylaws for forest management or to impose fines or other sanctions. The project remains, in the eyes of the communities, a project initiated, managed, and financed by an international organization, a welcome presence but not a local institution rooted in the community's history and values (Kassibo 2002).

Building on existing institutions is clearly not always appropriate where traditional sources of legitimacy are disintegrating, imagined, or inequitable. Creating new institutions may in some cases be a more appropriate strategy in a new context, but the process is difficult and time consuming. In Zanzibar, it took three years to establish JECA and MICA, the conservation associations around Jozani forest and on Misali Island. Four years later, in 2002, members of both associations were very conscious that their communities still perceived them to be a part of an externally initiated and funded project. JECA and MICA are still defining their role in Zanzibar's institutional landscape, but there is likely to be space for this new form of multicommunity representation complementing existing village-level institutions for the many villages affected by the designation of Jozani forest and Misali Island as protected areas.

The Capacity to Represent Communities' Interests in the Wider Social and Political Arena

The Kangra District Cooperative Forest Societies Union has taken its case for recognition of the cooperatives' rights to manage their forests to the High Court of the state of Himachal Pradesh and has appealed for assistance from a public-interest legal fund in the national capital, New Delhi. The thirty-six cooperative societies that formed the union in 1996 joined forces, believing that, on their own, individual cooperatives would not have the capacity to represent their interests in legal arenas located a long way from the forests whose control is under dispute. Recognizing that the cooperatives in their present form are not representative community bodies, their continued existence as local institutions—and the possibility that they might become more representative—now depends on their ability to engage with the wider political and legal world in which they are located.

The levers that control and influence the legal, market, and policy environments are located in urban centers and are in the hands of political interests, business leaders, and others, who barely acknowledge the existence of forest communities, let alone their rights to the resource. The formation of representative associations and alliances or participation in organized social movements is a powerful strategy for community groups to overcome their weakness in national and international political arenas.

The Federation of Community Forest Users in Nepal (FECOFUN) was established in 1995 as a channel for communication between the government and forest user groups taking part in the new community forest program. As the number of forest user groups expanded, FECOFUN has become a membership network strong enough that it is able to speak directly on behalf of its constituency without the need for a further intermediary (FECOFUN 1996; Hobley 1996; Uprety 2003).[10] FECOFUN now offers user groups a range of services, such as technical assistance, marketing, and training in administrative skills (Gautam, Shivakoti, and Webb 2004:141). FECOFUN has strengthened its ability to advocate for its members by building alliances with national environmental, labor, and women's organizations in Nepal and internationally.[11] By 2003, claiming a membership of five million, FECOFUN was able to play a leading role in defending forest user groups against the government's attempts to exact higher tax payments on forest income and to impose more stringent forest management regulations.

FECOFUN has acted as a second-tier organization in advocating for user groups that would otherwise have little chance of being heard in national policy-making. Comparable organizations can be found in many other countries, where they have been an effective force representing the interests of their members in pressing for policy or legal changes in the national arena. It has proven more difficult, however, for second-tier organizations working at an international or regional scale to find a balance between support for community-level activities and action through participation in international forest policy debates.

In Central America, a group of community organizations established the Asociación Coordinadora Indigena y Campesina de Agroforesteria Comunitaria Centroaméricana (ACICAFOC—the Central America Indigenous and Peasant Coordination Association for Community Agroforestry) in 1991 to advocate for land tenure and indigenous territorial rights in the context of forest management from an office in San José, Costa Rica.[12] ACICAFOC has been an effective regional network disseminating information and promoting exchanges between its members. Its involvement in international and intergovernmental bodies has, however, led to some criticism that it is remote from its members' interests (Colchester et al. 2003:37). At the same time, ACICAFOC and other international networks have found that direct advocacy is difficult in an international context where different legal systems and policy frameworks disperse lobbying efforts or limit them to matters of general principle that still need to be negotiated separately in each national context (Colchester et al. 2003:13). FECOFUN and ACICAFOC demonstrate the potential strength of membership networks as advocates for their constituents, but the experience of ACICAFOC is a reminder of the difficulty of representing the local across national and international boundaries.

Representing Communities' Interests in Securing Tenure and Access

In most parts of the world, CBFM involves a transfer of usufruct and access rights from a state agency to local institutions representing forest communities. Even where ownership of the land and resource is clearly vested in the community, as in Mexico, the state has, until recently, unilaterally allocated concessions for harvesting communal forestland to the commercial forest-products industry, denying communities the opportunity to exercise their ownership rights over their forests.

The nature of the rights transferred to a community varies around the world from outright ownership to a limited bundle of rights associated with one or more specific products such as timber, fuelwood, medicinal plants, or grazing rights. The bundle might specify times and seasons at which products can be gathered, who may gather them, and whether they may be marketed commercially. There may be constraints and obligations such as a requirement to plant trees of certain species, to patrol the forest to exclude poachers, or to market a commercial product such as rattan through a government purchasing agency.

Whatever the bundle of rights, they must be secure without arbitrary and unpredictable reversals of policy. National policy and legislation play a major role in securing—or undermining—tenure arrangements. In China, legislation and regulations have clearly defined rights to land and resources at any particular time between the revolution of 1949 and the present, but they have been subject to frequent and dramatic modification as national policies have steered an uneven course between individual and collective ownership of the means of production (Menzies and Peluso 1992). During the last twenty years alone, policies have shifted from the privatization of collectively owned "wastelands" through auctions (Grinspoon 2002) to support for community management of collective and state-owned forests and then in 1999 to a complete logging ban on state land in the Yangtze watershed—later extended to collective and leasehold forests (Hyde, Belcher, and Xu 2003b). The result has been growing levels of poverty in some forest communities (Sichuan Academy of Social Sciences 2001:23–29; Uchida, Xu, and Rozelle 2004) and a noticeable increase in illegal, environmentally damaging logging in places where sustainable timber production had been practiced previously (Mu, Su, and Zheng 2001; Zhao 2004).

Lobbying for a Supportive Policy Environment

Policies in many countries impose a heavy burden of bureaucratic procedures, restrictions on marketing, as well as taxes and fees on forest enterprises of all kinds. For communities with limited capital and without access to the technical, business, and marketing skills that are available to larger corporate enterprises, the regulatory environment makes forest management a daunting undertaking. National organizations such as FECOFUN in Nepal are well placed to hear directly from their membership about the barriers they face, and they have the capacity to lobby the relevant ministries and legislatures for change. FECOFUN has successfully brought the concerns and interests of large numbers of rural people to the attention of the media and mobilized the support of allies in other spheres of Nepal's civil society.

Communities' capacity to protect their interests or to have their concerns heard by policy-makers can be severely hampered by their limited ability to communicate their case to the public and policy-makers. Media exposure of these issues can build public support for communities through informal appeals to constituencies not specifically associated with forests and forestry. Where political expression is constrained or controlled by authoritarian governments, however, direct pressure through the media or through the actions of representative organizations such as FECOFUN or social movements such as the Rural Workers' Union in Brazil is not a feasible strategy. In these situations, research framed as scholarly enquiry may be a less dangerous and more effective channel to reach policy-makers. Researchers in some of China's most prestigious academic institutions have been instrumental in revealing the degree to which target-driven planning, arbitrary taxation, and local government interference, not farmers' ignorance, have been responsible for discouraging sustainable local forest management (Albers, Rozelle, and Li 1998; Liu and Landell-Mills 2003). Presented as case studies analyzing the state of the environment and the persistence of rural poverty, their work has succeeded in bringing the voices of rural people to the attention of provincial and central government officials, contributing to a slow move away from current bureaucratic regulation of timber harvesting toward a search for incentives to encourage local forest management.

The Technical Capacity to Manage the Resource

For well over a century, production in forest management has meant large-scale commercial timber production, a goal that was well suited to a resource controlled by one owner seeking to maximize profits over the long term. These conditions rarely apply to forest resources managed by communities for whom the forest is one among many elements in a diverse landscape. Investment in forest management competes for labor and capital with water management, staple crops, livestock grazing, and other land uses. Communal owners face diverse preferences for species and spacing of trees—to allow, for example, for forest grazing and gathering of NTFPs by different groups in the same community. An even and sustained flow of income may not meet the community's occasional but urgent calls for funds to meet unexpected needs such as reconstruction after a natural disaster or construction of a facility such as a school or clinic. As in the case of the Huron-Wendat, a cultural imperative such as increasing habitat for a totemic animal may be at least as important as generating income.

Forest management is a difficult undertaking, increasing in complexity as the range of goods and services being generated increases. Nevertheless, knowledge is already present in communities, although indigenous or traditional management systems that have proved their sustainability over time may still be rejected by resource management agencies because they involve techniques that are not recognized within conventional constructions of scientific knowledge.[13] Commercial cultivation of *Cunninghamia lanceolata* (Chinese Fir) for timber in southern China has a documented history of over three hundred years (Menzies 1988b). Since the 1960s, the state has enforced what it describes as a scientific management system of monoculture plantations, prohibiting the burning, intercropping, and coppicing that characterized the traditional system. Unlike the old systems, these plantations have suffered from soil fertility problems and reduced growth rates in successive rotations. Even today, the state forestry authorities are reluctant to concede that the traditional techniques may have scientific validity, although there is now greater flexibility in allowing communities to use them in collective or leasehold forests (Tapp and Menzies 1997).

Strengthening the technical capacities of communities to manage forest resources demands mutual recognition and respect for local knowledge as well as for conventional scientific knowledge, and it is still rare to find efforts to incorporate both into a set of tools and skills that is available and accessible to communities. Despite some innovations, there is still a desperate dearth of alternative technical options for small-scale production systems for community forest management. With few exceptions, conventional forest management does not offer communities more than scaled-down models of commercial timber and logging-oriented management technologies. Surveying the technologies offered to communities in JFM programs in India's Western Ghats, Saxena and Sarin observe:

> Silvicultural practices and management options need to be radically altered. ... Maximizing outputs of multiple products will require innovative and experimental silviculture, which must focus more on forest floor management to enrich the soil and encourage natural regeneration. Canopy manipulation, tending and thinning, etc., should be so adjusted as to optimize NTFP production. Unless such radical changes are made in the technical management of non-degraded forests, it is difficult to increase the stake of the villagers in forest management.   —SAXENA AND SARIN 1999:192

For all the international attention to CBFM, there has been little funding available for research, experimentation, and testing of silvicultural systems or management regimes adapted to community needs. Debate and advocacy have addressed the complexity of community institutions, politics, and power more than they have addressed forest ecology and production technologies. There has been little dialog between social scientists, natural scientists, and local people with empirical insight into the dynamics of the forests in which they live and work (Donovan 2001). Yet reaching a consensus on community priorities and implementing the community's decisions depend on the options from which priorities will be chosen in the first place. It is becoming urgent to design and test management systems that are rooted in local ecologies and meet local needs in order to expand the range of options available to communities.

Technical Capacities and the Barrier of the Forest Management Plan

Communities may have little flexibility in setting their management goals and options, often being obliged to operate within established agency frameworks and targets for reforestation, conservation, or forest condition. Even where communities do have some decision-making powers, regulations normally require the preparation of a forest management plan. In principle, the plan ensures protection of environmental values and sustainable use of the resource. In practice, it can become a bureaucratic barrier rather than a vision for the long-term health of the forest and its people. Preparation of a forest management plan may include requirements that few communities can meet on their own, such as the involvement of a professional forester, a forest inventory with estimates of timber volumes and species lists, and projections of annual harvesting rates over rotations of several years. It is easy to share the suspicions of forest user groups in Nepal that the real purpose of new regulations requiring formal forest management plans is to restrict their activities, not to protect the environment as the department of forestry claims: "There is a general concern about whether the forest department, which does not have experience with the successful implementation of any forest management in the past, will successfully do so in the near future . . . as envisaged by the new policy" (Gautam, Shivakoti, and Webb 2004:145).

The capacity to locate and invite assistance from individuals and organizations outside the community is one way to meet regulatory requirements as well as to challenge agency assumptions about communities' lack of technical skills. In one of the snapshots that opens chapter 1 of this book, the villagers of Old and New Ekuri in Nigeria received funding from an international donor and support from a local NGO to hire a forestry specialist who taught them how to carry out the inventories and forest transects that the forest department required as a precondition for accepting the village's own forest management plan. The forest department has now accepted this local adaptation of a scientific tool, opening the doors to negotiations on alternative options for forest management less damaging to wildlife and NTFPs.

Communities do not always have access to the technical support that can assist in identifying new and innovative opportunities from forest management. In some cases, it may be possible to invest in training their own staff to prepare management plans. In other cases, it may be more appropriate to explore ways in which the community can call on expertise and support from other sources. It is time, though, for state resource management agencies to move away from stringent procedural requirements for approving community plans for management toward an approach that builds on communities' local knowledge and technical capacities and ensures protection of the public interest in protecting the environment without acting as a barrier to community initiatives.

Some New Directions in Building Technical Capacities for Forest Management

The success of Old and New Ekuri in designing and carrying out their own forest inventory and transects demonstrates that it is possible to bridge the gap between local and professional knowledge. There are other examples of encouraging new initiatives enlarging the domain of forest management beyond a narrow focus on timber production and incorporating local and traditional knowledge into a more syncretic body of forest science. Over the last twenty-five years, agroforestry, the management of trees within predominantly agricultural landscapes, has entered the accepted vocabulary and practice of forestry. Forest management for products other than timber is being tested.

Local knowledge and experience are appearing more frequently as integral elements of new silvicultural systems, such as a new system for the regeneration of mahogany (*Swietenia macrophylla* King) in Mexico's Maya forest, which was the outcome of a collaboration between forest scientists from several research institutes and *ejido* forest workers with long experience of observing the growth and regeneration of mahogany after harvesting (Snook and López 2003; Snook et al. 2003).

Among the factors contributing to this greater openness to alternative models of management and local knowledge has been a critique of the paradigms of orthodox, institutionalized science and its methods. The scientific method claims a universal validity or objectivity from its very disengagement from the lived experience of ordinary citizens. It seeks answers to questions through testing under controlled, replicable conditions, a methodology that is severely challenged in the face of uncertainty and stochastic events (Leach and Fairhead 2000:54–56). People act on and modify forest ecosystems, using tools such as fire or grazing. Fire, storms, floods, and drought are perhaps more important in shaping forest composition and growth than controllable variables such as spacing, species composition, or harvesting rates. An outcome of the critique of orthodox, institutionalized science has been calls for a participatory and democratic "citizen science" or "civic science," which honors local and traditional knowledge in an equal partnership with institutionalized science in order to "ask the right questions, and answer the questions right" (Baker and Kusel 2003:156).

The concept of civic science presents interesting possibilities for reshaping the future boundaries of science, research, and resource management (Baker and Kusel 2003:155). Many communities, though, are looking for more immediate support in the search for alternative forest management systems. Canada's First Nations have been particularly active in articulating their goals and priorities and then negotiating with existing institutions to commission research and experimentation to develop management systems meeting their priorities. The agreement between the Huron-Wendat Nation and Laval University in Québec is only one of many such agreements, and the Canadian government is actively supporting such initiatives funding a First Nations forestry program, whose objective is "to enhance the capacity of First Nations to sustainably manage their forest lands."[14] At the same time, First Nations are encouraging and supporting young people to train as foresters in order to build capacity within their own communities to manage their resources without relying on outside support.

An alternative strategy is to adapt conventional tools and methods to make science more accessible to communities. With resource management agencies often demanding inventories and growth projections in forest management plans, there have been many efforts to design kits to assist villagers in measuring tree diameters and to prepare forest transects. Certain skills, however, may be of more importance than others. Rural communities can, for example, learn and use mapping skills, but it is unlikely that each village in a region needs its own trained specialist to carry out a task that may not be required very frequently. It may be more valuable to concentrate on training villagers in map-reading skills and in strategic uses of maps, looking at the same time for ways in which they can have ready access to trained technicians who will be fully accountable to the community. Finding channels that give communities access to technical skills may be at least as important a form of capacity-building as investing directly in training community members who already have many other commitments and demands on their time and labor (Anau et al. 2003).

The Capacity to Participate as Informed Actors in Markets

There is demand in local and global markets for all kinds of forest products and services, but the existence of markets is not sufficient to ensure that communities have access to them or that communities can benefit from them (Scherr, White, and Kaimowitz 2002). Legal obstacles may restrict access to markets, or discriminatory policies and subsidies may favor large, international enterprises over small, local businesses. Timber markets are usually tightly controlled, but communities are also often prohibited from marketing valuable NTFPs such as pine resin in India or products such as rattan and rare medicinal herbs destined for urban consumer markets. Even where there are no legal or regulatory barriers, the process of marketing requires skills in identifying sources of demand, processing and packaging, securing fair prices, transporting to the final destination, and locating suitable sales outlets. Few communities in the world are completely isolated from markets and trade exchanges, but few forest communities are well equipped to enter rapidly changing markets without some support to build their capacity to participate as informed actors.

Some characteristics of forest communities accentuate their difficulties in taking advantage of markets (Rozmeijer 2003:8; Wollenberg 1998a:5–9). Many forest communities are located in remote areas with difficult topography. Many forest products are gathered in small quantities over a wide area, making it difficult for members of one community to supply—or to influence—more than a very small portion of aggregate market demand. Transportation is slow and costly. Communications—and thus access to information on prices and market demand—are difficult. Where forest communities are composed of ethnic or cultural minorities, they rely on intermediaries and traders whose ability to work in the dominant language allows them to orchestrate collection, transportation, and selling in distant urban markets.

It is usually easier for a community to supply local markets than to enter and benefit from distant markets. They can monitor and respond quickly to changing demand and prices, and they may be able to bring their products directly to market without relying on outside entrepreneurs. Nevertheless, products from community-managed forests can compete in urban and global markets, particularly in rapidly developing markets for so-called natural products and for products such as herbal medicines and forest fruit (such as açaí from the várzea forests of Brazil) or in emerging sectors such as ecotourism. To benefit from these opportunities, communities need access to information about markets, business, and entrepreneurial skills—and the agility to join forces where appropriate with other producers to reinforce their position as small-scale suppliers or to identify opportunities for value-added processing.

Connecting the Local to the Global

In local markets, producers of forest products interact with consumers on a daily basis and quickly become aware of changing demand, preferences, and prices. They are likely to be the primary and perhaps only suppliers of foods and some processed products, such as agricultural tools and equipment, some textiles, and household objects. Moving beyond the sphere of the local, however, markets change dramatically. Producers in regional or global markets compete with others producing goods that can be substituted, forcing them to be competitive in pricing and quality and to adapt rapidly to changing demands—with little understanding how or why those demands change.

The rapid growth in the Japanese market for matsutake mushrooms has created unprecedented opportunities for income generation in Naidu—as well as in Korea, Mexico, the United States, Morocco, and Bhutan. Matsutake harvesters in Naidu confront bewildering changes in prices as buyers in Japan move from one source of supply to another. They are aware that matsutake is also harvested in other countries and believe—with some justification—that the buyers are playing one source of supply against another to keep prices as low as possible. Ironically, matsutake harvesters in the United States and in Mexico also believe that commercial interests in China are acting to keep prices low in order to shut out competition from other countries (author's field notes, Oaxaca, January 2000; Eugene, Oregon, June 2002). Improved access to information about how seasonality, freshness, and size affect prices in Japanese markets would benefit matsutake harvesters in all producing countries, although they would still not alter their weak position as small producers in a monopsonistic market.

Entering larger, regional, or international markets also entails responding to more stringent requirements for consistent quality and reliable delivery. In Naidu, again, prices for matsutake dropped from RMB 400 to RMB 40 over two days in October 2001, following reports in the Japanese media that one shipment had traces of pesticide contamination (He 2004:11). Without the capacity in village markets to test for chemicals, harvesters and buyers had no choice but to accept the claim and to formulate new rules quickly (prohibiting the use of plastic bags for gathering and storage) to guarantee continued access to the market.

Problems faced by community-based enterprises in meeting rigorous standards, production volumes, and delivery deadlines have dogged efforts to link them to international markets for certified timber. Although some large chain stores and multinational corporations have announced that they intend to purchase timber certified as sustainably grown under socially responsible conditions, few community forestry enterprises have been able to benefit. Even where they have received certification from an accredited body such as the Forest Stewardship Council (FSC), they do not have access to the trade fairs and marketing bodies in which transactions with large corporations take place. Operating at a relatively small scale, they are also unable to supply the volumes that the buyers require (Clay 2001:128–30; Klooster 1999). A community sawmill operator in Ixtlán, Mexico, recognized that although his enterprise had received FSC certification—with financial assistance from an international donor—he was not able to sell his timber at a premium. He added that the sawmill did not yet produce the volume of timber needed for access to those markets but hoped that it might be possible to join forces with other neighboring producers to step up production in the near future (author's field notes, Ixtlán, August 2004).

The difficulties that small-scale community producers face in producing the volumes needed to supply regional and international markets argue for an intermediary able to collect and assemble forest products from different locations. Producers' associations and federations can reduce the risk of unfair exploitation by middle-tier traders, a strategy adopted in Mexico by the Proyecto para la Conservación y Manejo Sustentable de Recursos Forestales (PROCYMAF), which offers marketing consultancy services on a demand basis to community forestry enterprises (Scherr, White, and Kaimowitz 2002:8).

Forest communities' cultural distance from global markets may be as insuperable a barrier as their physical distance. The tastes and preferences of global consumers for many other forest products can be mysterious and inexplicable to those who harvest and sell the products. The women's groups in the villages surrounding Jozani forest had hoped to earn some income from selling crafts to visiting tourists. Since the opening of a visitors' center at the entrance to

PLATE 7. Community-owned sawmill processing certified timber in Ixtlán, Mexico.

PHOTO: AUTHOR

the forest, they have watched in frustration, however, as visitors have bought T-shirts but shown less interest in the locally woven baskets in brightly dyed coconut fibers. Tourists, for their part, are surprised to see such "unnatural" colors on local crafts, which do not conform with their idea of Swahili culture. Professional expertise in designing crafts to appeal to the tastes of foreign visitors would assist the women's groups to transform their occasional sales of handicrafts into a viable business. Fair-trade organizations in the northern countries have played a role in providing design and marketing services to community groups, but it appears that markets for ethnic products are reaching a point of saturation, forcing the organizations to explore new design and sales strategies with artisans to adapt traditional products to wider consumer markets (Clay 2001:152–60).

Ecotourism is a form of nonconsumptive resource management that has been promoted as a subsector of the world's fastest-growing industry—tourism—that protects the environment while directly benefiting communities.[15] It has at the same time been accused of "greenwashing"—profiting from a fashionable trend, with little real commitment either to protecting the environment or to working with communities (Honey 1999). In response, NGOs representing communities involved in ecotourism, interested travel and tourism companies, and environmental organizations have worked to develop certification systems setting out guidelines for best practices governing the environmental, social, and economic impacts of ecotourism activities (Honey 2002).[16] Attracting visitors is a problem, though, when the appeal of prime ecotourism destinations is their very remoteness. Jozani forest has no problem attracting large numbers of visitors because it is on the main road from the capital to the main beach resort area in a very small country experiencing a boom in conventional tourism. Misali Island, on the other hand, is a small uninhabited island off the coast of Zanzibar's second island of Pemba, which has for a long time been an occasional destination for sailing tours from the Kenyan resort of Mombasa. The few visitors to Misali have, in the past, been used to landing and using the beach without paying any fees, and many now resent and refuse to pay for what they still consider to be an open access resource.

International travel companies are far better placed than communities to analyze the market and to advertise and sell tours, and they are also more likely to know visitors' expectations for levels of comfort and service. East Africa, a region with a long history of nature-oriented tourism, is perhaps a leader in exploring innovative partnerships in ecotourism. The Maasai community of Il Ngwesi in northern Kenya has an agreement with the neighboring, privately owned Lewa Downs Conservancy, through which they receive assistance in managing an ecotourist lodge as well as technical support in wildlife conservation.[17] In southern Kenya, a Maasai Group Ranch at Shompole has negotiated with a luxury safari company for several years to come to a more complex agreement. The agreement creates a shareholding company in which the safari company initially holds the majority of the shares. As members of the community receive training and skills in managing the lodge, shares will be transferred gradually to the community, which will ultimately own the company, leasing the facilities to the safari operator.[18]

Communities are doubly disadvantaged in the emerging regional and global markets for environmental services such as carbon sequestration, hydrological regimes, or conservation of biodiversity. First, there are still few accepted and easily understood procedures for compensation for services. Second, international treaties govern the mechanisms for allocation and disbursement of many compensatory payments, placing decision-making powers firmly with national and international agencies, not local people. Carbon sequestration programs are formulated by national governments together with the private sector (corporations involved in trading carbon emission rights), leaving little place for communities to have a say in the location of projects or in mechanisms for payments (May et al. 2004; Corbera and Adger 2004). Conservation of biodiversity and compensation for bioprospecting under the terms of the Convention on Biological Diversity have become extremely controversial. Contentious ethical issues have surrounded the articles of the convention that confer patentlike intellectual property rights to what has been traditional or ritual knowledge considered to be the cultural heritage of a people, not a tradable commodity (Posey 1996; Zerner 2000).[19]

To the extent that mechanisms have been put in place for communities to receive compensation for environmental services from the landscapes they manage, it has proven very complex to ensure that compensation reaches those who bear the costs associated with management.[20] A recent worldwide review of 280 schemes for payments for forest environmental services recognized that few forest communities have access to information, funding, and the legal advice that might strengthen their capacity to negotiate agreements for environmental services. It concludes with a call for "a market support centre that offers free access to market information, a contact point for potential buyers, sellers and intermediaries, and an advice bureau to support the design and implementation of contracts" (Landell-Mills and Porras 2002).

Building Capacity to Participate in Markets

It may not be possible to change the distance and relationship between members of a forest community and a wholesale purchaser of certified timber or signatories to an international agreement such as the Kyoto Protocol on climate change, but there are points of intervention and strategies that can build the capacities of communities to act as stronger, better informed players in markets. One approach is to find ways directly to increase income earned by producers by bringing as much control as possible of the marketing and processing chains to the community. Another is to make technical, legal, and business services readily available to community institutions at an affordable cost or to provide funding with which communities themselves can hire the expertise they need.

Marketing chain analysis indicates who is selling a product to whom, where sales and processing take place, through what kinds of markets, and at what price. It can help to identify where value is added or taken away and where communities rather than intermediaries might capture that value—or where the services of these intermediaries might be advantageous in bearing the risk of unstable prices or in organizing the collection and transport to markets of widely dispersed products such as fruit or mushrooms. In Namibia, an analysis of production and marketing of oil seeds and devil's claw (*Pagophytum*), a traditional medicine, led to a nested hierarchy of NGOs, starting with a women's cooperative (Eudafano) linked to not-for-profit technical service providers, processors, and finally to the Southern African Natural Products

Trade Association (SANProTA). SANProTA, also known as PhytoTrade Africa, operates as a private-sector conduit with the capital and business expertise to negotiate contracts to sell the oils and medicines in international markets. While SANProTA is, in effect, still an intermediary, it is a company legally owned by the rural producers and communities who are its members. It has a mandate to conduct business and to reinvest any income in improving outreach and service provision to its members.[21]

Recognizing that sustainable natural resource management by communities is in the wider public and global interest, governments, international donors, and the private sector are beginning to invest in funding technical and marketing organizations serving communities. SANProTA receives funding from IFAD, and its membership includes, among others, local offices of CARE International, the Dutch development agency SNV, and Zambia's National Technology Business Centre. To reach international markets and to keep informed about changing demand, the association participates in the Vitafoods International Exhibition, a large international trade fair held annually in Europe. A characteristic of institutions such as PhytoTrade Africa is that they work within existing market frameworks and structures to offer expertise in response to demands from communities, rather than seeking to build the full range of skills within each community.

The Capacity to Build Community Assets with Benefits Generated from Managing the Resource

Individuals and households set aside some surplus production or income to build assets as a buffer to meet contingencies such as a poor harvest or illness or social obligations such as weddings and funerals. In 1987 Chambers and Leach showed the importance of trees as assets to the rural poor in India. Trees represented a form of steadily growing capital for a low initial investment cost. With a ready market for wood, it is easy to meet contingencies by selling trees without putting other assets at risk. Chambers and Leach were looking at trees owned by individual households, but their observations hold true for community forests too. An important distinction, though, is that CBFM involves a common resource, arguing for the reinvestment of at least some of the income generated into building community assets such as a school, a clinic, or a credit scheme or to meet contingencies.

Devising mechanisms through which the benefits of forest management might contribute to building long-term community assets is unfamiliar, uncharted territory for most communities as well as for their partners. One reason that there are relatively few examples of benefits from forest management being used for community asset-building is that it is still not common to see a stream of benefits greater than the initial investment. Even where management activities are generating income, a closer look at the balance sheet often reveals that success in projects such as the Shompole ecotourism scheme or SANProTA has been achieved as a result of grant funding to launch the project or to subsidize training and other forms of technical assistance.

Where management is generating a dependable stream of benefits and income, it is still the case that they are usually lower than the community's expectations had been. Material interest may not be the only reason for community involvement in management—villagers at Ngezi considered that "reduced hassles" with the forest department would be an important benefit from their proposed community forest. Nevertheless, when divided between individuals or households in the form of a dividend—perhaps the most common form of distributing benefits—individuals may conclude that the meager income from management does not offer sufficient incentive to participate in the collective activity. Dissatisfaction is compounded if the distribution is perceived to be unfair and inequitable, which is likely if the community management institution itself is unrepresentative (Tucker 2004:575–76). Shifting from individual rewards to community asset-building could contribute to defusing such tensions and enhance the value of the resource as a vehicle for realizing both community and individual aspirations.

The most straightforward approach to community asset-building is to direct all the income from management, at regular intervals, toward specific projects for the benefit of the community. At Jozani, revenue from visitors' fees to the forest has been channeled in successive years to the construction of a mosque, a primary school, and a house for a doctor at the local clinic. Unfortunately, there are unlikely to be many projects about which there is widespread consensus, and a new strategy is usually soon required. The next step at Jozani was to consider depositing the income in a fixed time savings account, which has the advantage of requiring just one decision—to extend the deposit period—every six months and which would allow the community to build a buffer fund in the event of a downturn in tourism. Other communities where the state has reduced services to rural areas have used income to pay the salary of a teacher or a nurse. The strategy in all these cases has been to reduce the discretionary authority of the committee or other group managing income and to make transactions as accountable and transparent as possible: everyone can see whether the mosque has been built; anyone can ask the teacher or nurse whether she has received her salary.

In some cases, forest income is used to compensate some individuals for direct contributions of time and labor to management. At Ixtlán, Mexico, the community forestry enterprise employs forest technicians, sawmill workers, and some full-time management staff. After payment of salaries, any income earned from forest management is divided evenly between reinvestment in the enterprise, a dividend paid to each of the 380 members of the community, and a social and emergency fund managed by the Commission for Community Assets (*Comisario de Bienes Comunales*) (author's field notes, Ixtlán, August 2004). Distribution systems can be more refined, with further subdivisions according to the degree of participation in management or shareholding arrangements determining what proportion of the income any household will be entitled to. The scope for disagreement and dissension increases, however, with increasing complexity, with less transparent processes of distribution, using income increasingly to reward individuals rather than to build community assets.

More elaborate financial mechanisms are being tested in some places to use income from community management as a vehicle for local development. Credit schemes are often a component of integrated community development programs (ICDPs), but have typically been conceived of as a strategy to diversify local economies to reduce dependence on a threatened resource rather than as a strategy for community asset-building.[22] These schemes usually operate with subsidized interest rates and do not follow what have become established as best practices following the example of well-known programs such as the Grameen Bank in Bangladesh.[23] Whatever their impact in fostering conservation, they are unlikely to evolve into viable long-term financial institutions serving communities managing natural resources.

The credit schemes associated with Jozani forest and Misali Island in Zanzibar follow recognized best practices, including a viable and sustainable interest rate and disclosure of business practices through open account books and regular public meetings at which proposed business activities are scrutinized by all members. Operating as village financial institutions, the credit schemes provide a way to include in the program households that are not directly involved in activities in the forest or on the island—especially important at Misali where there are many more households in each village than there are fishers using the island. In 2002 the credit scheme was still dependent on capital funds injected by project donors, but the intention was to use some of the income from conservation to increase the capital available for lending. Women in the village are particularly interested in the scheme, which offers a way of working around customary gender roles, which restrict commercial forest activities or offshore fishing to men.

Credit schemes place control of investment and the redistribution of income in the hands of a community-level institution, requiring attention to transparency and accountability. They are complex institutions, maintaining a difficult balance between financial solvency and equitable provision of services to members. Existing community institutions and their likely partners from conservation and development NGOs may not possess the financial skills and experience of microfinance to grapple with group lending techniques, setting interest rates, and maintaining accurate accounting systems. There is, however, a rich body of experience around the world showing that rural communities can manage microcredit schemes when they have access to professional support and supervision. Microfinance institutions are, however, rarely invited to be partners in CBNRM, although their services could be valuable in translating income into an asset benefiting the whole community.

Capacity-Building for Forest Management: Some Concluding Thoughts

Managing forest resources requires technical skills, but involves more than just a grasp of technical skills. Knowledge and technical skills are the tools used to meet the objectives that are the outcome of collective decisions and negotiations between different interests. The capacity of communities to manage forest resources is enhanced where there is a legitimate representative body in which all interests are heard in the process of reaching a shared vision and allocating responsibilities for realizing it. Where existing inequities and power relations compromise the legitimacy of a community's institutions, outside mediation can facilitate in crafting procedures and safeguards to protect the interests of vulnerable and disenfranchised groups or even in establishing new institutions.

Forest management is an undertaking that calls on a wide repertoire of skills, from the capacity to negotiate and mediate with actors outside the immediate community to technical knowledge and an understanding of legal systems, markets, and financial institutions. Some skills and knowledge will exist locally within a community, and some may be located in nongovernmental institutions, government agencies, or academic research centers at a considerable physical distance from the forest. Legal, technical, and marketing services may be available but at high cost. Associations and networks that pool the limited resources of individual communities can play an important role in securing those services.

Community-level institutions need not assume the burden of carrying out all the functions and building all the capacities needed for effective forest and resource management. Multiple, nested institutions reaching from the local level to the global may take on different responsibilities, where each has a comparative advantage. It may be more important to secure timely and affordable access to sources of support and skills through such partnerships than to expend scarce human and financial resources in building them within each community. Partnerships are not inherently equitable or empowering, however, and the next chapter turns to the subject of partnerships as sites of continuing negotiation and renegotiation over the roles of the different institutions involved.

9

Negotiating Partnerships

WHOSE VOICE IS LOUDEST?

NGOs seem curiously unaware of the extent to which they are resented by local
level actors because of the way they substitute their voice for those of local people
or take over the political space of indigenous peoples and local communities.

—COLCHESTER ET AL. 2003:16

CBFM INVOLVES partnerships between communities, government
agencies, NGOs, the private sector, and a number of other possible
actors. Partnerships can expand the repertoire of skills and capacities dedicated to forest stewardship, provide a forum in which to search for common
ground, and negotiate toward a management regime that can be implemented,
monitored, and adjusted to meet changing demands on the resource. A poorly
negotiated partnership, though, can set the scene for misunderstanding, tension, and continued or renewed loss of forest cover. This chapter asks, Why
do partners have such different interests in forest resources? Who is setting the agenda in CBFM? How can partnerships become sites for the negotiation of differences to reach a shared understanding of future goals and
objectives?

The word *partnership* has entered the vocabulary of international development projects as a desirable attribute of almost any activity, which its advocates
choose to present as a voluntary collaboration between two or more equal
parties to achieve a mutually desired goal. Critics contend that *partnership*—
together with terms such as *participation* and *empowerment*—has become
one of the most overused and abused concepts in the development lexicon,
since few such relationships in fact involve institutions or individuals equally
endowed financially, organizationally, or politically (Fowler 1998:140; Cooke

and Kothari 2001; Maxwell and Riddell 1998; Harrison 2002; Sachs 1992:1–6). Uncritical use of these concepts deflects attention from the roots of inequality and obscures deep divisions in the motives and interests of the various actors involved in an activity such as forest resource management.

Equitable partnerships, in which all parties share decision-making authority and bear an equal burden of responsibilities, will better serve the needs of all those involved than will asymmetrical relationships in which one or more parties wield power through a monopoly over decision-making and access to information or financial and human resources. Respect for the principle of voluntary association and withdrawal enhances accountability and strengthens the resilience of a partnership in which partners' interests may shift over time. Layered alliances (Agrawal 1997:viii) or networks linking with other local groups or to organizations with wider regional or international constituencies are a powerful means to project the voices of forest communities into the public eye and policy arenas where historically they have been lost in the clamor of more powerful contending forces.

Partnerships in Practice

The story of community involvement in the management of Jozani forest, Misali Island, and Ngezi forest in Zanzibar is the story of a formal partnership among resource-dependent communities, an international NGO, and a government agency, with the financial support of a number of international donors (Hartley and Rijali 2003:5). CARE Tanzania has assisted in locating international funds through its parent organization, CARE International, for a conservation and development project in which it has mediated among the partners to reconfigure relations between them and to establish legally and socially recognized local institutions to manage the resource and the revenue generated from management. Each partner has played a well-defined and mutually complementary role: the Department of Commercial Crops, Fruits, and Forestry (DCCFF) supervises the conservation and forestry components of the work; the new community associations have been given the task of representing the voices of local interests; and CARE has been responsible for project management, training, and mediating to instill trust and collaborative relations between the communities and the government agencies.

At a time when tourism has been the fastest-growing sector in Zanzibar's economy, the offer of a share of income from visitor entry fees to Jozani forest and Misali Island has represented a sufficiently attractive alternative for the concerned communities that the search for common ground between the partners has centered more on negotiations over the allocation of revenue and modalities of distribution than on resolving disputes over the basic aims of conservation and establishing a national park. CARE has offered services valued by both its partners, without which it is likely that progress toward community-based conservation in Zanzibar would have been considerably slower and more contentious. Nevertheless, the communities have been the weaker partners with respect to DCCFF. Jozani and Ngezi were already reserved forests, and the fishers on Misali reacted to a threat originating outside their communities. Negotiations in all three locations concerned the implementation of conservation, not alternative uses for the land and resources. Donors have directed nearly all funding in the form of grants to CARE, with very little direct financial support to DCCFF and no direct financial assistance as of late 2004 to the two existing community associations (JECA and MICA).

CARE Tanzania has been unusually sensitive in its efforts not to dominate the partnership that it was instrumental in forming. Nevertheless, the community-based conservation projects in Zanzibar have followed a common trajectory in which the impetus for a development activity has come from an outside agent, with the "beneficiary community" invited to join a partnership in a project whose basic parameters have already been determined. The euphemism "beneficiary community" concisely captures the relations between even the best-intentioned partners, where lack of access to information, funding, and decision-makers is an overwhelming obstacle, particularly to people whose presence in or near rural forested landscapes makes them invisible or mere intruders with no rights in the eyes of more powerful claimants to the resource.

In Zanzibar, the partners have found that overcoming their differences over access rights and preferred uses of the resource to reach a shared understanding of the future of the resource is only the first step. The transition to the longer-term tasks of implementation, monitoring, and distribution of costs and benefits is imposing new demands on the relationship. After many years together, the partners believe that they have built sufficient trust and mutual respect that they can meet the challenges ahead. This is hardly the norm, though, and there are many examples of more fractious partnerships where powerful interests have dominated over their weaker, less articulate, or poorer partners.

The often lengthy process of developing and legislating a supportive environment for community-based resource management highlights the importance of partnerships for advocacy and lobbying as well as the sometimes fragile and fissured foundations for partnerships. In Thailand, more than a decade after the appointment in 1990 of the first government committee to draft legislative guidelines for CBFM, the country's parliament and senate have yet to agree on final passage of a bill. While there is widespread popular support for the principle of giving villages rights to manage local forest resources, bitter divisions have emerged between advocates of conservation and an alliance of the rural poor and human-rights activists on just what rights should be granted, to whom, and on what lands, with further disagreement about which agency should have ultimate supervisory control over community forests.

Following widespread protests at destructive commercial logging and public alarm at severe floods that were believed to have been triggered by deforestation, the Thai government imposed a ban in 1989 on logging in natural forests.[1] At the time, an alliance of local organizations, social and environmental NGOs, and academics argued forcefully that the Royal Forestry Department (RFD) had failed in its mission to manage the country's forests sustainably and that local people would be more responsible stewards of the land. RFD, for its part, redefined its role in terms of conservation, aggressively expanding the number of protected areas, forcibly expelling many communities in the newly proclaimed reserves and parks. As successive drafts of a community forestry bill made their way to the legislature, however, the earlier alliance split into groupings described by Thai observers as "light green" and "dark green."

Advocates of the light green approach to community forestry emphasized the need for social justice and communities' rights to make major management decisions about forested land. The dark green model upheld the importance of conservation and central control, insisting on the need to enforce the exclusion of humans from protected areas—even if they had only recently been designated and had a long history of human settlement and activity. Light green activists have mobilized national social movements such as the Assembly of the Poor to petition for a "people's version" of a community forestry bill. The bill was first submitted to Parliament in 2000 and again in 2001 after elections for a new Parliament. It was subsequently approved by Parliament, but rejected in 2003 and again in 2005 by the Senate. Dark green conservation NGOs, for their part, have allied themselves with student groups and ethnic Thai lowland villagers to press their case, describing highland ethnic minority people as destroyers of the forest who must be removed to protect the national heritage. Legislation continues to be stalled and held hostage to changing interests and shifting alliances—all claiming to be acting to realize the goal of legitimizing community forest management.[2]

These examples confirm that partnerships can be effective and can facilitate progress toward mutual understanding and agreement on how to move forward. They also raise serious questions to be considered in the following pages about the dynamics and the contingent nature of consensus within partnerships that are easily subverted or dismantled when a particular conjuncture of political, social, or economic conditions changes.

Why Do Partners Have Such Different Interests in Forest Resources?

Households living along the Igarapés near Mazagão in Brazil describe the forest surrounding their homes in terms that encompass the physical appearance of the vegetation, the degree of human manipulation, and the products that humans derive from the land (chapter 4, pp. 54–55). Although the sale of timber is an important source of income, land from which trees are most commonly harvested is known as *moradia do bicho* or the "residence of animals," and none of the four categories of land refers specifically to the presence of trees. The caboclo landscape is not the same place as the endangered haven of biodiversity that attracts the attention and funding of international conservation organizations. Nor is it the same landscape where thirty years ago IBAMA, the federal environmental agency, had seen tracts of valuable timber to be granted as concessions to forest-product corporations—and subsequently abandoned after harvesting.

Smallholders, scientists, and government officials each see something different on the same piece of land. They classify the landscape in terms of the properties and the values they associate with it. Any forest,[3] whatever its age, species composition, or location, is a product of its symbolic or religious importance, as well as of the relationships of power that govern access to it and the way it is used (Michon 2003). It would be unrealistic, then, to expect agreement in any society on a common vision of a single best and most appropriate goal for forest management beyond the broadest generalizations such as "multiple use" or "sustained yield." It is in the translation of such superficially inoffensive concepts into actions in the forest that contending interests clash and seek to exercise control over the management and use of the resource.

The reservation by states around the world of vast areas of the forest estate in the name of the public interest adds a further layer of contention and conflict over whose interests should prevail in determining management objectives and practices. In the United States, there is a strong belief that the national forests are an asset held in trust on behalf of all citizens. Many urban-based conservation organizations, in particular, take this to mean that no preference should be given to local interests or forest-dependent enterprises—even in places such as New Mexico, where the designation of national forests extinguished centuries-old Spanish land grants predating U.S. sovereignty.[4] Wherever, and under whatever political system, the national interest consistently appears to override or exclude the interests of communities in or near reserved forests.

Stakeholders play a prominent role in the rhetoric of participatory development. In reaction to discredited models of top-down decision-making, planners and decision-makers consult with individuals and groups of people expected to share an interest in the forest, in order to solicit their suggestions and responses to proposals. Projects and plans then proceed on the assumption that the process of consultation has highlighted the shared goals and objectives of the stakeholders and that, in securing their acquiescence, it has defused or resolved differences. Until recently, the U.S. Forest Service has relied on statements from participants attending public meetings to legitimate its planning process as being built on participation and consultation with stakeholders. Critics of this process reject the suggestion that the statements of participants in meetings represent an aggregate public interest. They question who has the time and resources to attend such meetings, noting that participants are often representatives of or backed by a powerful interest group such as the timber industry or well-funded urban-based conservation organizations. Many residents of forest communities, forest workers, and historically excluded minorities such as Hispanos, Native Americans,[5] or African Americans often have neither the time nor the resources to participate, and as a consequence their voices are not heard (Baker and Kusel 2003:50; Danks 2000; Noon 2003).

Without denying the significance of the invitation to the public to participate in decision-making, reference to stakeholder participation fails to capture the unequal relations between actors (Bousquet et al. 1999a; Colfer 1995; Edmunds and Wollenberg 2001). In the case of CBFM, it assumes that all the stakeholders have an interest in maintaining the condition of the forest and that they share a vision of what a desirable forest condition would be. Negotiations over forest management premised on parity between stakeholders may in fact "mask abuses of power and more structural, enduring inequity" (Edmunds and Wollenberg 2001:232). If negotiations proceed instead with a recognition from the outset of different interests in the forest and an explicit goal of strengthening the bargaining power of disadvantaged groups through strategic alliances and improved access to information (Agrawal 1997:29), the outcome is ultimately more likely to be accepted by all actors, making it more enforceable and resilient in the face of changing circumstances.

Partners and Their Interests

Political economists analyze society in terms of three sectors: the state or public sector, the market or private sector, and civil society or institutions such as NGOs. The prominence of one sector over another in international development has changed in concert with evolving political ideologies and policy frameworks from a reliance on the market in the decades following the Second World War to targeted state interventions to achieve social goals during the

1960s and 1970s (Rist 1997; So 1990; Uphoff 1993). By the 1980s civil society, local institutions, and NGOs came to the fore as "falling living standards . . . focused attention on immediate survival and on the substitution possibilities which civil organizations could offer to what the state (public goods and welfare) and the market (jobs) were no longer able to deliver" (De Janvry, Sadoulet, and Thorbecke 1993:565). The political and economic breakdown into three sectors represents the channels through which different actors pursue their interests, but it oversimplifies the relations between the contending interests that converge over forest resources. Whichever sector conventional wisdom privileges at any point in time, none of them is a closed, monolithic sphere of interest, and forest management is inevitably the outcome of some degree of involvement from institutions in all three sectors.

Government agencies pursue differing mandates—for example, the Himachal Pradesh Cooperatives Development Union has aligned itself with the Kangra District Cooperative Forest Societies Union in their civil suit against the state Forestry Department. Corporations compete nationally and internationally. There are sharp divisions within the environmental NGO community over the most effective strategies for conservation. Some organizations demand the complete exclusion of all human activity in protected areas (Terborgh 1999; Redford and Richter 1999; Van Schaik and Kramer 1997). Others promote integrated programs linked to local development in the belief that conservation will be successful only if local people derive some benefits (Borrini-Feyerabend 1996; Schwartzman, Moreira, and Nepstad 2000; Western, Wright, and Strum 1994).[6] Communities, for their part, share an interest with at least some segments of the private sector in building and maintaining viable enterprises marketing forest products, locally, nationally, and internationally.

The public sector, the private sector, and civil society do not exist and function in separate, unrelated spheres. It is important when considering how they pursue their interests in forest resources, to evaluate the degree to which each is involved in setting objectives, decision-making, and implementation of decisions over land and resource management. It is in the course of negotiations around these choices that different interests press their claims and in which alliances and partnerships will form, play themselves out, dissolve, and reform (Ostrom 1993; Springate-Baginski 2004).

The State, Communities, and International Development Agencies

The most fundamental partnership at the heart of CBFM is between communities and the state agencies mandated to manage forest resources. Moves to involve communities in management challenge the monopoly of power and authority over resources previously claimed by the state agency. CBFM aspires to redistribute rights, responsibilities, and incentives for management between partners rather than continuing to enforce a division between a sovereign authority and subordinate, voiceless subjects. The degree to which the relationships between the state agency and communities have actually been reconstituted varies, but unequal relations generally still prevail. With few exceptions, the agency that is now charged with fashioning collaborative partnerships and working with communities is the same state agency—or its postcolonial successor—that had previously reserved the forests and extinguished the rights of resident communities, transforming them into encroachers or illegal squatters. As one international practitioner remarks: "This really raises the question of whether or not forestry departments are the best possible 'partners' for communities" (Davis-Case 2001:10).

As the main interlocutor with government in the partnership, the community is not only the weaker partner politically, but also has to contend with reconciling the diversity of interests within its own physical and social boundaries. As discussed in the preceding chapters, local institutions struggle with questions of legitimacy, accountability, and representation that are not easily resolved. Where a partnership serves as a forum for negotiations over the terms of engagement and cooperation between the state agency and the community, the question of who is the community and who legitimately represents its interests remains a live issue. Formal institutions of local governance, informal but established and respected village associations, and new bodies created with a specific mandate to manage resources on behalf of the community may all claim to represent local interests. A partnership needs a structure and procedures that give it flexibility to accommodate different community voices in a dialog without degenerating into a confrontational platform from which to pursue factional interests.

Not only is it the case that neither government nor community is monolithic and homogenous, but it is also difficult to draw a sharp line dividing government from community. Local representatives of government agencies are in daily contact with residents of the community—and are likely to be from the community themselves. It is often at this level that the first steps have been taken to encourage community participation, with representatives of the state forestry department or equivalent agency agreeing to experiment with or simply to tolerate creative local solutions to conflicts for which national policies have no solutions (Joshi 1999). At the same time, the efforts of individuals who have earned the trust and respect of their community in working to develop and promote those creative solutions may be recognized through appointment or popular election to office in local government. In Yunnan Province in China, leaders of nongovernmental village-based community resource management programs have been elected as village head or mayor—the only level of administration where open elections are currently permitted in China (Zhu 2004).

The dominance of state and agency interests is reinforced in CBFM by the intervention of international donors and development institutions. The aid and technical assistance they offer is directed toward programs and projects formulated in consultation with national governments to resolve problems defined to fit the changing priorities of both parties. The hierarchical structures of large international agencies discourage participatory decision-making, compromising their capacity to press for change in the national institutions they support.[7] Despite a discourse of community empowerment, donors do not have mechanisms to provide financial and capacity-building support directly to community-level institutions. Funding is nearly always channeled through national governments and intermediaries such as international consultancies or NGOs, whose claims to represent the interests of communities are open to question. "'Beneficiaries' seldom have the right to accept or refuse a project, to identify needs and set the goals for the activities or to exert some control over funding decisions, procedures, timing and information flows" (Hoskins 2002:4).

Civil Society and NGOs

International development agencies have turned to partners from civil society—NGOs in particular—as an alternative to government channels, which are often accused of being unduly bureaucratic or corrupt (Uphoff 1993). NGOs bring together like-minded people committed to taking action to realize a shared goal they believe to be in the public interest. Operating outside conventional bureaucratic structures, they can respond more rapidly and nimbly to the concerns of their partners, and there have been some expectations that they might offer an alternative pathway for development.

The term NGO has come to be used to describe a diversity of organizations that coexist under the broad heading of civil society.[8] Uphoff warns: "This category [NGO], without refinement, puts self-help membership associations in the same category with paternalistic, philanthropic organizations. Such heterogeneity lumps together a village savings club in Peru and the Rockefeller Foundation, which might study or subsidize this association" (1993:609).

To avoid such "lumping together," it is useful to distinguish between partnerships with representative organizations and partnerships with intermediary NGOs. In Brazil, the residents' associations along the Igarapés near Mazagão have chosen to be members of the Amapá Rural Workers' Union (SINTRA) to represent their interests in arenas where they would otherwise be powerless. FECOFUN in Nepal unites otherwise small and scattered community forest user groups, building alliances to press for favorable policies for its members. Representative organizations such as these are by no means immune to authoritarian or abusive internal governance and corruption, but their members do at the very least have the option of withdrawing from the association or joining a different movement—as some forest users have done in Amapá, choosing to join the Rubber Tappers' Union (CNS) rather than SINTRA. The right of free entry or withdrawal from a partnership is an important check on its legitimacy, ensuring a minimum level of accountability with respect to the weaker and less articulate partners.

During the 1990s flows of international aid slowed, but the proportion of funds channeled through NGOs increased (Fowler 1998:138). As a result, NGOs find themselves in an uncomfortable role as intermediaries, chosen to fill the gap left by the limited reach and capacities of overextended states (Edwards and Hulme 1997; J. Nugent 1993; Uphoff 1993). Many Latin American NGOs in the field of rural development emerged in the course of popular struggles against military dictatorships, and their transition from resistance to the role of service providers and implementers of programs initiated by the state or international agencies has triggered a crisis of legitimacy and identity. Some now face criticisms from popular social movements, such as associations of farmers or indigenous people, that they have distanced themselves from the poor to become contractors or instruments of the establishment (Bebbington 1997; García-Guadilla 2002:19–20). Reliance on donor funding creates an unequal relationship between the NGO and the donor as well as between the NGO and its partners in rural communities, undermining the chances of building a relationship that respects the autonomy and identity of local people and institutions (Chapin 2004; Fowler 1998:140–45; Hoskins 2002; Sundar and Jeffery 1999:29–34).

As designated intermediaries and facilitators, development NGOs enjoy a degree of power that allows them to shape agendas and to determine the representation of stakeholders—leading to criticism that some of them have become unaccountable gatekeepers filtering access to funding and technical assistance (Edmunds and Wollenberg 2001:240; Harrison 2002; McCarthy 2000:119). NGOs' legitimacy lies in their claim *not* to be agents of the government and to represent the interests of constituents and stakeholders, although their accountability is, in practice, to the funders who have chosen them, rather than to the local people and institutions that they purportedly represent (Colchester et al. 2003:15–19; Igoe 2003; Li 2002:276; Sundar and Jeffery 1999:33).

The role of NGOs in partnerships can become distorted if they substitute their own interests or ideological biases for the broader priorities and interests of the communities where they work. There is a need for advocacy on behalf of local interests, for facilitation between them and national or international forces, and for intermediaries that can offer services and support that the state and markets are unable or unwilling to provide. NGOs can meet those needs as partners in a diverse civil society, but their legitimacy and credibility in playing this role depends on their accountability to their partners, not on the pursuit of their own interests and agendas.

The Private Sector

In northern industrialized countries, as in the south, the private sector has failed to demonstrate that market forces alone will ensure environmentally sustainable utilization of forest resources, stable and prosperous communities, or equitably distributed generation of wealth. Commercial logging operations have possibly triggered more conflict and confrontation in forests than any other activity. Industrial timber producers that have benefited from state control over forest resources are therefore more likely than other forest-based businesses to resist the changes in their practices that would be the likely consequences of accepting communities as partners in forest management.

Policies favoring community participation in forest management and certification programs incorporating criteria for social responsibility have led in some places to constructive negotiations and partnerships between communities and timber corporations. A global review of fifty-seven such partnerships[9] concluded that some of them, though not all, did bring real benefits, including employment and income generation, although there were also negative environmental impacts from logging and questions emerging from inequitable distribution of benefits within communities (Mayers and Vermeulen 2002). In the Amazon, legal recognition of indigenous territories and extractive reserves has involved the private sector in a growing number of business partnerships with communities. Despite some difficulties, these arrangements appear to have more positive social and environmental outcomes than previous arrangements under government concessions, particularly where civil society organizations have been able to assist in brokering deals, providing technical assistance, and monitoring compliance (Morsello 2004; Johann Zweede, personal communication).

Private-sector interests in forest resources extend from large international timber corporations to individual entrepreneurs, such as those who buy matsutake mushrooms in a village for resale to wholesalers in the county town. Large or small, the private sector links communities to markets. Partnerships with the private sector are as important as those with the state and civil society for communities managing forest resources. The interests of the private sector and of forest communities converge most nearly in the marketing of non-timber forest products (NTFP), handicrafts, and services such as ecotourism. These are activities where communities can benefit from the business and marketing skills of entrepreneurs who depend in turn on community involvement either in collecting and processing products or in receiving and hosting visitors. As discussed earlier (chapter 8), converging interests do not ensure equitable relations, but support from state or nongovernmental intermediaries can assist in brokering and monitoring contracts, in locating financial skills, and in providing training to build entrepreneurial skills.

Who Is Setting the Agenda?

A project evaluation from Yen Bai Province in Vietnam claimed that the project would significantly reduce regulatory costs for the government, reduce the "dependency and passivity" of the local people, and help to pay for forest protection (Vu 2001, quoted in chapter 7, pp. 103–104). This argument for CBFM leaves no doubt over which partner is in control of determining the project's goals. The project marks a significant change from past practice in the process of consultation with the community and recognition that restrictions on land use should be balanced with the incentive of a share of the benefits. The outlines of an acceptable forest management plan are, however, predetermined and must include "effective production and high productivity" (Vu 2001:8) with detailed silvicultural standards for rehabilitating forest cover and maximizing the production of timber and NTFPs (Vu 2001:9–10). The communities in the project have some space for negotiation that they did not enjoy before, but the state has taken care to stake out the boundaries of that space.

There is a jarring note to the discourse of partnership and participation when CBFM is introduced as a development project, accompanied by a consultation process incorporating tools such as participatory rural appraisal (PRA)—but where the concerned communities are fully aware that the decision to implement a CBFM project has already been taken. In a forum for an exchange of views between communities managing natural resources in East Africa, representatives from Tanzania observed that the donors supporting a mangrove management project planned for, not with, the community. They complained of the degree of control wielded by the donors:

> The community reported that it is not allowed by its current donors to prepare project proposals and submit them to other donors. Similarly, the community prefers to plant certain mangrove species, which they believe are better suited to the areas and also have a higher market value. However, the donor agencies

have rejected the community's ideas and in turn the species provided by the donor agencies are not flourishing.   —WATKIN 2001:27

The risk of conflicting agendas is greater where environmental protection and conservation are the stated or unstated objectives of a proposed partnership. The many strands of the contemporary international conservation movement still come together in a commitment to setting aside and protecting land from human disturbance to preserve endangered species or habitat. Indigenous people counter that in many parts of the world the remaining islands of biodiversity are places with a long history of human use, and they dispute the assumption that conservation can be achieved only through the exclusion of local people and the imposition of restrictions on their access and utilization. From the community perspective, it often appears that conservationists see any presence of people as a concession, not as an essential component of conservation. Negotiations within the partnership concern what the community may or may not do, not what conservation agencies and their staff may or may not do (Lima 1999:248–49).

A History of Dispossession and Exclusion: Racism and Inequity in Forest Partnerships

There may be no easy solution to striking a balance in conservation between strategies of exclusionary preservation and sustainable utilization, and advocates of different perspectives defend their case with passion and conviction. In some arguments for the primacy of preservation, there is, however, a disturbing undercurrent of racism, especially painful where forestry and conservation are themselves associated with a history of dispossession and disenfranchisement.

In "Lifeboat Ethics: The Case Against Helping the Poor," American ecologist Garrett Hardin wrote in 1974 of the danger posed to the environment by overpopulated developing countries, arguing both against international aid and against immigration as a threat to environmental and economic survival. Hardin was not by any means the first or the last writer to blame environmental degradation on the poor and the "other"—usually racial minorities.[10] His unwavering focus on demographic pressure and the assumed ignorance of the poor, to the exclusion of economic or political forces driving environmental change, conforms to the conventional narrative of forest and resources degradation justifying the exclusion of local and indigenous people. It continues to resurface even where there is an ostensible commitment on the part of environmental organizations to community-based conservation (Chapin 2004).

PLATE 8. Harvesting wild coffee in Kibale Forest National Park, Uganda.

PHOTO: WENDY STONE/CORBIS

Before its designation as a national park in 1993, Kibale forest in Uganda had been a forest reserve where the government assigned concessions to timber companies for logging. The forest has become known for what is said to be the highest density of primate species in the world, with twelve different species, including chimpanzees. In the late 1990s the Global Environmental Facility, through the World Bank, funded a program to explore the possibility of allowing surrounding communities to harvest the wild coffee that grows inside the forest for sale in the United States as "wild forest coffee." The intent was to market the coffee with an explicit link to the conservation of chimpanzees and other species in the park, charging buyers a premium and using the revenue to create a fund that communities would use for local development programs.[11]

An important element of the marketing strategy was to secure the endorsement of influential environmental organizations in the United States such as the Sierra Club. A member of the Sierra Club's leadership invited to visit Uganda to learn about the project was reluctant to endorse it on the grounds that national parks are designated to protect the biodiversity of pristine ecosystems and that any form of commercial utilization would compromise this mission. Challenged to justify his position in a place where logging had taken place since the 1960s and where several thousand residents had been moved out of the forest at the time it was gazetted, he said that the Ugandan government should have considered the potential difficulties at the time the decision had been made to gazette the national park. In insisting that Uganda had to live by its choice of conservation as strict protection, he chose to ignore the pressures that the Ugandan government had faced when gazetting Kibale Forest National Park in 1993 as an environmental component of a large internationally funded economic restructuring package. Coerced conservation, not publicly debated and mandated choice, was the background to the proposed program to compensate local people for the livelihoods they had lost. The wild coffee project continues, but is struggling to find the assured market that endorsement from the Sierra Club might have given it.

Racial and nationalist undertones are common in environmental discourses demanding the removal and resettlement of people—usually from ethnic minorities—said to destroy forests. Few of Thailand's upland ethnic minority people—the "hill tribes"—enjoy Thai citizenship. As debate over the country's proposed Community Forestry Bill has become increasingly polarized, dark green environmental groups have linked upland people with a vaguely defined threat to national security, demanding that they be removed and excluded from protected areas in order to protect the nation's environmental heritage (Laungaramsri 2001:106–20; Lohmann 1999; Makarabhirom 2000).

Conflict between some conservation organizations and local or indigenous people is not in defense of material interests but of deeply held value systems. Accommodation over economic values is easier to negotiate than it is over the cultural and symbolic values of land and resources. Unfortunately, misunderstanding and misrepresentation of traditional cultural values are common, leading sometimes to bitter recriminations when romanticized constructions of "ecologically noble natives" confront the realities of people and cultures struggling in the face of dispossession, marginalization, and poverty (Edmunds and Wollenberg 2001:241; Li 2002:270; Ramos 1994). In the United States, many environmental organizations draw analogies between their values and the spiritual heritage of Native Americans (La Duke 1996; Mander 1992; Taylor 1997) but recoil vociferously when modern Native Americans apply for permits for ritual hunting of whales or the capture of sacrificial golden eagle chicks under the terms of their treaties with the United States or federal legislation guaranteeing rights of religious freedom and traditional cultural practices.[12]

The hostility generated by these fractured alliances between environmental organizations and local communities is demonstrated by the verbal and physical violence—including at least one bombing attempt—that surrounds the contested plan to allow Hispano communities to carry out timber harvesting on the Vallecitos Sustained Yield Unit of the Carson National Forest in New Mexico.

The Forest Guardians, one of the environmental groups appealing against the plan in the courts, has presented itself as a contemporary heir to the American civil-rights movement. The claim is rejected with outrage by local activists who took part in the civil-rights marches of the 1960s, had been arrested for their actions, and now view the Forest Guardians as privileged white residents of the cities that are the state's most profligate consumers of scarce natural resources (Kosek 2004b:145–46; Mathews 1999). The Forest Guardians' appropriation of a local history of struggle for rights and their rejection of any possibility of distinct local interests or cultural values in the forest have perpetuated the dispossession of communities from lands they lost more than a century ago and reduced the likelihood of partnership between environmental organizations and communities to counter the influence of large corporate interests over timber management on the national forests in the United States.

Hijacking: Community Management or Someone Else's Project?

CBFM is most visible in the international public eye as the subject of project reports and a prolific literature of research papers, monographs, and unpublished "grey literature." Outside the world of development projects and agency-driven programs, however, communities are taking the initiative to craft their own ways to regulate access and utilization of resources to respond to shortages of fuelwood, changing flows of water in their streams, or market demand for forest products (Sarin et al. 2003:17–23; Turner 1999). In Kenya, Uganda, and Tanzania, a concerted effort to contact communities managing natural resources identified more than thirty local initiatives in each country—organized by villages, churches, and women's groups—receiving no funding or assistance or recognition from any outside source (Watkin 2001). A similar picture is emerging in Mexico, where a recent survey found at least twice as many community-based forestry enterprises than the previous estimates of less than one thousand (Antinori, Bray, and Rojo 2004).

East African communities used the term *hijacking* to describe what happened to local initiatives where an outside partner became involved. They described instances where a community group involved in a focused activity with modest ambitions such as tree-planting for more accessible firewood entered into a partnership with an outside agency in the hope of getting access to financial and technical assistance or of improved linkages with government agencies—only to find decision-making powers shifting to the new partner: "Once the external agency hijacked [the] project, it expanded to become a big project and soon failure was looming" (Watkin 2001:28).

Hijacking of local initiatives by a donor-funded program can provoke a reaction that not only undermines the new project, but also runs counter to the original intentions of the community-initiated action. The Worldwide Fund for Nature (WWF) has collaborated since 1994 with the Zanzibar department of fisheries to implement a community-based marine conservation program involving seventeen villages surrounding Menai Bay on the opposite coast of Unguja Island from Jozani forest (Levine 2004:21–24). Fumba village had established a village conservation committee some ten years before the WWF project began, using their own funds to patrol the area to stop destructive fishing practices. At the request of WWF, Fumba agreed to dissolve its committee and participate instead in a new program centered in Kizimkazi village on the other side of the bay. Since then, Fumba has watched as funding and public attention have flowed to project headquarters in Kizimkazi, while they have witnessed an increase in illegal fishing, which they ascribe to reduced patrols by project boats reluctant to serve the more remote Fumba communities. Fumba residents have vented their anger in the Zanzibari press and admit to acts of resistance such as disabling project equipment. Their reaction to the project is captured in one fisher's complaint: "People in Fumba were the first to protect the environment. Here we were teachers for other areas, but the project removed us ... now people from here have had their hearts broken—they don't continue [to work to protect the environment]" (Levine 2004:23).

On Misali Island, local initiative appears to have succeeded in building a more equitable and supportive partnership with CARE International and DCCFF than did its counterpart with comparable objectives at Menai Bay. The idea for creating a conservation area first came from the fishers, not from their prospective partners. It was the fishers of Misali who came to the conclusion that they could benefit from the organizational assistance of an international NGO as well as political backing from the government agency. Words convey subtle but important messages. At Menai Bay, people talk of "project" patrol boats and of village committees under the project, while at Misali, reference is to MICA (the Misali Island Conservation Association) setting rules for fishing and monitoring compliance. All those involved recognize that MICA has yet to establish itself as a fully legitimate and effective community institution, but it does seem to have a voice and an identity as a partner in the program rather than as an instrument of a project.

Conclusion: Partnerships in an Unequal World

In CBFM, asymmetrical relations between partners are almost inevitable, given that communities are seeking to regain access to land and resources they have lost or to have a locally devised initiative given official recognition.

Disadvantaged groups do not enter negotiations over CBFM as equal stakeholders, but they can redress the balance to some extent by forming networks and alliances to broaden political support and to help build their own capacity to articulate and advocate for their position (Edmunds and Wollenberg 2001). Based on the principle of voluntary association, these alliances widen communities' perspectives and bring them greater visibility without appropriating their own initiatives and agendas.

Agreements and rules that emerge from the interaction between partners have legitimacy to the extent that they are the outcome of a dialog giving voice to different understandings of the present and visions of the future (Bousquet et al. 1999b:119). The process of negotiation itself therefore demands commitment, mutual respect for the different interests represented, and continuous questioning to ensure that understandings are shared and that dissenting views have not been muffled. Under these conditions, bargaining can construct a framework for positive change that is acceptable to all the partners (Agarwal 2001:1641; Lima 1999:260–61).

Whatever its institutional form, a partnership should provide a space in which to reach a common vision and pool the skills and capacities of all participants to allow them to progress toward that vision. Power and structural inequities may endure in CBFM partnerships, but they can be countered if efforts are made to incorporate certain organizational features into their structure and operations:[13]

- voluntary association—the ability to choose or reject partners and activities and to invite new partners who might provide skills that are otherwise missing
- ethical relations—symmetry in access to information, rights and responsibilities, and funding
- transparency and honesty about whose interests individuals and organizations can genuinely claim to represent
- mechanisms for accountability
- open and respectful communication
- adaptability and respect for the principle of contingency by keeping access open to those who are not yet partners

Earlier in this chapter, I quoted a passage from a study by Marilyn Hoskins of FAO's involvement in community forestry in which she asked some basic questions about partnerships. Does the community—"the beneficiary"—have any choice in choosing or rejecting its partners and the project being proposed by the partner? Does the community exert any control over funding decisions, procedures, timing, and information flows? Are demands for accountability reciprocal? (2000:2). Partnerships in which the answer to these questions is yes would serve all those involved, rather than operating as arrangements entrenching the domination of one interest over the others. They might not guarantee the success of community-based management, but they would make it more likely that the strengths of each partner are brought to bear on the task they have taken on together and that mutual respect makes the resolution of differences a possibility.

10

Governance and Empowerment

Nagarahole is a lush tropical forest on the edge of Coorg, where the coffee bushes give way to bamboo thickets on either side of the road. . . . Bandits have made the place their Sherwood Forest. The infamous Koose Muniswamy Veerappan, known for a long run of kidnappings, is reputed to have funded operations from woodland spoils, and has eluded capture by disappearing among the trees.

—*TIME ASIA* MAGAZINE, 16 SEPTEMBER 2002

In the terrain that poachers—even Veerappan had been there once upon a time—trudged across in search of . . . forest wealth, the khaki-clad guards of the jungle have climbed down their erstwhile ivory towers to reach out to the original inhabitants of the land, armed with a plethora of developmental schemes, in lieu of their participation and cooperation in the protection of forests.

—*NEWS TODAY* (CHENNAI), 12 OCTOBER 2004

VEERAPPAN WAS killed in a police ambush on 19 October 2004 after a lifetime of kidnappings and crime, dealing in poached ivory and sandalwood. His death has only served to burnish his legend as a daring—albeit fearsome—outlaw fighting for the poor from deep in the forests of south India. Veerappan's forested domain was home to tribal people whose presence the state only tolerated while excluding them even from gathering honey, medicines, or foods such as tubers and fruit from ancestral lands it now claimed as its own. Dispossession and alienation had made them receptive to the appeal of a charismatic outlaw and of rebel movements such as the Naxalite guerillas. The state is now granting some access rights and introducing development projects, hoping to transform the ungovernable space of the forest into a harmonious, productive landscape in which the tribal communities will play a new role as protectors of the forest, replacing exclusion with participation and inclusion.

The story of Veerappan and the outlaws of Nagarahole forest is only a recent iteration of a story that has been played out countless times over the centuries, as states have struggled to extend their control over forests. In the English tradition of Robin Hood, the forest was where the good outlaws hid from the tyrannical sheriff of Nottingham. In the almost contemporaneous Chinese novel, *Outlaws of the Marsh* (*Shui Hu Zhuan*), the geography was reversed.

The 108 bandits heroes lived on a mountaintop. The emperor's evil underlings held sway over the lowlands. The forest was a no-man's land between the two, a wooded lair from which to launch ambushes and raids on the imperial forces and a shadowy, tangled wilderness in which the outlaws showed their bravery in fights with wild animals or in rescuing their companions from the clutches of corrupt officials.[1] Even today, in the United States, people in search of an alternative lifestyle choose to move away from urban areas to settle in small secluded communities in or around the national forests, while some of the more remote and inaccessible recesses of the forests are a haven for former hippies tending illegal but lucrative plots of marijuana.

CBFM is a commitment to a realignment of power and decision-making authority, to reordering the relations between government and the governed in forests. In the context of resources management, governance refers to who participates in decision-making, the procedures and rules by which decisions are made and consensus is reached, as well as mechanisms to hold decision-makers accountable for their actions. Improved governance should give communities the strength and authority to formulate and implement a forest management regime and the power to negotiate and to defend their own interests against others. There is a growing consensus that political representation and the downward accountability of elected representatives to their constituencies are important conditions for effecting the devolution of tenure, access, and authority that make it possible for the primary users of natural resources to take on the responsibilities of long-term stewardship (Alden Wily 2001; Gibson, Ostrom, and McKean 2000:233–34; Larson 2004; Mandondo and Mapedza 2003:2–4; Murphree 2000:7; Ribot 2002).

International attention to governance has shaped a favorable political environment for CBFM, although there is an inherent contradiction in the phenomenon of international trends molding and driving policies and programs that purport to empower the local.[2] There is also considerable, justified skepticism about the degree to which agencies have opened their formerly exclusive preserves of decision-making and enforcement to forest communities (Anon. 2002b; Dove 1995; Elías and Wittman 2004; Kaimowitz et al. 1998; Lele 2002; Murphree 2000; Ribot 2002; Sarin et al. 2003; Wollenberg 1998a). A critical review of the impacts of community-based natural resources programs in the Philippines goes so far as to claim that they have been "in reality a mis-named continuation of central control. Well-intentioned policies have unfortunately contained fundamental defects . . . and this has enabled self-interested bureaucracies to inhibit the sharing and transfer of power" (Gollin and Kho 2002b:19).

More positively though, there is evidence from places such as Naidu and Jozani and from formerly disenfranchised peoples such as the Huron-Wendat

Nation in Québec or the Zapotec members of UZACHI in the Oaxaca highlands that some local people, at least, have been able to secure their communities' rights of access to resources and rise to the challenge of shaping their futures. Changed institutional arrangements in the context of CBFM can empower local resource users to be a part of governing the forest, not just governed subjects in the forest—although their new rights are often fragile and need to be anchored in wider national institutions of accountable governance.

Much of the literature on CBFM and governance mirrors the international development community's continuing preoccupation with processes of devolution and decentralization. While acknowledging the importance of understanding how and why states are redistributing power and authority, I will step back from detailed analysis of devolution as one particular strategy for improving governance to look more broadly at the search for an allocation of powers between the diverse interests in forest resources, which empowers local voices and increases the capacity of local institutions to implement sustainable and equitable management regimes (Elías and Wittman 2004; Mandondo and Mapedza 2003). This chapter addresses the association between improved governance and CBFM, asking how—and if—one advances or enables the other. It considers what the role of governments and states might be in the altered relationships of power and decision-making that are being proposed. Finally, it questions the extent to which change has empowered local institutions and strengthened their capacities for equitable and sustainable resource management.

Better Governance Through CBFM?

Some governments and international development agencies have promoted CBFM as an institutional framework for conflict mediation and resolution. The outcome of improved governance through CBFM is expected to be a collaborative process through which different interests might reach agreement on the "collective choices that will orient action for the long term future" (Bousquet et al. 1999a:7), a process that is essential to the long-term sustainability and survival of the resource itself (Buckles 1999).

The significance of improved governance in CBFM is greater, however, than its potential for reducing conflict. The passage of time and the certainty of change demand resilience and flexibility in management regimes. Centralized authoritarian systems are ultimately as fragile as the legitimacy of the state regimes that impose them (Mosse 2004:646). Throughout history, ordinary people all over the world have engaged in "everyday acts of resistance" (Scott

1987) against perceived injustice. If the outcome of negotiations over forest resources is to be respected by all the parties, neither the process of negotiation nor their conclusions can be imposed. The invitation to the local stewards of natural resources to take their place in the negotiations and decision-making that determine future actions and uses of forest resources is perhaps CBFM's most significant innovation in governance, signaling a readiness to redistribute significant powers that states have appropriated to themselves in the past.

Community-based resource management is situated within the dynamics of national political systems. In calling for transparency, equity, and accountability in the process of negotiation and in the implementation of their outcomes, good governance of forest resources becomes more than a hopeful approach to resolving age-old conflicts in the forest. It takes its place as an element in a more far-reaching interrogation of long-standing patterns of relations between states and citizens and of the distribution of roles and powers between the different institutions of the state and society (Li 2002:273; Murphree 2000:7). CBFM has prised open space for local voices to be involved in the planning and management of local affairs, which had formerly been claimed as the exclusive preserve of bureaucratic and often autocratic agencies (Brown et al. 2002). In Mexico, CBFM appears to have encouraged a more respectful government engagement with communities, lower levels of conflict over forest resources, and an active, commercially viable community-based forestry sector (Bray and Merino-Pérez 2002; Klooster 1999). Even in more closed political systems, CBFM has introduced new practices, such as open candidacies in elections for forest management committees in Vietnam (Manor 2004:195) or challenges from respected leaders of forest committees to officially selected candidates in local government elections in China (see chapter 9, p. 00).

In most cases, the redistribution of powers has stopped at collaborative agreements in which the community gains access rights and a share of revenue, but which fall short of a complete transfer of the ownership of the resource from the state to the community. In some countries, the state has taken the step of ceding full ownership to communities. The process of "reconstructing the meaning of collaborative management" (Alden Wily and Dewees 2001:20–27) is perhaps most advanced in Tanzania, partly as a consequence of the government's recognition that it is unable to pay the increasing costs of policing what was becoming an ever-expanding area of reserved forests and protected areas.

Examples of an effective transfer of powers to forest communities in some places are matched by strong critiques of governments in other places holding on to the most important levers of control. In Kangra, the Himachal Pradesh Forestry Department has refused to pay grant-in-aid payments for the preparation of forest working plans and the *haq chuharram* shares of income from the sale of trees, disabling the CFSs by depriving them of their principal source of income. In many countries, technical requirements for the preparation of forest management plans restrict the communities' choices to conventional scenarios of conservation, subsistence use, or commercial timber harvesting (chapter 8, pp. 138–39).

A persistent criticism of CBFM's failure to empower local institutions has been that it is in fact unusual for community institutions to be entrusted with control over forests. It is more common for the powers of the state agency to be assigned to the lower rungs of government administration such as the county or township in China (Xu and Zuo 2003), the municipality in Guatemala (Elías and Wittman 2004) and Bolivia (Kaimowitz et al. 1998), rural councils in Senegal (Ribot 1999), or communes in Mali (Kassibo 2002). Whether or not these levels of administration are representative and accountable democratic institutions, they remain branches of state authority, prompting one observer to remark that "since community turns out in practice to be a lower level of government rather than new local institutions . . . it is more useful to regard such measures as rearrangements of the way in which rule is accomplished" (Li 1997:74).

A counterpoint to this critique has been a concern that in countries moving toward more representative and accountable local government, donor- or government-directed resource management programs have bestowed powers and decision-making rights on independent committees or NGOs acting outside or parallel to emerging democratic processes (Manor 2004:200–201; Kassibo 2002; Ribot 2004:36–42) or on unrepresentative and unaccountable traditional authorities (Ribot 2002; Kepe 1998). Parallel or overlapping institutions can offer multiple channels for action where bureaucratic inertia blocks new initiatives and defends its turf, but there is a danger that they can create confusion instead (Vasavada, Mishra, and Bates 1999). In Kangra alone, so many committees have been established to oversee development projects over the last half century, that few people can remember them all, and it has taken careful research and scholarship to trace their genealogies and histories (Vasan 2001). Furthermore, when local authorities are not a part of the realignment of powers between the state and communities, they may deliberately ignore communities' new rights or act directly to block the passage of relevant legislation at the national level. After more than a decade of experimentation in the form of internationally funded projects, Botswana's CBNRM legislation had not yet been approved by late 2004, partly as a result of the lack of support from local authorities (Rozmeijer 2003:7).

Communities near Jozani, Misali, and Ngezi (chapter 4) and other communities managing forests in Tanzania have taken advantage of the provisions in national law that allow then to embed the community's forest management institutions and rules as legally enforceable local bylaws. Communities in other countries such as Mexico or the former trust lands of Namaqualand in South Africa (chapter 7, pp. 116–17) have used similar approaches to embed local statutes in national legislation and administrative structures. Other strategies might include bringing the community forest management institution into the structure of local government as a specialized working group or committee or giving legal recognition to a defined community forest users' group with normal fiscal responsibilities in the form of tax on earned income (Murphree 2000:11). It is important to acknowledge the complementarity of local government and CBFM institutions and to give each the authority and resources it needs to play the role for which it has the competence and the capacities.

Decentralization, Devolution, and the Changing Roles of Government

Decentralization and devolution have entered the discourse of natural resource management, often deployed almost as a synonym for good governance. While there is more to improved governance and CBFM than policies of decentralization and devolution, there is value to considering how those processes of political reform are shaping and changing the roles of local governments.

Assessments of devolution and decentralization in forest and resource management echo the frequently voiced criticism that states have usually transferred to communities the burdens of patrolling, monitoring, and planting or regeneration, while resource management agencies continue to claim ownership of the land itself and remain firmly in control of basic decisions about management goals and objectives, technical standards, or finance and accounting systems. Transposed into the idiom of devolution and decentralization, the argument is that the transfer of powers and authority has not been complete since states have reserved important powers of oversight and even veto for themselves, nor has it been a devolution to accountable institutions representing the interests of the local actors involved in day-to-day decisions about managing resources (CIFOR 2004; Lind and Cappon 2001; Ribot 2004; Shackleton et al. 2002).

While acknowledging the importance and the pertinence of the critique that devolution in natural resource management has been incomplete, I will not retrace an already extensive literature on the subject here,[3] but will concentrate on some aspects of the debate that cast light on the changing relations between states and citizens in CBFM. A fundamental question is whether states are devolving powers to new local institutions or dispersing them among lower levels of existing administrative structures. A related issue concerns representation and the accountability of the institutions to which power is devolved. I conclude with the proposition that it is more important to place the locus of decision-making about forest management with those who are directly engaged in and affected by its outcomes than it is to devolve formal jurisdiction over the resource to a level of the administrative hierarchy determined a priori by the stipulations of a national agenda of devolution and decentralization.

The impetus for devolution in natural resource management comes from the assumption that the inclusion of local people improves decision-making where local knowledge, information, and experience are relevant, as they are in the management of forest ecosystems. It is also assumed that people who have been a part of making the rules for management will enforce them more rigorously and that incorporating resource users into forest governance will promote more equitable development when they are in control of the distribution and disposal of revenue. These assumptions about efficiency and equity presuppose the right to make and implement decisions without undue constraints (Ribot 2002:21). They also demand that the decision-making bodies should operate in an open and transparent manner and that they should be directly accountable to the resource users in order to respond to their concerns and aspirations.

Initiatives in which decision-making authority is reassigned from government officials in the central government to their counterparts in the lower levels of administration have been referred to as deconcentration since they retain power in the state apparatus but disperse it more widely (Ostrom, Schroeder, and Wynne 1993:168; Ribot 2004:9). Devolution and decentralization themselves may be analyzed as different phenomena—with decentralization described in comparable terms to deconcentration as the delegation of limited powers to subordinate levels of the government hierarchy (Murphree 2000:5). Others have preferred to distinguish between administrative devolution and democratic devolution, where powers are transferred to representative and accountable local institutions (Larson and Ribot 2004:3). Referring to the common phenomenon of assigning the burdens of management to local people but only a minimum of authority and a modest share of benefits, Alden Wily (1996) has talked of states divesting responsibilities rather than devolving authority. These distinctions serve as a reminder that where administrative reorganization devolves responsibility within existing hierarchical structures or to local institutions without authority and entitlement, it only replaces the preferences of central government with those of local governments and is co-optive, not empowering (Murphree 2000:5). Murombedzi observes, skeptically: "The implementation of CBNRM tends to strengthen local government in the same way that native administration was strengthened by various colonial property laws that placed ownership of communal property rights in the hands of the 'Tribal Trusts'" (2003:137).

During the 1990s Uganda transferred a part of its forest estate to the four traditional kingdoms, which were taking on some local governance responsibilities. In the Bunyoro-Kitara Kingdom, the king himself appointed a forest trust to manage the forests. During the years that followed, the trust sold concessions to commercial loggers, leading to concerns on the part of the national forestry authorities and resistance on the part of local villagers, who resorted to setting forest fires in concessions. Surveys show that nearby forests controlled by elected local councils have, by contrast, maintained or improved forest cover and successfully implemented regulations obliging landowners to maintain at least 10 percent of their land in forest or planted trees (Ribot 2004:32). Devolution—or decentralization—of powers to institutions with the autonomy and authority to make decisions serves only to bring arbitrary rule and domination closer to people unless the institutions are also representative and accountable to local populations. If local institutions are autocratic, appointed, hereditary, or otherwise not accountable to citizens, they are unlikely to act in the longer-term interests of local people.[4]

Local institutions are, of course, subject to manipulation and capture by powerful interests in the same way that local government can be. Gendered structures of power or the division of labor exclude women and other marginalized groups, entrenching inequalities within communities. The proliferation of user committees set up in successive development projects has in some places given new opportunities for domination by local elites, who are better educated and have more free time to participate than less privileged members of the community. None of these acknowledged weaknesses is unique to local institutions and politics, however, and it is possible to guard against them with mechanisms to monitor performance, ensure transparency in actions, and sanction abuses. The Mexican community of Ixtlán de Juarez in the state of Oaxaca, for example, is managed by a Commission for Community Assets (*Comisario de Bienes Communales*) elected by the General Assembly of all 380 *comuneros* or members of the community.[5] The commission supervises several community forestry enterprises and its operations are monitored in turn by an independent Supervisory Council (*Consejo de Vigilancia*) that reports back to the assembly (author's field notes, Ixtlán de Juarez, August 2004).

If good governance is simply equated with devolution or decentralization, it diminishes the importance of CBFM in the evolution of governance—especially in places where autocratic states allow little political space for open political expression and for citizens to exercise their rights. Devolution is just one strategy in continuing efforts to improve governance—to harness the energies and resources of a nation's citizens by drawing them more closely into the political processes that shape and implement a vision of their future. In the context of CBFM, decision-making should be situated as close to the sources of those energies and resources as possible if the realignment of powers is to encourage communities to build equity in the resource through sustainable management (Murombedzi 2003:144). The challenge for governance in forest and resource management is not to determine which level of administration should receive devolved jurisdiction over the resource, but to empower accountable institutions representing those who have a direct interest in management and are most affected by its outcomes.

Government Roles in CBFM

A common apprehension among the staff of forest management agencies is that if CBFM becomes a reality and if local institutions receive full authority to make and implement decisions about the future of their forests, there will be no future role for government and government agencies. At the same time, some advocates for CBFM argue that a significant retreat of government from local affairs is a precondition for communities to make an investment in forest management. Both opinions, coming from opposite poles of a spectrum, suggest a withdrawal of the state to make way for local empowerment. It is not appropriate, though, to conceive of state and local as mutually exclusive entities. State agencies represent a channel through which local people make demands to secure government services (Li 2002:268), while local institutions facilitate the exchange of information and resources between state agencies and citizens. There is a distinction between a government agency accountable primarily to higher levels of administration and a local institution accountable primarily to constituents below it. The two do not exist in separate realms, however. The realignment of powers in CBFM does not mean the removal of the state but a change in its role.

The implementation of CBFM does not preclude the need for direct management by specialized agencies in specific places where important resources, endangered habitats, or species are under exceptional threat or where intervention may be necessary to guarantee flows of public goods and services such as water, flood protection, energy generation, and soil protection. Even in these cases, though, principles of social justice demand full and prompt compensation to affected communities for the costs not only of any alienated land but also of the rights of access and utilization they are losing, accompanied by full consultations to consider which rights they can continue to enjoy without threatening the object of protection. The process by which Jozani forest became Zanzibar's first national park did take at least some of these principles into account, including lengthy consultations with surrounding villages on boundaries and compensation for crop damage from the growing population of red colobus monkeys, as well as negotiations over continued use rights for certain forest products.

Conventional resource management and conservation policies have cast the state in the role of planner, implementer, and overseer. The state has claimed jurisdiction over land and resources in the public interest. Where the special circumstances described above do not apply, though, the public interest may be better served if the state were to facilitate communities managing natural resources to get access to technical support and extension services, to coordinate between local managers, and to serve as intermediaries between localities and higher levels of government or in mediating disputes.

Supporting Capacity-Building in Communities

Few, if any, forest communities inherently possess all the skills and abilities that are involved in forest management (chapter 8). Communities may have limited capacities at the outset, but the new responsibilities of management can weaken even those capacities by adding to or multiplying the inherent uncertainties of day-to-day life (Mehta et al. 1999:10). To argue, however, that community management must wait until communities can demonstrate that they possess all the necessary skills is little different from the colonial denial of civil rights to local people until some day far in the future when they could be "trusted" with the exercise of power. Instead, it is important that the process of shifting powers and authority to community institutions should be accompanied by support for building their own capacities or in locating sources of assistance.

CBFM has an advantage over strict management by one sectoral agency in that community institutions may draw on a wider range of skills, not only from the relevant agency, but also from other sectors, the NGO community, and elsewhere.[6] The villagers of Naidu have received marketing advice from the County Foreign Trade Corporation, which the forestry department would have been unable to provide. In the snapshot from Oregon (chapter 1), the Lakeview Stewardship Group has formed a coalition focused on restoration of the forest to which U.S. Forest Service staff contribute as professional foresters in collaboration rather than in confrontation with conservation scientists, environmental activists, ranchers, and representatives of the timber industry (Hanscom 2004). Staff in state resource management agencies have skills and training to contribute to building capacity within community management institutions, but they must be able to respond to expressed needs and demands from community managers. Both resource management agencies and communities can adapt to their new roles, and in managing forests sustainably they can also strengthen the community.

Coordination, Scale, and Fragmentation

Since the boundaries of ecological units such as a forest or a watershed usually extend beyond the jurisdiction of a single community, there is a risk that multiple community-based management institutions may create a "fragmented array of disjointed local enterprises" (Murphree 2000:10). An area such as the Serengeti ecosystem straddles the international boundary between Tanzania and Kenya and incorporates several national parks, conservation areas, private tourist and hunting concessions, state-owned forests reserves, municipal governments, pastoral communities (organized as different political units in the two countries), and large, privately owned agricultural estates and plantations. State agencies have a role to play in facilitating coordination between local management units, whether they are at the scale of several communities adjacent to one forest or of the many different state, private, and communal institutions with an interest in an area the size of the Serengeti.

Scale is a major challenge in implementing any program of improved governance and is even more so in the case of environmental governance. Some form of coordination between overlapping institutional and administrative jurisdictions is necessary both to maintain the ecological integrity of the landscape and to minimize the risks of disputes or conflict. Coordination across several communities and administrative entities calls for procedures to assist in harmonizing management regimes, to mediate in cases of disputes, and to monitor changes such as forest regeneration, wildlife movements, or hydrological cycles that extend across the boundaries of each unit. The task is not easy since it involves an actor from a higher level of administration promoting complementary, sometimes uniform, policies and practices without compromising the local knowledge, social bonds, and networks that are the strength of community management.

State agencies may be tempted to resort to familiar patterns of authoritarian control in the name of coordination, but it is possible to avoid the danger that they will impose their agenda over local priorities. Agreements between all the parties might define the scope of activities delegated to the coordinating agency and procedures to appeal against arbitrary actions through agreed channels such as the courts or another intermediary. Government intervention may not necessarily be through the resource management agency, and some communities may devise their own mechanisms for coordination. At Duru-Haitemba in Tanzania, for example, the eight villages with rights to

PLATE 9. Village government meeting in Ayasanda Village, Duru-Haitemba, Tanzania.

PHOTO: LIZ ALDEN WILY

the forest have chosen to take disputes and disagreements through the local primary courts under the Ministry of Justice, while the five villages managing the nearby Mgori forest have set up their own coordinating committee (Alden Wily 1997b:11).

If an agency succeeds in making the transition from being perceived as an adversary to being accepted as a source of guidance and technical assistance, its staff may find themselves enjoying a new rapport with forest communities. Relieved of the burden of policing unenforceable boundaries and enforcing punitive rules, district foresters from Nepal and Tanzania report that communities are asking them for advice on wider issues of local development and even trusting them to act as impartial mediators in boundary disputes and other conflicts (Alden Wily 1997b:13).

State Agencies as Intermediaries with Central Government

Early international interest in devolution came about because of the failure of large infrastructure projects designed and implemented in a top-down mode by central governments (Ostrom, Schroeder, and Wynne 1993:164–68). During the intervening decades, divesting central planning and transferring authority to local institutions has become associated more with service provision or sectors—such as resource management—where the ability to mobilize local information, knowledge, and human resources is essential to effective performance. Planning and provision of infrastructure such as roads, energy, and communications have tended to remain at higher levels of government administration, despite the growing importance of privatized services.

As actors in national development, state agencies are in a position to contribute to the success of CBFM by representing local concerns in formulating policies to reduce the barriers to management. Burdensome permit procedures or technical requirements for management plans, restrictions on marketing, and arbitrary and punitive taxation have all had limited effectiveness in the past and tend to invite evasion rather than to act as incentives for wise management. Weak community tenure rights expose locally managed resources to the possibility of takeover by well-financed and well-connected outside interests such as commercial plantations, mining, or environmentally damaging tourist developments. State agencies can act as intermediaries for their forest community partners in assisting to shape policy reforms that put in place secure and supportive, not restrictive, legal and administrative environments for community-based management.

Community institutions are not inherently democratic, equitable, and inclusive. Earlier sections on community (chapter 7) and on capacity-building (chapter 8) have observed that long-standing divisions within a community and culturally constructed identities such as gender or ethnicity are easily reproduced and entrenched in local institutions. States have a very sensitive role to play in building principles of equity and diversity into the institutions that will take on responsibility for forest management. NGOs and other actors in civil society can also assist local institutions to address their shortcomings while also acting as a check against "state-aligned actors' predilection for overwhelming dominance" (Mandondo and Mapedza 2003:5).

Empowerment: The Power to Engender Aspirations

One outcome of good or improved governance should be empowerment—the power to "engender aspirations" (Mosse 2004:6), to make and act on decisions about the future trajectory of development. At the Twelfth World Forestry Congress in Québec City in 2003, an African speaker challenged a workshop on poverty to demonstrate that CBFM is not just another strategy to impose Western constructs of conservation-as-preservation on rural

Africans, forcing them to renounce development and to live in perpetual poverty. The answer to the challenge is that development must increase, not decrease, choice (Murphree 2004:5). CBFM puts local communities in the position of decision-makers, where previously they had been subjected to the decision and choices of others—usually of government agencies. After meeting with members of Jozani Environmental Conservation Association (JECA) in Zanzibar, the program officer responsible for governance in the Ford Foundation's East Africa office remarked that it was the first time that he had met with villagers who had such a clear sense of what their expectations were for the future and the confidence that they had the material and human resources to make it happen. In the eight villages surrounding Jozani, people were coming to believe that they could engage with development on their own terms and be a part of conservation, rather than watch passively as a new national park expanded the area of forest from which they were already excluded to protect endangered species of significance to global biodiversity.

Not all communities would accept that they have experienced empowerment through their participation in CBFM. Many might argue to the contrary. A report on CBNRM in the Philippines proposed that the implementation of community-based management plans would be an indicator of empowerment both in planning and in the capacity to take action. If this were the case, however, it would appear that there is very little empowerment in the Philippines, since by 2002, out of more than 4,000 registered CBFM communities, no more than 98 even had a management plan, and fewer still were acting on them (Gollin and Kho 2002a:21). Visions of poor marginalized communities empowered by participation in CBFM are not entirely unfounded, but they often misread participation as a proxy for empowerment—and fail to examine closely what is happening when people "participate" in an organized activity such as a development project or forest management.

Participation in Development

Participation appeared in the vocabulary of international development in the late 1950s and became prominent in the late 1970s when development planners concluded that top-down planning was the cause of failed projects and an ever-widening gap between rich and poor. Based on elements of democratic theory that stress the importance of participation by local people in the operation of their own public affairs (Nelson and Wright 1995; Uphoff and Esman 1974), it was logical to look for ways to restructure planning to incorporate the participation of local people.

Since then, participation has become an inescapable element of development rhetoric and practice. On the positive side of the ledger, it is no longer acceptable to design and launch new initiatives and projects without at least the appearance of consultation with the people who have now become "partners" in, not "objects" of, development. The need to bring the voices of the poor and disenfranchised into an interactive process of strategy formulation and project planning for development has generated innovative methodologies such as participatory rural appraisal (PRA), which gives rural people a flexible set of tools to analyze their livelihoods and to articulate their priorities and pathways for future change (Barahona and Levy 2002; Chambers 1995, 2002; Shah, Kambou, and Monahan 1999). On the other hand, the ostentatious embrace of the discourse, if not the practice of participation by even the most authoritarian regimes, has opened it to the criticism that it is manipulative, a way to create the illusion of popular support for a modernizing process that creates needs that ultimately reinforce or perpetuate dependency and extend government control over even the poorest and most marginalized citizens (Cooke and Kothari 2001; Rahnema 1992:118–19).

Pimbert and Pretty have proposed a useful typology of seven forms of participation, ranging from the perfunctory "being told what is going to happen and what has already happened" to the empowering "people participate by taking initiatives independent of external institutions to change systems" (1997:309–10). Participation can inspire and motivate people only when it is free and informs the formulation of planning or decision-making. It makes little contribution to good governance or empowerment if people participate under duress or overwhelming political pressures—as has often been the case, for example, with mass campaigns to "transform nature" or to plant trees in China (Ross 1988; Shapiro 2001). Nor will participatory planning for CBFM inspire communities to invest in long-term stewardship of the forest with its attendant costs in terms of time, labor, and possible benefits foregone, if the process is a formality to give the stamp of popular approval to an agenda that has already been determined by a government agency or a conservation organization.

Meaningful participation involves a process that reaches to all groups within the community, includes them in decision-making at all stages of planning and implementation, and honors their rejection of proposed activities, not only their endorsement (Drijver 1992:134). Where participation includes the diverse voices in a community and gives them a chance to shape decisions about their future, it can become a vehicle not just for more sustainable forest management, but also for better governance. In practice, though, it is still common for participation to be little more than an invitation to comment on and perhaps to offer minor suggestions for the modification of plans whose contours and principal components cannot be questioned. As with devolution, participation can empower only if it brings decision-making closer to citizens (Mandondo and Mapedza 2003:3).

Empowering Communities to Set Their Agenda

Empowerment cannot be conferred on the powerless in an act of patronage by those in power—a gesture that only perpetuates existing inequities. It involves strengthening citizens' abilities freely to set their own agenda for the future or to "explore the possibilities of action" (Rahnema 1992:122). Secure and enforceable users' rights empower forest-dependent communities with the confidence of assured long-term access to the resource and its benefits.

Users' rights include the right to decide who is allowed to utilize the resource, when and at what rate, as well as rights to market forest products and to receive and to dispose of a share of the income (Gollin and Kho 2002b:114). In Mazagão, these powers are, to a great extent, in the hands of the producers' associations—where it is interesting to note that they have been conceded to the associations by residents. It is residents, not an outside agency, who have the authority to make any changes in this alignment of powers. In Naidu, the village has reclaimed its rights to its forests after years of struggle. As a legally recognized administrative entity, the village is now, like Mazagão, responsible for setting and enforcing the rules for harvesting and marketing as well as for the disposal within the community of revenue from fines and fees. In both places, empowerment has come about as a result of the communities' own initiatives and efforts, not by the design of any project.

A fundamental means of empowerment is to grant authority for planning, taxing, and implementing, together with the legal and fiscal powers for discharging such authority. In many community-based resource management programs, the most significant financial benefits do not accrue to communities. Devolution of authority over natural resources has not been accompanied by the fiscal authority or budgetary measures that would allow municipalities to break with long-standing patterns of raising revenue from the sale of concessions to harvest timber and to give communities full authority to develop and implement their own forest management plans (Elías and Wittman 2004; Kaimowitz et al. 1998; Larson 2004).

Many governments retain control over rights to sell or benefit from the most lucrative forest products, such as timber, leaving only secondary, or subsistence, products to local people (Dove 1993; Li 2002). In Zimbabwe, the greater share of revenue from community-based wildlife management in the CAMPFIRE program is divided between rural district councils and the safari industry, which is still mostly the preserve of white Zimbabwean businesses. Communities living with the wildlife receive a small share of the revenue and the possibility though not the assurance of employment with the safari companies that have concessions on communal lands (Murombedzi 2003:141–48). In the same region, however, communities that register as community-based organizations (CBOs) in Botswana's Wildlife Management Areas do have significant financial autonomy. Subject to approval by the Department of Wildlife and National Parks of a constitution for the CBO and a wildlife management plan, communities may enter into contractual partnerships in their own right with the private or commercial sector and are then responsible for their own financial management and the allocation of benefits to members, including the reservation of funds for administration and reinvestment (Rozmeijer 2003).

A less tangible but equally important aspect of empowerment concerns the generation and production of knowledge. From the definition of the broad parameters of what constitutes development, sustainable use, or conservation to the determination of what is "scientific" or acceptable forest management, the exclusion of local voices is a barrier to empowerment. Policies may call for the participation of local people in resource management, but obsolete dualistic categories persist with little integration of new learning either from scientific research or from local experience and knowledge. Conservation and protection are separated from utilization. Thailand's stalled community forestry legislation has stumbled over a rigid vision of conservation being possible only in strictly protected areas emptied of humans, despite the evidence that many of the remaining islands of forest surround the settlements and hillside swidden fields of minority communities.

Research is changing conventional understandings of the dynamics of vegetation change, stability, and disturbance in ecosystems, as well as of the interactions between human populations and the environment. The use of fire in forest management is a disputed issue that reveals the tenacity of the claim that knowledge and its application are the preserve of scientific institutions and trained staff in professional agencies. Generations of foresters around the world have learned that one of their most important tasks is to protect the forests in their care from the ravages of fire. The stigmatization of swidden cultivation has been partly due to the purportedly destructive use of fire. Over the last fifty years, a rich body of both ecological and ethnographic research has revealed the importance of fire and deliberate burning by humans to the regeneration of certain ecosystems, to the maintenance of some forest types, and to the prevention of devastating wildfires. Although this body of knowledge has entered the mainstream by now, many forestry departments still firmly resist incorporating it into modifications of their policies of excluding people and prohibiting burning (Leach and Fairhead 2000). In other places, prescribed burning has become a part of agency policy, even as local traditional techniques of fire management are still prohibited or restricted. Several Native American groups in California continue to press unsuccessfully for approval of their fire management plans based on customary practice, even though they are situated in the heart of an ambitious program of prescribed burning and thinning under recent federal and state programs for fuel and fire hazard reduction.[7] Empowerment will be an elusive property of community-based management as long as the knowledge deployed in shaping policy does not honor and embody the experience of local people.

Conclusion

Good governance and community empowerment trace a channel along which the instrumental and the social-justice streams of CBFM converge. Divesting the responsibilities for management while conceding only a share of revenue is some compensation to communities for their loss of access to resources, but it does not give them the vested interest that turns passive beneficiaries into active managers. Management involves taking risks and deciding on and choosing between options. Good governance involves the art of negotiating the distribution of powers and authority needed to frame and to make informed decisions about the options. Situating those powers in equitable and accountable institutions representing those most affected by the decisions is instrumental in establishing conditions for assuming responsibility for effective long-term management less marked by contention and conflict than has been the case in the past. At the same time, it empowers the community to look forward to the possibility not only of setting its own agenda for the future, but also of having the capacity and resources to make it a reality.

The realignment of powers and authority proposed in CBFM is not without risks. At one level, it is quite possible that the decisions of empowered communities will reflect local priorities for improved livelihoods through increased revenue, rather than maintaining forest cover or conserving biodiversity. The practice of negotiating conservation easements with private landowners offers a possible model for compensating forest communities for the opportunity costs of any restrictions to their preferred management regime in those cases for which there is a compelling and demonstrated larger national or global interest to be protected. At another level, there is also a danger that in detaching resources management from wider issues of local governance and representation, single-purpose CBFM institutions will reproduce existing hierarchies and fragment grass-roots participation, undermining wider processes of democratization that might be taking place. CBFM institutions are complementary to, not in opposition to, local government and gain in strength from being recognized as a part of national structures.

CBFM offers the promise of a new framework for relations between government and forest communities where confrontation and tension have formerly been the norm. To realize the promise, communities need the powers and authority to make and enforce management decisions. Governance and empowerment enter into the construction of the new framework in terms of the redistribution of powers between the state and the community and in terms of accountable, transparent, and democratic principles guiding forest management institutions and their relations with government agencies. Good governance is an important measure of what sets CBFM apart from past practice in forest management, and equity and accountability, which have been conspicuously absent in the past, are important measures of good governance.

11

Conclusions

The achievement of sustainable forest management, nationally and globally, including through partnerships among interested Governments and stakeholders, including the private sector, indigenous and local communities and non-governmental organizations, is an essential goal of sustainable development. This would include actions at all levels to:

... Recognize and support indigenous and community-based forest management systems to ensure their full and effective participation in sustainable forest management.

—WORLD SUMMIT ON SUSTAINABLE DEVELOPMENT 2002,
PLAN OF IMPLEMENTATION §45(H)

Natural resource management in southern Africa has been interpreted to mean the management of natural resources through some formal project or programme, rather than everyday interactions between people and natural resources in their daily struggle for livelihoods.

—MUROMBEDZI 2003:142

 THIS STUDY has had the dual ambition of capturing the diversity of CBFM while asking how and under what circumstances communities and their partners have moved from a history of exclusion and confrontation to a negotiated accommodation of interests over access to and utilization of forests. The stories it has told and the analysis of community, capacity-building, partnerships, and governance conclude that the "full and effective participation in sustainable forest management" that the World Summit on Sustainable Development (WSSD) called for in its plan of implementation has yet to be realized.[1] Communities, government agencies, and their partners all over the world are still struggling to find answers to basic questions of representation and decision-making, building or gaining access to skills and capacities for effective management, and the negotiation of an equitable distribution of powers and responsibilities.

Achievements and Challenges

The snapshots, stories, and other examples that have appeared in the preceding chapters show that there are many places in which communities are managing healthy forests, using their forest resources sustainably, and regenerating degraded land. The collective forest at Naidu is visibly healthier than the neighboring state-owned forest. In Oaxaca, UZACHI was one of the first community-managed forests to receive certification from the Forest Stewardship Council. In Lakeview, Oregon, the focus of management has been the restoration of land damaged by past logging practices. In many places, CBFM is proving to be an effective and ecologically beneficial approach to forest management.

In many places, too, secure access to forest resources has allowed individuals and communities to derive tangible benefits contributing to livelihoods and building community assets, which in turn allows communities to begin to map out their own vision of development and to invest in making it a reality. In Zanzibar, revenue from tourists visiting Jozani forest has been used to improve infrastructure and services in participating villages as well as to contribute to the village banks whose reach extends beyond the population most directly affected by the new national park. The Igarapé associations of Mazagão now supply up to 60 percent of the timber in the state capital, using the income to support local schools and to assist their members at times of special need.

Empowerment is more difficult to measure. The Igarapé associations empowered their members when they joined forces to open the markets of Macapá to community-owned sawmills. In mastering the technical skills needed to prepare an inventory of their communal forest, the villagers of Ekuri in Nigeria were able to implement their own forest management plan rather than to watch, powerless, as the state forestry department assigned harvest quotas to outside commercial interests. The Huron-Wendat Nation of Québec is slowly regaining access to its traditional lands and addressing unemployment among its young people with a forest management program focusing on generating jobs during the winter months. All these people, who had been overlooked, ignored, or dispossessed of their territories in the past, are a real and acknowledged presence now, taking their place as articulate stewards of the land and committed to managing the forests that shape their lives and identities.

CBFM challenges the claims of state agencies to be the sole arbiters of the public interest in forested land. State control and management have not prevented extensive loss of forest cover over the last century or more. Forest communities have responded to exclusion with conflict and resistance. From the 1970s an upsurge of popular movements around the world demanding social justice converged with heightened global concern about the state of the environment, favoring experiments with new partnerships and realigning the relations between the state, communities, and other actors with an interest in forest resources.

Communities are not equally empowered partners in these new relationships. States have been reluctant to transfer essential decision-making authority, preferring benefit sharing to power sharing. NGOs and other intermediaries from civil society have the resources and connections to use CBFM partnerships to pursue their own agendas if they wish to. In privileging their goals, they can undermine the communities' stake in maintaining healthy forests. Communities that are able to forge alliances with wider networks and social movements can, however, redress the balance and take advantage of CBFM to realize their own vision of an improved future.

Conditions Favoring CBFM

At the close of chapter one, I proposed to subject the four stories at the heart of this study to an enquiry along three lines:

- What are the dynamics that have caused states to move from excluding communities from forest resources in the name of the public interest to invoking communities in the name of more effective sustainable forest management?
- How do different expressions of the goals of CBFM shape the partnerships in CBFM and their outcomes?
- What conditions strengthen communities' capacities to improve their livelihoods and to maintain or improve the health of forest ecosystems through the management of forest resources?

The narrative that emerged from the stories, reinforced by the evidence of other examples of CBFM from around the world, demonstrates that CBFM reflects the global diversity of forest ecosystems, communities, and national systems of governance in the diversity of its stated objectives and institutional arrangements. Communities' growing role in forest management is driven both by a utilitarian recognition that state agencies have failed to demonstrate their ability to manage forests sustainably and by demands for social justice and the restoration of rights of access to forest resources expropriated in the past by the state. In an undertaking as complex as CBFM, where each forest and each community is the product of a unique ecology and history, predicting the specific outcomes of any particular model of CBFM is likely to be little more than speculation. The observations and lessons in this study do, however, indicate that there are some conditions that favor management by communities. Few, if any, places enjoy all seven conditions proposed here, but the more that are present, the greater the chances of an outcome that benefits the community while maintaining or improving the health of the forest:

1. Institutions for management have legitimacy in the eyes of the whole community with mechanisms to balance plurality of interests against the cohesion of shared norms and values within a community.

2. The community enjoys decision-making authority and a share of benefits commensurate with the burden of responsibility it takes on.

3. The community has access to appropriate technical options and skills to manage forests and to market its products and services.

4. The community can choose its partners and whether to enter or to leave the partnership, fostering accountability between the parties.

5. Partners transcend their sectoral interests and resist counterproductive rules and constraints designed to advance their own agendas.

6. The community has access to wider networks, social movements, and other sources of external political support.

7. The community's rights of access and utilization are embedded in formal governance and legal systems, and it has access to the police powers of the state if necessary to impose sanctions on those who break the rules.

These seven conditions do not function as a simple formula for success. They embody principles learned from the emergence and evolution of CBFM, and each one plays a part in shaping a favorable context for CBFM.

1. Institutions for management have legitimacy in the eyes of the whole community with mechanisms to balance plurality of interests against the cohesion of shared norms and values within a community.

The "forest community" is a heterogeneous entity encompassing diverse interests that nevertheless recognize a shared experience of and interest in a common space—the forest. Geographic and social boundaries of the community are not fixed, nor are they always the same as the administrative boundaries on which CBFM projects are often constructed. Wealth, rank, gender, education, age, and caste are just a few of the different but overlapping interests within a community. Mobile populations, migration, and changing demographics in rural areas are all reminders of the fluid boundaries of community—although participation in managing forest resources can in itself build the values and reciprocal relationships that constitute social capital in a community.

Communities face the challenge of building legitimate institutions that balance plurality of interests and the cohesion of shared norms and values in order to identify common ground and to make and implement decisions. They should be based on initiatives coming from within the community, not designed and imposed from the outside. Elites and powerful interests wield influence and dominate decision-making bodies even where traditionally excluded groups such as women, the landless, or minorities are guaranteed representation. Community institutions are more effective where they incorporate mechanisms to help counter inequalities of power and influence. The presence of a third party as observer or mediator can redress the balance to some extent. In Zanzibar, CARE International has exercised its influence as a respected NGO to strengthen the role of women in the newly formed environmental conservation associations and to advocate for the interests of communities in negotiations with the Department of Commercial Crops, Fruits, and Forestry. In Kangra, the Himachal Pradesh Cooperatives Development Union has played a comparable role, although its efforts to date have not succeeded in legitimizing the CFSs in the eyes of the Forestry Department.

Within forest management institutions themselves, procedural mechanisms and rules can at least dilute the influence of powerful interests. Opportunities for women, the landless, or other disadvantaged groups to meet and deliberate separately in order to formulate a common platform that is recognized as the expression of the interests of the whole group can bolster the position and confidence of otherwise isolated representatives. Tenure limits and regular rotation of office holders restrict the time in which individuals can exploit a position for personal gain. Established and transparent procedures for the use of collective assets can minimize the degree of discretion and thus opportunities for patronage or corruption in their distribution. In Naidu, income from fines is used to cover the costs of holding the annual community meeting with accompanying entertainment—and the accounts are open to all for inspection. Many Mexican communities specify how income from forest operations is to be distributed between community funds and services. Mechanisms such as these will not eradicate long-standing or recent sources of inequality on their own, but they can help community institutions to function better as fora in which to identify common ground and negotiate toward a shared vision of the future.

2. The community enjoys decision-making authority and a share of benefits commensurate with the burden of responsibility it takes on.

A basic premise of CBFM is that communities with a long-term stake or equity in the future of a resource will manage it sustainably. The benefits derived from a forested ecosystem must therefore be commensurate with the burden of responsibility accruing to a community taking on the task of management.

The communities in the four stories of this study have acted to guarantee the flow of benefits derived from the forest or to safeguard a perceived threat to their access to both material and spiritual values. The people of Naidu and Mazagão receive tangible incomes from the sustainable harvest of both timber products and NTFPs. The communities using Misali Island took action not only to protect their livelihoods but also to prevent the loss of a religious site. In Kangra, one of the main points of contention between the remaining CFSs and the Himachal Pradesh Forestry Department is the loss of what are perceived to be long-established customary rights to revenue from the forests.

Management includes responsibility for making decisions about goals and objectives, not just about contributing labor. States have taken steps to give communities a stake in forest management, with the expectation that inclusion rather than exclusion will reduce conflict and foster a sense of stewardship over the resource. Few states have been willing, however, to consider entrusting communities with the degree of decision-making rights associated with full ownership, although there is evidence from places such as the Duru-Haitemba forest in Tanzania that fears of unchecked and accelerated loss of forest cover in the absence of government control are misplaced. The greater danger is that communities bear the burden of responsibilities such as patrolling and protecting or labor-intensive planting and regeneration without enjoying a corresponding level of decision-making. A restrictive regulatory environment with predetermined objectives and negotiations limited to bargaining over the share of revenue accruing to the community serves only to buy compliance with someone else's rules and lasts only as long as income does not fall below expectations. In the words of a Chinese villager in Yunnan Province, "When it is all responsibility with no benefits, then why should we be interested?" (author's field notes, Anwang, April 1990).

3. The community has access to appropriate technical options and skills to manage forests and to market its products and services.

CBFM encompasses management by, among others, long-established village communities resident in or around forests, by user groups within communities, clans, women's groups, by religious organizations, and by the spiritual guardians of sacred groves. Communities manage forests in joint committees with state agencies, as residents' associations, cooperatives, land trusts, contracted leaseholders, and even commercial enterprises. CBFM has enriched the institutional landscape of forest management with innovative forms of collective and joint tenure, new partnerships adapted to local contexts, and endorsement of some existing arrangements previously not recognized by law.

The diversity of institutions engaged in CBFM is yet to be matched, though, with a comparable choice of technical options to meet the many demands for products and services of value to communities. Harvested products such as matsutake mushrooms, wild coffee, or pine resin are the major source of income for many communities, but the forestry profession continues to treat them as minor NTFPs. Timber trees are often an opportunistic source of capital to meet contingencies and special needs, such as reconstruction after a natural disaster, or to build a community asset, such as a mosque or schoolhouse. Silviculture based on the principle of managing for a "nondeclining even flow" yield does not serve the interests of these communities. Technologies designed to reduce costs by replacing labor with machinery are of little relevance to communities such as the Huron-Wendat, with limited access to capital and a problem with unemployed youth.

Conventional forest management continues to undervalue local knowledge, although the long history of locally devised silvicultural systems and techniques such as coppicing and pollarding, intercropping, and enriched fallows indicates that they are ecologically sound, with the flexibility and resilience to meet the needs of their users through changing economic and political times. Nevertheless, many forest communities are located far from consumers in increasingly regional and global markets. They are poorly placed to learn about new opportunities outside their experience, and they have limited access to information and skills to take advantage of them. The rules for harvesting matsutake that the residents of Naidu have put in place are designed to prevent damage to the mushrooms and are based on experience accumulated since the recent emergence of a market for a product that had previously been of little interest. Harvesters know little about ongoing research into the ecology of matsutake, which might suggest ways in which to improve the harvest. Trained professionals and their skills could make an important contribution to the future of CBFM, but there is an urgent need for investment in reorienting and expanding their technical repertoire.

4. The community can choose its partners and whether to enter or to leave the partnership, fostering accountability between the parties.

Equitable partnerships have the potential to bring together the skills and resources of different actors and are more likely than single-agency management to offer a framework for negotiation over conflicting interests in land and resources. Most CBFM partnerships, however, reproduce long-standing unequal relations of power in which the state or other interests such as the commercial forestry sector or environmental movements determine the rights they will grant to communities and their representatives. Each partner has a role to play and a contribution to make, but the weaker and less articulate voices are easily overwhelmed unless specific measures are in place to ensure that the stronger partners do not act only in pursuit of their own agenda.

Intermediaries such as NGOs have advocated successfully for community participation in forest management, and they have helped community institutions get access to services and support to build their capacities for management. With few exceptions, though, communities remain the beneficiaries, not the principals, of these efforts. NGOs do not have any formal accountability to communities, and to accentuate the asymmetry in the partnership, it is usually the NGO, not the community, that receives donor funding to implement CBFM.

Even self-initiated community management activities have difficulty in identifying and working on their own terms with partners whose skills and contacts strengthen rather than undermine local capacities. Where outside funding supports a CBFM project, communities do not have the opportunity to choose, reject, or change their partners from civil society. The right of free association and free withdrawal would be a powerful mechanism to foster accountability, but it is rarely encountered. Inequality between the partners in CBFM is inescapable, but it is possible to avoid inequity if principles of voluntary association, respectful communications, ethical relations, transparency, and accountability govern relations between them.

5. Partners transcend their sectoral interests and resist counterproductive rules and constraints designed to advance their own agendas.

Explicit articulation of a set of goals for CBFM—such as poverty alleviation, watershed protection, or social justice—tends to be a product of formal projects and programs, usually initiated from outside the community. Despite the rhetoric of participation, project goals often diverge from the community's own interest in managing forest resources. The villagers of Naidu have formulated regulations to maintain the quality and volume of the matsutake crop in order to increase their incomes, not to conserve biodiversity or to alleviate poverty.

In the pursuit of their expressed goals, CBFM projects shape what level of decision-making is conceded to the community as well as the institutional structures and outcomes of community management. In seeking to improve livelihoods, a project may draw the physical and social boundaries of the community in terms of economic status, gender, place of residence, and ethnic or cultural identity. It may place a greater emphasis on alternatives to management and utilization of forest ecosystems than on finding and testing alternative forest management systems adapted to the needs and capacities of communities. The objective of social justice may be secured with the restoration or recognition of rights of tenure or access to forest resources, while the community still struggles to build technical and institutional capacities for management.

It is important for external partners in CBFM to transcend their own interests, to resist imposing counterproductive constraints in order to pursue their agenda, and to ensure that communities have the skills and resources they need to make informed choices, to implement decisions, and to monitor the outcomes. This is particularly important in and around protected areas, where the goal is conservation or the preservation of biodiversity with its high cost to communities in terms of opportunities foregone. Where there is a demonstrated global interest in protecting a threatened resource, it is incumbent on the global community to accept its share of the costs, to act on its obligation to compensate local communities fully for the access rights they are being asked to give up, and to ensure that agreements negotiated with communities are not just a means to buy their acquiescence, but that they offer a real incentive to choose conservation.

6. The community has access to wider networks, social movements, and other sources of external political support.

Communities are weak and vulnerable compared to other actors with an interest in forests. Membership of networks, alliances, and larger national or international social movements can strengthen their position in negotiating the terms of CBFM with more powerful and articulate interests. In Latin America, in particular, labor movements have a history of activism on behalf of the rural poor, and they have been a powerful force in advocating for the rights of forest communities to regain control of their forests and to resist the encroachments of destructive logging concessions. They have also taken on an important role in securing technical support and access to markets for their members. Membership in SINTRA (the Rural Workers' Union of Amapá), for example, has allowed the Igarapé associations of Mazagão to negotiate access to the timber markets of Macapá and to make the case to the federal authorities that their harvesting practices are sustainable and should be accepted in officially recognized forest management plans.

Alliances between community-level groups such as FECOFUN in Nepal and with wider social and political movements such as SINTRA in Brazil or the Assembly of the Poor in Thailand strengthen the voices of marginalized forest communities in national and international arenas. In contrast to partnerships with intermediaries such as NGOs, there is less chance that a representative organization will substitute the community's agenda with its own. There is at least a minimum degree of accountability since the community can choose to accept or reject membership and since the option to withdraw remains open if the anticipated benefits or advantages of participation do not materialize.

7. The community's rights of access and utilization are embedded in formal governance and legal systems, and it has access to the police powers of the state if necessary to impose sanctions on those who break the rules.

CBFM institutions are not isolated, autarkic, independent entities. They exist and function within a dynamic political space in which funders' priorities change, allies in government agencies are transferred or lose influence, and markets for forest products fluctuate unpredictably. Several communities may have jurisdiction over adjacent tracts of the same forest, where the actions of one community will affect the condition of a neighbor's forest.

Rights of access and utilization are fragile when they are contingent on a special dispensation such as the demands of a donor or when they are granted as an exception to normal policy and practice. They are hollow if they cannot be enforced or defended when contested. Embedding CBFM institutions within the structure of local governance and the legal system promises greater security from the vagaries of development fashions that otherwise make the long-term survival and thus sustainability of projects precarious, and it gives recourse to the state's powers of arbitration and enforcement if needed.

The ability of communities managing resources to monitor and enforce compliance with the regulatory regime they have agreed on is seriously compromised if they do not have the power to detain offenders or the authority to take punitive actions such as imposing fines and seizing illegally harvested timber and other forest products or straying livestock. Prevailing against encroachment from outside the community stretches the capacities of most community institutions and is likely to be beyond their capacity without the further backing of the police powers of the state when confronting powerful commercial or politically connected interests. The state must be prepared to break with past practice and to reverse the purpose of law enforcement with respect to forests from the exclusion of communities to safeguarding their rights in the forest.

The Future: Moving Past Benefit Sharing

Ultimately, it is the ability to adapt in response to changing circumstances that gives a management system the resilience to be sustainable. Murphree observes that "conservation cannot be properly understood in terms of fixed, predictable states; it is better perceived of as resilience in a complex, evolving biophysical-cum-social system comprised of structures which interact across scales of place and time and which move through adaptive cycles of growth, accumulation, restructuring and renewal" (2004:7). The certainty of change, growth, and renewal applies not only to the specific case of conservation, but to resource management in general. Conflict and contending interests are the norm, and community-based management will not eliminate them. CBFM offers a way to link the resource more closely to the social system that interacts most directly with it, putting in place mechanisms for negotiation, not only to reach accommodation between different interests in the present, but also to cope with change in the future.

Coercive exclusionary policies for conservation of forests and biodiversity are costly financially and socially and have not been very effective. The appeal of CBFM to some state agencies is the expectation of reduced costs with the transfer of responsibility to communities for labor-intensive tasks such as patrolling, regeneration, and monitoring compliance with regulations. Effective CBFM is not, however a cheap option, since it involves not only the transfer from the agency to the community of costly responsibilities, but also an investment in building skills and capacities, a meaningful redistribution of revenue and benefits, and research into new, alternative technologies for forest management. The costs to both society and the environment of continued conflict and contention are, however, almost certainly higher.

Community-based management is not the answer to all conflict over forests. It is one among many possible models of management that is particularly relevant where there is a history of state appropriation of forested lands and exclusionary policies. It may not be appropriate for specific instances where endangered species or habitats are under immediate threat from dramatic and rapid changes in land use (such as conversion to commercial plantations or resettlement projects) or the collapse of local institutions. In these places, a more active state role in protecting biodiversity may be justified, although due process of consultation and compensation to local people remain critical for success. In other forested landscapes, however, CBFM can break with an adversarial past to assist in restoring the connections between human systems and ecological systems. To do so is a complex undertaking demanding a level of trust and confidence between the partners that is usually lacking at the outset. It carries the weight of the multiple expectations of many interested actors, leading at times to contradictory objectives and, as a consequence, to contested assessments of what constitutes success and failure.

Government and donor interest in CBFM has focused on projects to reduce conflict and to put more effective management systems in place. Negotiations have centered on bargaining over the revenue or product from management rather than on a realignment of authority and control. Bargaining over benefit sharing rather than over user rights carries the risk that if income is more modest than expected or is subject to unpredictable changes in markets, as is the case with tourism for example, it compromises the primary incentive for compliance. A more balanced agenda would also seek to strengthen communities' powers and capacities to manage, anchoring them securely in supportive national legal and political structures. Negotiating new roles and partnerships, hearing the voices of diverse actors and interests, and exploring alternative ways of using a resource require steady support over a long period of time. It remains to be seen whether policy-makers and the funders of international development can learn to give time for just and equitable stewardship of resources to take root in communities and to offer support rather than to impose their own counsel.

Notes

1. Introduction

1. I am grateful to Chief Edwin Ogar of the Ekuri Initiative for bringing me up to date on developments at Ekuri since my visit there in 1999.
2. I would like to thank Louis Lesage, coordinator of Forest and Wildlife Management for the Conseil de la Nation Huronne-Wendat in Wendake, for the time he spent with me discussing the history and vision for the future of Huron-Wendat forest management.
3. I have chosen to use the term *community-based forest management* from among the many terms in current use. See pp. 9–10 on the terminology applied to the many models of community involvement and participation in resource management. I accept the power of words to shape ideas and discourse, but I believe at the same time that communities managing forest resources face similar challenges even where there are nuances in the details of the institutions and management regime with which they are working. For consistency, I will use the term CBFM and occasionally the more general term *community-based natural resource management* (CBNRM) where communities managing forests, water, or other natural resources are addressing similar issues.
4. Mencius is the Latinized rendering of the Chinese name that is written as Mengzi or Meng-tzu in the two most widely used romanization schemes.

2. Naidu Village, Yunnan Province, China

1. Other sources of matsutake for the Japanese market include Korea, Mexico, the Pacific Northwest in the United States, Bhutan, and the Atlas mountains of north Africa. See Richards and Creasy 1996 for the United States, and Namgyel 2000 on Bhutan.

2. The village committee (formally known as the administrative village) is the lowest rung of the administrative hierarchy in China, extending from the central government to the province, prefecture, county, township, and village committee. The elected village committee usually has jurisdiction over several "natural villages" or hamlets, each under an elected village head. The staff and leaders in levels above the village committee are appointed, and branches of the Communist Party of China exist in parallel to the government administration at all levels.

3. On the administrative history of southwest China, see Herman 1997.

4. For discussions of forestry administration in China, see Richardson 1990:159–69; Xu and Ribot 2004:155–57; and Harkness 1998.

5. Matsutake (*Song rong* in Chinese) has always been known as an edible fungus in China. It is rather bland in taste and has not traditionally been valued in Chinese cuisine. Japanese consumers, however, believe that matsutake has medicinal properties, which has made it a valuable species in Japan. Depletion of matsutake in Japan itself led to the search for alternative sources of supply in the 1970s and 1980s (see Yeh 1998 and 2000 for more background on the matsutake in Yunnan). See also He 2004 for a study of the matsutake marketing chain from the village level to the provincial level.

6. TRAFFIC is an international program associated with the Worldwide Fund for Nature (WWF) and IUCN/The World Conservation Union, which monitors and controls international trade in threatened and endangered species. For details, see the TRAFFIC Web site: http://www.traffic.org/.

7. It is not clear what has caused the decline in prices between 2001 and the time of writing in 2004. Some sources believe that there has been an increase in supply, with matsutake now being exported to Japan from several new sources, including Bhutan and Morocco. Others believe that prices have deliberately been manipulated by Japanese buyers, who claimed in 2002 that one shipment of Chinese matsutake was contaminated by pesticides. Others believe that overharvesting has resulted in a decline in quality and a corresponding drop in prices. A similar collapse in prices affected the U.S. matsutake market in the summer of 2004.

8. Restricting sales of products from community-managed forests to one location is an effective strategy to ensure compliance with community rules about harvesting seasons, allowable quantities, and acceptable quality. In an interesting parallel to Naidu, the villages of Old and New Ekuri in Nigeria (see chapter 1, p. 2) restrict sales of all NTFPs from their forest to certain days in a central market.

9. Details of the Shusong project—supported by the Worldwide Fund for Nature—are from an interview in Shusong (author's field notes, 4 August 2002).

3. Jozani Forest, Ngezi Forest, and Misali Island, Zanzibar

1. For information on Misali and the Sacred Gifts to the Earth program, see the relevant Web pages of the Alliance of Religions and Conservation (ARC) and the Wordwide Fund for Nature (WWF).

2. On the history of Zanzibar, see Sheriff 1987 and 1994.

3. See Honey 1999: chap. 8 for a discussion of the impacts of mass tourism in Zanzibar.

4. Zanzibaris may be the only people in Africa to cultivate and enjoy southeast Asian fruits such as the rambutan (*Nepthelium lappaceum*) and the durian (*Durio zibethinus*). On

agroforestry in Sumatra, see de Foresta et al. and Michon 1994. On fruit cultivation in Java, see Suryanata 1994. On the political ecology of durians and other forest fruits in Borneo, see Peluso 1996.

5. Siex and Struhsaker (1999) conclude that their research showed that harvests of coconuts were not affected by red colobus predation. They suggest that it was the perception of loss, not any objectively determined impact on yields, that mattered to farmers and led to complaints.

6. For the story of the tourist development at Mnemba, see Honey 1999:273–75.

7. See Hale et al. 2000 for an optimistic assessment of the project. My observations between 1997 to 2002 suggested that the program had failed to take root in the target communities, but that it had perhaps been important in encouraging the Zanzibari authorities to explore new approaches and new partnerships in linking communities, environmental protection, and development.

8. A *shehia* is the lowest level of local government in Zanzibar, consisting of one to three villages.

9. As of November 2002 village conservation committees had been established in the villages surrounding Ngezi, but there had not yet been any moves to establish a local equivalent of JECA or MICA.

10. As an autonomous entity within the United Republic of Tanzania, Zanzibar maintains jurisdiction over its natural resources with its own policies, legislation, and regulations.

11. A report prepared for CARE Tanzania in 2001 recommended this double monitoring system both as a mechanism to control commercial harvesting in the forest and as a means to empower the community to make important management decisions (Dubois 2001: §3.1.1).

12. These details of the contents of a community forest management agreement are based on the Charawe Community Forest Management Agreement of 2001, a copy of which DCCFF in Zanzibar kindly made available to me. The Charawe agreement follows the format established under the Forest Resources Management and Conservation Act of 1996.

13. This is a classic act of passive resistance. I have heard wood gatherers in forest communities in China, India, and eastern and southern Africa talking about techniques to make sure that wood is "dead and downed" and have heard of similar responses in many other countries.

14. I am grateful to Thabit Masoud of CARE Tanzania (Zanzibar) for explaining the details of the revenue-sharing agreement and the legal procedures preceding the gazetting of the national park (personal communication).

4. The Várzea Forests of Mazagão, Amapá State, Brazil

1. See Lima 1999:258–59 for a discussion of the origins, construction, and cultural representations of the caboclo identity. Also S. Nugent 1997 and Smith 2002.

2. Açaí is a thick beverage made from the fruit of the açaí palm (*Euterpe oleraceae*), eaten together with granulated cassava as a staple in várzea communities and increasingly popular in cities such as Macapá and Belém, where a local identity associated with caboclo culture is emerging. Bicho are small animals hunted and trapped in the forests around homesteads (see the description of caboclo homesteads and land use later in this chapter).

3. "O Manejo Communitário dos Recursos Naturais e as Políticas Públicas" was organized by IPAM (Instituto de Pesquisa Ambiental da Amazônia). I am grateful to the IPAM staff for inviting me to attend the workshop as an observer.

4. Under Brazilian law, in areas subject to tidal movements (defined as diurnal variation in water levels of more than five centimeters), land up to thirty-three meters inland from the median point of the highest and lowest water levels is considered to be *terreno da marinha*. Remaining land is termed *terreno alocial* and may be allocated to private owners by local authorities. In the estuarine várzea, nearly all land is covered at high tide—that is, it is within thirty-three meters from the median point. I would like to thank José Benatti of IPAM in Belém for providing this information during his presentation at the Belém workshop on Community Management of Natural Resources held in April 2003.

5. See Pinedo-Vazquez et al. 2001:30–34 for a detailed description of the smallholder land use systems of the tidal várzea.

6. Managing trees as "natural capital" is important to farmers all over the world and has been for a long time. See Chambers and Leach 1987 for India; Menzies 1994, chap. 6 for China.

7. The distinction between extracted products and cultivated products is important. Taxes are levied only on cultivated products, not on extracted products. The Rural Workers' Union of Amapá is fighting on behalf of caboclos to have more forest products classified as extracted. See the discussion below on the role of SINTRA.

8. The calculations of income in these two papers are not directly comparable. Anderson and Ioris (1992) calculate income from all sources in a community near Belém. Pinedo-Vazquez et al. (2001) calculate income from timber production alone in a community near Mazagão. Nevertheless, both measures demonstrate incomes significantly above the average for rural people that have been maintained over the ten years between publication of the two papers.

9. The following description of the institutional setting of the smallholder forest management system around Mazagão is based on my discussions with a number of people in the Mazagão area and in Macapá during April 2003.

10. These rules are all informal community-based rules since legally all land comes under state or federal jurisdiction (see the section above describing tenure in the estuarine várzea). Even where land is not flooded, the constitution authorizes the state government to allocate it permanently or to lease it to concessionaires for commercial management. In practice, few if any residents had title, and IBAMA (Instituto Brasileiro do Meio Ambiente e dos Recursos Naturais Renováveis), the national agency responsible for forest management, has allocated large areas as concessions for commercial management.

11. The important role that SINTRA plays in caboclo life will be discussed later in this chapter.

12. See Pinedo-Vazquez et al. 2001 for a detailed discussion of the heritage of the timber boom of the 1960s and 1970s and of the ways in which the small-scale sawmills have opened new markets and opportunities for smallholder forest management.

13. I would like to thank Johann Zweede of FFT in Belém for the time he spent with me discussing smallholder forest management in the Amazon.

14. See note 7 above.

15. Amália's story is based on my field notes written the day after a long informal conversation in her home on one of the Igarapés near Mazagão. I have not used her real name in order to maintain her privacy.

16. The original statement made at the April 2003 conference on community-based re-sources management in Belém was "Inserção da mentalidade de produtor florestal nas populaçõess rurais amazônicas." Similar statements were made by a number of speakers, referring specifically to the long-time rural populations in the Amazon, not to recent settlers in colonization programs about whom the statement may be more applicable.

17. The Quilombolas of the Rio Trombetas in the northeastern Amazon, near the Suriname border, have been struggling for many years to avoid being evicted from a proposed bioreserve. Ironically, the forest that the reserve is supposed to protect is the result of several centuries of occupation and management by the Quilombolas, who were first brought there by the Portuguese to work on plantations of sugar, cacao, tobacco, and cotton cleared from the original forest (Acevedo and Castro 1998).

18. Both SINTRA and CNS oppose colonization schemes imposed by government pro-grams. They are both struggling to formulate responses to the demands for social justice articulated by the Landless Workers' Movement (Movimento dos Trabalhadores Rurais sem Terra [MST]), which has organized occupations of so-called unused or unproductive land.

19. The Maisons Familiales Rurales (MFR) movement is based on the principle of divid-ing students' education between a period of activity in their social and professional environment and a period in the school environment. For details see http://www.mfr .asso.fr.

20. Raffles (2002: esp. chaps. 3 and 7) has explored the many layers and fractures of com-munities along the Igarapés of Amapá and Pará.

5. Kangra Valley, Himachal Pradesh, India

1. There are several detailed studies of the Kangra CFSs. I have drawn extensively on this work, complemented with my own observations and discussions with members of some of the forest cooperatives during a visit to Kangra in July 2002. I wish to thank Ashwini Chhatre and Rajeev Ahal, in particular, for their generosity in allow-ing me to draw on the results of their research and for time spent in conversation or in e-mail discussions to fill me in on details about the origins and experiences of the cooperatives.

2. This account of the initiation of the experiment with the CFSs draws on the two, almost identical histories outlined in Chhatre 2000:15–18 and Ahal 2002:7–13. Both studies quote the text of relevant sections of the 1937 report of the Punjab Government Forest Commission (also referred to as the Garbett Commission).

3. *Chil* is the term used in Kangra for the tree more commonly known in India as *Chir* Pine (*Pinus roxburghii*), from which resin is extracted for use as turpentine and other industrial products.

4. This history of the cooperative movement in Kangra is based on a July 2002 con-versation with Ajit Kumar of the Cooperative Transformation Initiative (CTI) of the Kangra-based NGO Navrachna, which seeks to revitalize the cooperative movement in the area.

5. The issue of the grant-in-aid has proved to be particularly contentious. Chhatre and Ahal interpret the grant-in-aid to be a fund to cover costs of forest management where income did not cover those costs. Over the last thirty years, the Forestry Department has stated that the grant-in-aid "means the income from Forest produce being prop-erty of Govt. surrendered to the Cooperative Forest Societies under the provisions of

Kangra Forest Societies rules" (Sharma n.d.:4). This interpretation is strongly contested by the remaining CFSs and some NGOs working with them.

6. In India, forest and water resources come under the purview of the states, not the central government. On the grounds of historical ownership, the Punjab retains control, even today, over some of the resources inside Himachal Pradesh, such as water for electricity generation.

7. Springate-Baginski 2001:49 gives a detailed account of the activities of one functioning CFS in the mixed-caste village of Sarah.

8. The issue of equity and class- or gender-based exclusion will be discussed further in this chapter and in later chapters. See Agarwal 2001 for a rich discussion of how the "participatory" institutions of community forestry in India and Nepal often in fact exclude women and other disadvantaged groups within the community. See also Berry 2001 for a discussion of how women's organizations in Himachal Pradesh can reproduce the social and class hierarchies in their communities when they are called on to represent women in institutions such as JFM committees or CFSs.

9. The dilemma of balancing security within the existing structure of local government against the risk of factional politics is a recurring problem for village-based resource management institutions and has already been alluded to in the discussion about Zanzibar in chapter 3.

10. "Application . . . for Grant of Permission to Sue" (High Court of Himachal Pradesh 2000: §3).

11. This question is by no means unique to India or to developing countries. See chapter 6 on contested narratives of the public interest in forests.

12. See the discussion in Chhatre 2001:20–21 on debates within the imperial forestry establishment in the 1850s on the ecological implications of allowing or excluding grazing in Himalayan forests.

13. Commenting on a similar situation in the state of Orissa, Sarin et al. (2003:13) point out that §28 of the Indian Forest Act specifically permits the state government to designate any reserve forest as a village forest to be managed by the community.

6. The Community Narrative of Forest Loss and Degradation

1. The phrase comes from Jack Westoby's eloquent 1987 collection of essays questioning the impacts of forestry activities in international development programs since the 1950s.

2. It is impossible to say how many studies there have been of CBFM. An Internet search on 9 March 2005 using the Google search engine produced 7,230,000 raw hits to "community forest management" in English alone.

3. In discussing the use and abuse of narratives later in this chapter (pp. 97–98), I will consider how the narrative of degradation has been deployed as justification for excluding people from forests and its power to persist in the face of evidence that contradicts its basic premises.

4. For a detailed study of how industrial interests were able to claim ownership and to introduce management regimes that transformed the physical structure of forests in northern France during the eighteenth and nineteenth centuries, see Dornic 1984.

5. The persistence of colonial models of administration into the postindependence period is a subject that has generated a rich vein of scholarship in its own right. For Africa, see Mamdani 1996. For a focus on natural resources, see Peet and Watts 1996.

6. Some observers have referred to this kind of extension of state control through the demarcation of forests as a form of internal colonialization. Within the United Kingdom, for example, the Forestry Commission in Scotland (which owns and manages 8.7 percent of the land) has been described as colonial in form and practice (Inglis and Guy 1997; Ritchie and Haggith 2004).

7. White and Martin 2002:6 calculate that 37.8 percent of the forested land in the United States is administered directly by the government, with a further 5.9 percent "reserved" for Native American groups but controlled by the BIA. All remaining forestland is in industrial or smallholder private ownership.

8. See Harkness 1998 for a review of Chinese forestry policy and practice fifty years after the revolution. See also Hyde, Belcher, and Xu 2003a for an appraisal of the impacts of the reforms of the 1980s and 1990s.

9. See Lee, Field, and Burch 1990 for a critique supported by several case studies of the ways in which the discourse of sustained yield has dominated and continues to dominate U.S. Forest Service planning, despite strong evidence of unsustainable harvesting practices and of fragile, unstable forest-dependent communities left behind in the wake of a highly cyclical forest economy.

10. Klein (1995) has reviewed the genealogy and competing meanings of the concept of "master narrative" in postmodern theory.

7. Invoking the Community

1. Little (1994:349–54) traces the linked paths of evolving development discourse and the growth in international interest in community-based resource management.

2. As noted in chapter 1 (p. 11), this study focuses on regimes of CBFM in which state control over forests is giving way to community involvement in management. The arguments for CBFM represented here do not, therefore, include the views of communities with their own, long-standing, legally recognized forest management institutions or of communities with more recent, self-initiated management systems.

3. See Castle 2002 for a critical review of the concept of social capital.

4. Agrawal was referring in this case to the Van Panchayat community forest management councils in Uttar Pradesh. His remark is equally applicable to the Kangra cooperatives.

5. Although, as discussed in chapter 5, as of late 2004 the Forestry Department had yet to act on the agreement to include the CFSs in the JFM program.

6. Chapter 9 will address the subject of negotiating partnerships.

7. The legislation did not explicitly exclude women from membership in the cooperatives, but since few if any women could hold land, gender was in practice a determinant of membership.

8. This account is based on an informal evening discussion with five members of the women's group, with the assistance of a male interpreter, the retired village primary school teacher (author's field notes, August 2003).

9. The word *Hua* is the term used in the local language, not (Han) Chinese.

10. See chapter 2, p. 19, for details of the different categories of forest tenure in China.

11. Used as litter in pigpens, then added as manure to the fields.

12. For an account of the negotiations between the South African national parks and the Makuleke community in the northern Kruger National Park, see Reid 2001.

13. In a sixth area, the process of public consultation had been so difficult that a referendum could not be held. The Surplus People Project (SPP), an NGO facilitating the process, recommended to the Department of Land Affairs that the minister should appoint a facilitator to resolve the deadlock (Harry May, personal communication). For information about the consultations surrounding the Transformation of Certain Rural Areas Act (TRANCRAA), see Van Ryneveld 1996 and Surplus People Project 2000.

14. In his analysis of the 1994 Rwandan genocide, Mamdani warns, however, of the potentially tragic consequences of constructing ethnicity with reference to assumed cultural differences and prior occupation of territory (2001).

15. See Agarwal 2001 for an analysis of "participatory exclusions, community forestry, and gender."

16. Chapter 8 looks at capacity-building with communities, while chapter 9 considers the kinds of partnerships that might best serve the interests of communities managing natural resources.

8. The Capacity to Manage

1. Thorough studies of the history of forest management and the emergence of the paradigm of scientific forestry can be found in Agnoletti and Anderson 2000; CNRS 1987; Corvol-Dessert et al. 2004; James 1990; Miller and Staebler 1999; and Peyron and Maheut 1999.

2. See also Peluso and Ribot 2003 for a further theoretical analysis of access.

3. On the Huron-Wendat forest, see the snapshot at the beginning of chapter 1. For accounts of a similar reorientation of management priorities and technologies on the Menominee Reservation in the United States, see Davis 2000; Mater 1998; and Pecore and Nesper 1993.

4. The Forest Trends survey *Who Owns the World's Forests?* found that in sixteen countries for which data were available a total of 396 million hectares has been allocated as concessions to the timber industry, in excess of 150 million acres more than was allocated to communities in the same countries (White and Martin 2002:8).

5. Saxena's paper is, in fact, a review of what has happened since such restrictions were loosened in 2000. His conclusion, however, is that the undeveloped markets that were the outcome of the earlier system of monopolies and parastatal control have been dominated by many of the same people who had been its beneficiaries and that local producers have so far not been able to take advantage of more open markets.

6. The evidence of continued degradation under community management has fueled a vocal movement to revert to more authoritarian or coercive policies for conservation. See, for example, Linden, Lovejoy, and Phillips 2004; Oates 1999; and Terborgh 1999. See Wilshusen et al. 2002 for a response to these arguments.

7. For a review of conflict resolution in community forest management, see the special issue of *Unasylva* entitled "Accommodating Multiple Interests in Forestry" (1998).

8. The five communities involved signed a Memorandum of Understanding in December 2001 with the Kenyan forestry department and the Kenyan wildlife service to establish the Ngare Ndare Forest Trust (NNFT). See http://www.lewa.org/ngare_ndare_forest _reserve.php.

9. For a study of a conservation project in the Russian far east, see Herrold 2002:272–397. For an example of attempts to reorient the forestry sector in Kyrgyzstan, see Carter et al. 2003.
10. Political changes in Nepal are putting some of the achievements of the country's community forestry program at risk. In 2003 FECOFUN mobilized its members to resist a government plan to impose a 40 percent tax on community forest income, a move that could undermine one of the major incentives for communities to invest in managing forests (Poudel 2003). As of late 2004 these efforts had succeeded in making the new tariff unenforceable.
11. The FECOFUN Web site gives details of the federation's structure and objectives and has a list of its national and international partners; see http://www.fecofun.org/.
12. For background on ACICAFOC, see the association's Web site at http://www.acicafoc .net.
13. One notable exception is perhaps the case of agroforestry, which gained recognition in the international scientific research establishment with the founding in 1978 of the International Centre for Research in Agroforestry (ICRAF)—now the World Agroforestry Centre—in Nairobi, Kenya.
14. See also Anderson et al. 2000 and Berkes et al. 2002. The quotation is from the First Nations Forestry Program Web site: http://www.fnfp.gc.ca/.
15. The International Ecotourism Society (TIES) defines ecotourism as "responsible travel to natural areas that conserves the environment and improves the well-being of local people" (TIES Web site, under "What Is Ecotourism": http://www.ecotourism.org/). Reports and documents from the International Year of Ecotourism can be found at the World Tourism Organization (WTO) Web site: http://www.world-tourism.org/ sustainable/IYE-Main-Menu.htm.
16. For an example of a certification system, see the eco-rating scheme developed through the Ecotourism Society of Kenya: http://www.esok.org/?q=node/view/26.
17. See the Il Ngwesi/Lewa Downs Web site at http://www.lewa.org/ilngwesi.php.
18. For a brief report on the negotiations leading to the Shompole agreement, see the African Conservation Centre (ACC) Web site: http://www.conservationafrica.org/ Reports.htm.
19. See the special issue of Nature, 9 April 1998, entitled "The Complex Realities of Sharing Genetic Assets."
20. For a set of case studies from Costa Rica, Mexico, Brazil, El Salvador, and the United States (New York State), see Rosa, Kandel, and Dimas 2003, accessible at http://www .prisma.org.sv/pubs/csa_s.php?idioma=es.
21. I am grateful to Tony Cunningham of the People and Plants Initiative for telling me the story of the marula oil and devil's claw marketing chain. SANProTA had yet to make a profit at the time of writing (2005) and still depended on financial support from the International Fund for Agricultural Development (IFAD). Information about Eudafano can be found at http://www.thebodyshop.com.au/upload/CT_Marula. doc; and about SANProTA and PhytoTrade Africa at http://www.phytotradeafrica .com.
22. For a detailed analysis of the impacts of a credit scheme on communities and on conservation of wetland resources in China, see Herrold 2002:205–13.
23. The Consultative Group to Assist the Poorest (CGAP) has developed eleven principles of microfinance, with the objective of establishing sustainable microfinance

institutions offering convenient, flexible, and affordable services to the poor. See the CGAP Web site for these key principles of microfinance: http://www.cgap.org/keyprinciples .html.

9. Negotiating Partnerships: Whose Voice Is Loudest?

1. Dove points out that catastrophic events such as the floods in Thailand and similar events in India or the 1973/1974 Sahelian drought can "seize the public imagination and catalyze its commitment to change" (1995:324). Blaikie (1985) and Thompson and Warburton (1985) have analyzed how interpretations of such events have been used to scapegoat the weak and powerless.

2. For reviews and analyses of Thailand's efforts to pass a community forestry bill, see Laungaramsri 1998; Makarabhirom 2000; and Rajesh 2002.

3. There is not even consensus on what constitutes a forest. Fruit orchards are included in statistics for forest cover in China, while Korea specifically excludes fruit orchards. In the Philippines any untitled land with a slope steeper than 18 percent is classified as forestland. In Belgium each of the country's three linguistic and political regions has a different legal definition of a forest. For an exhaustive review of definitions of forest around the world, see Lund 2004: §2.3.2.

4. The Spanish land grants were, of course, superimposed over earlier Native American land use systems. See chapter 6, pp. 93–94. Also Coward 2004 and Kosek 2004a. The belief that the national forests are held on behalf of all citizens also ignores the history of displacement and dispossession of Native Americans, which preceded the reservation of the forests.

5. In the United States, many Native American groups refuse to be consulted as "stakeholders" on the grounds that the forestland in question were originally theirs and that negotiations should be on a nation-to-nation basis (Renée Stauffer, personal communication).

6. See Wilshusen et al. 2002 for a critical review of the two contending paradigms in international conservation.

7. For a review of how the bureaucratic structures of the U.N. Food and Agriculture Organization (FAO) together with an institutional culture of inertia prevented its Forest, Trees, and People, Program (FTPP) from reaching its objectives, see Colchester et al. 2003:34.

8. For a review of the diverse institutional forms, practices, and functions of NGOs, see Fisher 1997.

9. It should be noted that not all of the fifty-seven partnerships described in the review are with community groups. Some of them are between timber corporations and individual households in a community growing timber in a contractual arrangement with the corporation.

10. For a review of "race and environmental history" in the United States, see Merchant 2004. See also Moore, Pandian, and Kosek 2003. On Africa, see Adams 2003 and Leach and Mearns 1996. On the Amazon, see Hecht and Cockburn 1989.

11. For a brief description of the project (now associated with the Global Environmental Facility [GEF] through UNDP), see the GEF Web site section for Uganda: http://www .undp.org/biodiversity/biodiversitycd/practiceUganda.htm.

12. The Makah Tribal Council in Washington State has received permits for its ritual whale hunt, which began again in 1999 in the face of strong condemnation from some (but not all) environmental organizations in the United States and internationally. For a summary of the Makah story, see Dark 1999. The Hopi have permits to collect sacrificial golden eagle chicks for use in religious ceremonies from some national forests in Arizona. Their request to collect them from the Wupatki National Monument, which they consider to be a sacred site, is opposed by several environmental organizations (CNN 2000; U.S. National Parks Service 2001).

13. This list is my own reformulation of thirteen organizational features for ethical partnerships proposed by Fowler 1998.

10. Governance and Empowerment

1. *Shui Hu Zhuan* has also been translated as "The Water-Margin" and "All Men Are Brothers." It is one of China's best loved epic novels, attributed to Shi Nai'an (1296–1370?). It tells of the deeds of 108 outlaws and their leader Song Jiang fighting against oppression and corrupt officials during the Song Dynasty (960–1279).

2. The ways in which the international discourse of good governance together with treaty obligations, particularly World Trade Organization rules relating to free trade, limit national sovereignty and options for governance over the environment and natural resources is an intensely contested issue, the subject of extensive research, documentation, and public debate beyond the scope of this study. See, for example, Cashore 2002; Conca 2001; French 2000; Sampson 2000; and Voon 2000.

3. For an earlier review of the origins of the concepts of decentralization and devolution in the context of decolonization in the 1950s and its revival in the 1970s and 1980s, see Ostrom, Schroeder, and Wynne 1993: chap. 8. For a more recent review of its application to natural resource management, see Larson and Ribot 2004 and the special issue of the *European Journal of Development Research* they edited (volume 16.1 [Spring 2004]).

4. It is important to recognize that excluding customary or traditional authorities can also endanger a local institution since they are influential in their communities and have important symbolic and cultural roles. Shackleton and Campbell (2001:9) have proposed that traditional leaders may contribute most positively to local resource management institutions as patrons or ex officio members, while the local institutions themselves should be constituted democratically through an open electoral process.

5. The municipality of Ixtlán de Juarez has a total population of more than 5,000 residents. Of these, only 380 are "commoners" (*comuneros*). To qualify as a *comunero*, a person must be born in the municipality, must be willing to follow the rules of the community, and must be accepted as a member by a meeting of the assembly (author's field notes, Ixtlán de Juarez, August 2004).

6. This observation does presuppose that the community institution has the capacity to represent its interests and build partnerships in the wider social and political arenas beyond its boundaries (chapter 8).

7. See Huntsinger and McCaffrey 1995 for the Yurok. Other groups facing similar difficulties include the Karuk (Renée Stauffer, personal communication) and the Mountain Maidu (author's field notes, Quincy, September 2005). See also the Redlodge Clearing

214 10. GOVERNANCE AND EMPOWERMENT

House Web site at http://www.redlodgeclearinghouse.org/stories/maidustewardship .html#contact.

11. Conclusions

1. The full text of the WSSD Plan of Implementation is available at http://www.un.org/ esa/sustdev/documents/WSSD_POI_PD/English/POIChapter4.htm (accessed 22 December 2004).

References

Books and Articles

Acevedo, Rosa, and Edna Castro. 1998. *Negros do Trombetas: Guardiães de Matas e Rios.* Belém: Cejup/UFPA-NAEA.

Acworth, James, Henry Edwoge, Jean-Marie Mbani, and Grace Ntube. 2001. *Towards Participatory Biodiversity Conservation in the Onge-Mokoko Forests of Cameroon.* Rural Development Forestry Network Paper 25d. London: Overseas Development Institute.

Adams, William M. 2003. Nature and the Colonial Mind. In William M. Adams and Martin Mulligan, eds., *Decolonizing Nature: Strategies for Conservation in a Post-Colonial Era,* 16–50. London: Earthscan.

Adams, William M., and Martin Mulligan, eds. 2003. *Decolonizing Nature: Strategies for Conservation in a Post-Colonial Era.* London: Earthscan.

Agarwal, Bina. 2001. Participatory Exclusions, Community Forestry, and Gender: An Analysis for South Asia and a Conceptual Framework. *World Development* 29, no. 10: 1623–48.

Agnoletti, Mauro, and Steven Anderson. 2000. *Forest History: International Studies on Socio-Environmental Change.* Report no. 2 of the IUFRO Task Force on Environmental Change. Wallingford: CABI.

Agrawal, Arun. 1997. *Community in Conservation: Beyond Enchantment and Disenchantment.* CDF Discussion Paper. Gainesville, FL: Conservation and Development Forum.

——. 1999. Community-in-Conservation: Tracing the Outlines of an Enchanting Concept. In Roger Jeffery and Nandini Sandar, eds., *A New Moral Economy for India's Forests? Discourses of Community and Participation,* 92–108. New Delhi: Thousand Oaks/London: Sage.

Agrawal, Arun, and Clark C. Gibson, eds. 2001. *Communities and the Environment: Ethnicity, Gender, and the State in Community-Based Conservation.* New Brunswick: Rutgers University Press.

Ahal, Rajeev. 2002. *The Politics of Cooperative Forest Management: The Kangra Experience, Himachal Pradesh.* Talking Points 3/02. Kathmandu: International Centre for Integrated Mountain Development.

Albers, Heidi, Scott Rozelle, and Guo Li. 1998. China's Forests Under Economic Reform: Timber Supplies, Environmental Protection, and Rural Resource Access. *Contemporary Economic Policy* 16, no. 1: 22–33.

Alden Wily, Liz. 1996. Moving Forward in Community Forestry: Getting to Grips with the Critical Issue—Who Has Control? Paper presented to the Eleventh World Forestry Congress, Antalya, Turkey.

——. 1997a. *Finding the Right Institutional and Legal Framework for Community-Based Natural Resources Management: The Tanzanian Case.* CIFOR Special Publication. Bogor: CIFOR.

——. 1997b. *Villagers as Forest Managers and Governments "Learning to Let Go": The Case of Duru-Haitemba and Mgori Forests in Tanzania.* Forest Participation Series no. 9. London: International Institute for Environment and Development.

——. 2001. *Forest Management and Democracy in East and Southern Africa: Lessons from Tanzania.* Gatekeeper Series no. 95. London: International Institute for Environment and Development.

Alden Wily, Liz, and Peter Dewees. 2001. *From Users to Custodians: Changing Relations Between People and the State in Forest Management in Tanzania.* Research Paper no. 2569. Washington, DC: World Bank Policy. http://econ.worldbank.org/resource.php?type=5.

Alden Wily, Liz, and Sue Mbaya. 2001. *Land, People, and Forests in Eastern and Southern Africa at the Beginning of the 21st Century.* Nairobi: IUCN-Eastern Africa Regional Office.

Ali, Abdullah, Ali Said Hamad, Mbarouk Ali, and Robert G. Wild. 2000. Misali Island, Tanzania: An Open Access Resource Redefined. Paper presented at Constituting the Commons: Crafting Sustainable Commons in the New Millennium. Eighth Conference of the International Association for the Study of Common Property, Bloomington, IN, May 31–June 4. http://dlc.dlib.indiana.edu/archive/00000193/.

Alliance of Religions and Conservation. n.d. Tanzania: Fishermen Say No to Dynamite—Using Islamic Environmental Principles. http://www.arcworld.org/projects.asp?projectID=170 (accessed 13 November 2003).

Anau, Njau, Jon Corbett, Ramses Iwan, Miriam van Heist, Godwin Limberg, Made Sudana, and Eva Wollenberg. 2003. *Do Communities Need to Be Good Mapmakers? Integrated Approaches to Participatory Development Bibliography.* http://www.iapad.org/bibliography.htm (accessed 6 September 2004).

Anau, Njau, Ramses Iwan, Miriam van Heist, Godwin Limberg, Made Sudana, and Eva Wollenberg. 2004. Negotiating More Than Boundaries in Indonesia. In Carol J. Pierce Colfer, ed., *The Equitable Forest: Diversity, Community, and Resource Management,* 19–41. Washington, DC: Resources for the Future/Bogor: CIFOR.

Anderson, Anthony B., and Edviges M. Ioris. 1992. Valuing the Rain Forest: Economic Strategies by Small-Scale Forest Extractivists in the Amazon Estuary. *Human Ecology* 20, no. 3: 337–69.

Anderson, David G., and Richard Grove. 1987. *Conservation in Africa: People, Policies, and Practice.* Cambridge: Cambridge University Press.

Anderson, David G., Robert Wishart, Ara Murray, and Derek Honeyman. 2000. Sustainable Forestry in the Gwich'in Settlement Area: Ethnographic and Ethnohistoric Perspectives. University of Alberta Sustainable Forest Management Network, Project Report 2000-9. http://sfm-1.biology.ualberta.ca/english/pubs/en_pubssac.htm (accessed 14 June 2004).

Anon. 1999. Hear Us and Know Us: Voices and Perspectives from Old Ekuri and New Ekuri Akamkpa L.G.A., Cross River State, Nigeria, Ekuri. Prepared as a contribution to Conservation by Communities. Community Forestry Management in Sub-Saharan Africa, Obudu, March 5–9.

Anon. 2000. *Community-Based Resource Management: The Experience of UZACHI and ERA: Oaxaca.* Briefing handbook for Ford Foundation program officers' visit to UZACHI, February 10.

Anon. 2002a. Misali Island Conservation Association. Informational brochure prepared for distribution to visitors to Misali Island. Wete: MICA.

Anon. 2002b. Moving Towards Good Forest Governance in Asia and the Pacific. Draft position paper submitted as past of the Indonesian People's Forum for PREPCOM IV of the World Summit on Sustainable Development. RECOFTC Working Paper 2002/01. Bangkok: Regional Community Forestry Training Center. http://www.recoftc.org/03region/materials/pub_series/greyzone.html (accessed 15 October 2004).

Antinori, Camille, David Bray, and Juan Manuel Torres Rojo. 2004. Mexican Community Forestry: Enterprise Organization and Regulatory Frameworks. Paper presented at the workshop on Community-Based Forestry in the Next Decade: Towards an "Agrarian" Approach? Berlin: Humboldt University, Junior Research Group on Postsocialist Land Relations, October 8–9. http://www.agrar.hu-berlin.de/wisola/ipw/plr/.

Arnold, J. E. M. 1990. *Social Forestry and Communal Management in India.* Rural Development Forestry Network Paper 11b. London: Overseas Development Institute.

Atencio, Ernie. 2002. Working Toward 89,000 Acres of Common Ground on the Valles Caldera. *La Jicarita News* 7, no. 3 (March).

Baker, Mark. 1994. Rhythms of the Kuhls: Persistence and Change within the Communal Irrigation Systems of Kangra Valley, Himachal Pradesh. PhD diss., University of California, Berkeley.

Baker, Mark, and Jonathan Kusel. 2003. *Community Forestry in the United States: Learning from the Past, Crafting the Future.* Washington, DC: Island Press.

Ballabh, V., and K. Singh. 1988. Managing Forests Through People's Institutions: A Case Study of Van Panchayats in Uttar Pradesh Hills. *Indian Journal of Agricultural Economics* 43, no. 3: 296–304.

Ballard, Heidi. 2004. Local Ecological Knowledge and Management of Salal (*Gaultheria shallon*) by Mobile Forest Workers in Olympic Peninsula, Washington, USA. Paper presented at the Tenth Meeting of the International Association for the Study of Common Property, Oaxaca, Mexico. http://www.iascp.org/conference.html (accessed 8 September 2004).

Banwari. 1992. *Pañcavaṭī: Indian Approach to Environment.* Delhi: Shri Vinayaka.

Barahona, C., and S. Levy. 2002. *Participatory Methods for Generating Credible Statistics.* Statistical Services Centre, University of Reading.

Barraclough, Solon L., and Krishna B. Ghimire. 1996. Deforestation in Tanzania: Beyond Simplistic Generalizations. *The Ecologist* 26, no. 3 (May/June): 104–9.

Barton, Greg. 2002. *Empire Forestry and the Origins of Environmentalism.* Cambridge Studies in Historical Geography 34. Cambridge: Cambridge University Press.

BBC News World Edition. 2004. Admirers Flock to Indian Brigand's Grave. Report filed by Habib Beary, BBC correspondent in Bangalore. http://news.bbc.co.uk/2/hi/south _asia/3975155.stm (accessed 2 November 2004).

Bebbington, Anthony. 1997. New States, New NGOs? Crises and Transitions Among Rural Development NGOs in the Andean Region. *World Development* 25, no. 11: 1755–65.

Becker, Laurence C. 2001. Seeing Green in Mali's Woods: Colonial Legacy, Forest Use, and Local Control. *Annals of the Association of American Geographers* 91, no. 3: 504–26.

Bensted-Smith, Robert. 1990. An Environmental Policy and Program for Zanzibar. Report to the Zanzibar Integrated Land and Environment Project of the Commission for Lands and Environment.

Bercé, Yves-Marie. 1986. *Histoire des Croquants: Étude des Soulèvements Populaires au XVIIe Siècle en France.* Paris: Seuil.

Berkes, Fikret. 1999. *Sacred Ecology: Traditional Ecological Knowledge and Resources Management.* Washington, DC: Taylor & Francis.

Berkes, Fikret, Iain Davidson-Hunt, Tracy Ruta, and John Sinclair. 2002. Scientific and First Nation Perspectives of Non-Timber Forest Products: A Case Study from the Shoal Lake Watershed, Northwestern Ontario: NCE-SFMN Project Combining Scientific and First Nations' Knowledge for the Management and Harvest of Traditional and Commercial Non-Timber Forest Products. University of Alberta Sustainable Forest Management Network, Project Report 2002-4.

Berry, Kim. 2001. The Group Called Women in Himachal Pradesh. *Himalayan Research Bulletin* 21, no. 2: 62–69 (published April 2003).

Bertrand, A. 1985. Les Nouvelles Politiques de Foresterie en Milieu Rural au Sahel: Réglementations Foncières et Gestion des Ressources Ligneuses Naturelles dans les Pays de la Zone Soudano-sahélienne. *Revue Bois et Forêts des Tropiques* 207:23–40.

Bigombe, P. 1998. Towards Decentralization of Forest Management in Cameroon: The Dynamics of the Contest Between the Forester State and the Construction of Participatory Management of Forest Resources. *Forest, Trees, and People Newsletter* 15–16:2–12.

Bisong, Francis. 1999. Conservation by Communities: Community Forestry Management in Sub-Saharan Africa: Report of a Workshop on Community Forestry Management in Sub-Saharan Africa Held in Obudu Cattle Ranch, Cross River State, March 5–10. Lagos: Ford Foundation.

Blaikie, Piers. 1985. *The Political Economy of Soil Erosion in Developing Countries.* New York: Wiley.

——. 2001. *Is Policy Reform Pure Nostalgia? A Himalayan Illustration.* Berkeley Workshop on Environmental Politics, Working Paper 01-9. Berkeley: Institute of International Studies.

Blasco, F., and A. Weill, eds. 1999. *Advances in Environmental Modelling.* Paris: Elsevier.

Bliss, John, Greg Aplet, Cate Hartzell, Peggy Harwood, Paul Jahnige, David Kittredge, Stephen Landowski, and Mary Sue Sascia. 2001. Community Based Ecosystem Monitoring. In Gerald Gray, Maia Enzer, and Jonathan Kusel, *Understanding Community-Based Forest Ecosystem Management,* 143–67. New York: Haworth.

Boissau S., J. C. Castella, Nguyen Hai Thanh. 2001. *La Distribution des Terres de Forêt au Nord Viêt Nam: Droits d'Usage et Gestion des Ressources.* SAM Paper Series 9. Hanoi: Vietnam Agricultural Science Institute.

Borch, M. 2001. Rethinking the Origins of Terra Nullius. *Australian Historical Studies* 117:222–39.

Borrini-Feyerabend, G. 1996. *Beyond Fences: Seeking Social Sustainability in Conservation.* 2 vols. Gland, Switzerland: IUCN.

Bousquet, François, Olivier Barreteau, Christophe Le Page, Christian Mullon, and Jacques Wéber. 1999a. *Advances in Environmental Ecological Modelling.* Paris: Elsevier.

——. 1999b. An Environmental Modelling Approach: The Use of Multi-Agent Simulations. In François Bousquet et al., *Advances in Environmental Ecological Modelling*, 113–22. Paris: Elsevier.

Bray, David, and Leticia Merino-Pérez. 2002. *The Rise of Community Forestry in Mexico: History, Concepts, and Lessons Learned from Twenty-Five Years of Community Timber Production.* Mexico City: Ford Foundation.

Bray, David, Leticia Merino-Pérez, Patricia Negreros-Castillo, Gerardo Segura-Warnholtz, Juan Manuel Torre-Rojo, and Henricus Vester. 2002. Mexico's Community-Managed Forests as a Global Model for Sustainable Landscapes. *Conservation Biology* 17, no. 3: 672–77.

Briggs, Charles, and John R. Van Ness, eds. 1987. *Land, Water, and Culture.* Albuquerque: University of New Mexico Press.

Bromley, Daniel W., and D. P. Chapagain. 1984. The Village Against the Center: Resource Depletion in South Asia. *American Journal of Agricultural Economics* 66:868–73.

Bromley, Daniel W., David Feeny, Margaret A. McKean, Pauline Peters, Jere Gilles, Ronald Oakerson, C. Ford Runge, and James Thomson, eds. 1992. *Making the Commons Work: Theory, Practice, and Policy.* San Francisco: ICS.

Brosius, Peter. 2004. Seeing Natural and Cultural Communities: Technologies of Visualization in Conservation. Manuscript presented at the Environmental Politics Colloquium, Berkeley, February 2.

Brown, David, Kate Schreckenberg, Gill Shepherd, and Adrian Wells. 2002. *Forestry as an Entry Point for Governance Reform.* ODI Forestry Briefing no. 1. London: Overseas Development Institute.

Bryant, D., D. Nielsen, and L. Tangley. 1997. *The Last Frontier Forests: Ecosystems and Economies on the Edge.* Washington, DC: World Resources Institute.

Buckles, Daniel, ed. 1999. *Cultivating Peace: Conflict and Collaboration in Natural Resource Management.* Ottawa: International Development Research Center/World Bank.

Bunker, Stephen. 1985. *Underdeveloping the Amazon: Extraction, Unequal Exchange, and the Failure of the Modern State.* Urbana: University of Illinois Press.

Burnham, Philip. 2000. *Indian Country, God's Country: Native Americans and the National Parks.* Washington, DC: Island Press.

Byron, N., and J. E. M. Arnold. 1999. What Futures for the People of the Tropical Forests? *World Development* 27, no. 5: 789–805.

Carlson, Alvar. 1990. *The Spanish American Homeland: Four Centuries in New Mexico's Rio Arriba.* Baltimore: Johns Hopkins University Press.

Carr, David. 1986. *Time, Narrative, and History.* Bloomington: Indiana University Press.

Carruthers, Jane. 1995. *The Kruger National Park: A Social and Political History.* Pietermaritzburg: University of Natal Press.

——. 1997. Nationhood and National Parks: Comparative Examples from the Post-Imperial Experience. In Tom Griffiths and Libby Robin, eds., *Ecology and Empire: Environmental History of Settler Societies*, 125–38. Seattle: University of Washington Press.

Carter, Jane, Brieke Steenhof, Esther Haldimann, and Nurlan Akenshaev. 2003. *Collaborative Forest Management in Kyrgyzstan: Moving from Top-Down to Bottom-Up Decision-*

Making. Gatekeeper Series no. 108. London: International Institute for Environment and Development.

Cashore, Benjamin. 2002. Legitimacy and the Privatization of Environmental Governance: How Non-State Market-Driven (NSMD) Governance Systems Gain Rule-Making Authority. *Governance* 15, no. 4: 503–30.

Castle, Emery N. 2002. Social Capital: An Interdisciplinary Concept. *Rural Sociology* 67, no. 3: 331–49.

Castro, Alfonso Peter. 1995. *Facing Kirinyaga: A Social History of Forest Commons in Southern Mount Kenya.* London: Intermediate Technology.

Chambers, Robert. 1995. *Poverty and Livelihoods: Whose Reality Counts?* Brighton: Institute of Development Studies.

———. 1997. *Whose Reality Counts? Putting the Last First.* London: Intermediate Technology.

———. 2002. *Relaxed and Participatory Appraisal: Notes on Practical Approaches and Methods for Participants in PRA/PLA-Related Familiarisation Workshops.* Brighton: Institute of Development Studies, Participation Resource Centre.

Chambers, Robert, and Melissa Leach. 1987. *Trees to Meet Contingencies: Savings and Security for the Rural Poor.* Rural Development Forestry Network Paper 5a. London: Overseas Development Institute.

Chapin, Mac. 2004. A Challenge to Conservationists. *Worldwatch Magazine* (November/December): 19–31.

Chhatre, Ashwini. 2000. Forest Co-Management as if History Mattered: The Case of Western Himalayan Forests in India. Paper presented at the biennial conference of the International Association for the Study of Common Property, Bloomington, IN, May 31–June 4. http://dlc.dlib.indiana.edu/documents/diro/00/00/02/34/index.html.

———. 2001. Territorialization, Resistance, and the Mirage of Permanent Boundaries: Forests of the Western Himalayas, 1876–1897. *Himalayan Research Bulletin* 21, no. 2: 15–25 (published April 2003).

China CITES Office. 2002. Yunnan Sheng Songrong Ziyuan Ji Maoyi Xianzhuang Yanjiu [A Study of Matsutake Resources and Trade in Yunnan Province]. Report prepared by the Matsutake Study Group of the Leique Academy for Nature Conservation. Kunming: People's Republic of China CITES Office, Kunming Bureau.

Churchill, Ward. 2002. *Struggle for the Land: Native North American Resistance to Genocide, Ecocide, and Colonization.* San Francisco: City Lights.

CIFOR. 2004. Decentralization, Federal Systems in Forestry, and National Forest Programs: Report of a Workshop Co-organized by the Governments of Indonesia and Switzerland. Paper presented at the Interlaken Workshop on Decentralization in Forestry, April 27–30, Interlaken, Switzerland. http://www.cifor.cgiar.org/int/_ref/events/swiss/background.htm (accessed 21 November 2004).

Clay, Jason. 2001. *Community-Based Natural Resource Management Within the New Global Economy: Challenges and Opportunities.* New York: Ford Foundation.

Cleary, David. 2001. Towards an Environmental History of the Amazon: From Prehistory to the Nineteenth Century. *Latin American Research Review* 36, no. 2: 65–96.

CNN. 2000. Hopi Eagle Hunt Raises Hackles. CNN Environmental News Network Report, November 7. http://archives.cnn.com/2000/NATURE/11/07/eagle.hunt.enn/ (accessed 19 October 2004).

CNRS. 1987. *Les Eaux et les Forêts du 12e au 20e Siècles.* Paris: CNRS.

Colchester, Marcus, Tejaswini Apte, Michel Laforge, Alois Mandondo, and Neema Parthak. 2003. *Bridging the Gap: Communities, Forests, and International Networks.* CIFOR Occasional Paper no. 41. Bogor: CIFOR.

Colfer, Carol J. Pierce. 1995. *Who Counts Most in Sustainable Forest Management?* Working Paper no. 7. Bogor: CIFOR.

——, ed. 2004. *The Equitable Forest: Diversity, Community, and Resource Management.* Washington, DC: Resources for the Future/Bogor: CIFOR.

Colfer, Carol J. Pierce, and Yvonne Byron, eds. 2001. *People Managing Forests: The Links Between Human Well-Being and Sustainability.* Washington, DC: Resources for the Future/Bogor: CIFOR.

Commission for Natural Resources, Zanzibar. 2001. *National Forest Policy for Zanzibar (1995).* Zanzibar (Tanzania): Government Printer.

Conca, Ken. The WTO and the Undermining of Global Environmental Governance. *Review of International Political Economy* 7, no. 3: 484–94.

Conroy, Czech, Abha Mishra, and Ajay Rai. 2000. Learning from Self-Initiated Community Forest Management in Orissa, India. *Forest, Trees, and People Newsletter* 42 (June): 51–56.

Conservation International. 2003. *Critical Ecosystem Partnership Fund: Eastern Arc Mountains and Coastal Forests of Kenya and Tanzania.* CEPF Factsheet. Washington, DC: Conservation International. http://www.cepf.net/xp/cepf/where_we_work/eastern_arc _mountains/eastern_arc_mountains_info.xml (accessed 10 November 2003).

Cook, Annabel Kirschner. 1995. Increasing Poverty in Timber-Dependent Areas in Western Washington. *Society and Natural Resources* 8, no. 2: 97–109.

Cooke, Bill, and Uma Kothari. 2001. *Participation: The New Tyranny?* London: Zed.

Corbera, Esteve, and W. Neil Adger. 2004. The Equity and Legitimacy of Markets for Ecosystem Services: Carbon Forestry Activities in Chiapas, Mexico. Paper presented at the Tenth Biennial Conference of the International Association for the Study of Common Property, Oaxaca, Mexico. http://www.iascp.org/conference.html.

Corvol-Dessert, Andrée, Pierre Gresser, François Duceppe-Lamarre, and Daniel Berni. 2004. *Les Forêts d'Occident du Moyen-Âge à Nos Jours: Actes des XXVIes Journées d'Histoire de l'Abbaye de Floran.* Toulouse: Mirail.

Coward, E. W. 2004. Making and Unmaking Property in the Taos Valleys: Processes of Displacement, Impoverishment, and Development in the Southern Rocky Mountains. In G. Pena Devon and Ruben O. Martinez, eds., *Voces de la Tierra: Four Hundred Years of Acequia Farming in the Rio Arriba, 1598–1998.* Phoenix: University of Arizona Press.

Croll, Elisabeth, and David Parkin, eds. 1992. *Bush Base: Forest Farm: Culture, Environment, and Development.* London: Routledge.

Cronkleton, Peter. 2004. Gender, Participation, and the Strengthening of Indigenous Forest Management in Bolivia. In Carol J. Pierce Colfer, ed., *The Equitable Forest: Diversity, Community, and Resource Management,* 256–73. Washington, DC: Resources for the Future/Bogor: CIFOR.

Cronon, William. 1992. A Place for Stories: Nature, History, and Narrative. *Journal of American History* (March): 1347–76.

Danks, Cecilia M. 2000. Community Participation in National Forest Management: The Role of Social Capital and Organizational Capacity in Collaborative Efforts in Trinity County, California. PhD diss., University of California, Berkeley.

Dargavel, John. 1995. *Fashioning Australia's Forests.* Melbourne: Oxford University Press.

Dark, Alx. 1999. The Makah Whale Hunt. Report for Native Americans and the Environment. http://www.cnie.org/NAE/cases/makah/ (accessed 19 October 2004).

Darlington, Susan. 1997. Not Only Preaching: The Work of the Ecology Monk Phrakhu Pitak Nantakhun of Thailand. *Forest, Trees, and People Newsletter* 34 (September).

——. 1998. The Ordination of a Tree: The Buddhist Ecology Movement in Thailand. *Ethnology* 37, no. 1: 1–15.

Davis, Thomas. 2000. *Sustaining the Forest, the People, and the Spirit.* Albany: State University of New York Press.

Davis-Case, D'Arcy. 2001. The Reflective Practitioner: Learning and Teaching in Community-Based Forest Management. *Conservation Ecology* 5, no. 2, art. 15. http://www.consecol.org/vol5/iss2/art15.

DeBuys, William. 1985. *Enchantment and Exploitation: The Life and Hard Times of a New Mexico Mountain Range.* Albuquerque: University of New Mexico Press.

de Foresta, H., and G. Michon. 1994. Agroforests in Sumatra: Where Ecology Meets Economy. *Agroforestry Today* 6, no. 4: 12–13.

De Janvry, Alain, Elisabeth Sadoulet, and Erik Thorbecke. 1993. State, Market, and Civil Organizations: New Theories, New Practices, and Their Implications for Rural Development. *World Development* 21, no. 4: 565–75.

Denevan, W. M. 1992. The Pristine Myth: The Landscape of the Americas in 1492. *Annals of the American Association of Geographers* 82:369–85.

Department of Commercial Crops, Fruits, and Forestry. 2001. *Charawe Community Forest Management Agreement.* Zanzibar: DCCFF.

Devon, G. Pena, and Ruben O. Martinez, eds. 2004. *Voces de la Tierra: Four Hundred Years of Acequia Farming in the Rio Arriba, 1598–1998.* Phoenix: University of Arizona Press.

Dhiman, D. R., and Kiran Bhatia. 1990. Joint Forest Management Strategies in Himachal Pradesh. Paper presented at the Workshop on Sustainable Forestry, September 10–12. New Delhi: Indian Environmental Society/Ford Foundation.

Diegues, Antonio Carlos. 1991. The Role of Cultural Diversity and Communal Participation in Wetland Management in Brazil. *Landscape and Urban Planning* 20:61–66.

——. 1997. *Deforestation and Livelihoods in the Brazilian Amazon.* São Paolo: NUPAUB/Research Center on Human Population and Wetlands, University of São Paolo.

Donovan, D. G. 2001. Where's the Forestry in Community Forestry? In M. Victor and Andrew Barash, eds., *Cultivating Forests: Alternative Forest Management Practices for Community Forestry: Proceedings of an International Seminar,* chap. 1. RECOFTC Report no. 17. Bangkok: Regional Community Forestry Training Center. http://www.recoftc.org/03region/materials/conference_reports/international2.html#Cultivating.

Doornbos, Martin, Ashwani Saith, and Ben White, eds. 2000. *Forests: Nature, People, Power.* Oxford: Blackwell.

Dornic, François. 1984. *Le fer Contre la Forêt.* Rennes: Ouest-France.

Dove, Michael R. 1993. A Revisionist View of Tropical Deforestation and Development. *Environmental Conservation* 20, no. 1: 17–24, 56.

——. 1995. The Theory of Social Forestry Intervention: The State of the Art in Asia. *Agroforestry Systems* 30:315–40.

Drijver, Carol A. 1992. People's Participation in Environmental Projects. In Elisabeth Croll and David Parkin, eds., *Bush Base: Forest Farm: Culture, Environment, and Development,* 131–45. London: Routledge.

Dubois, Olivier. 2001. *Facilitation of the Participatory Review of the Joint Forest Management Component of the CARE/DCCFF Jozani–Chwaka Bay Conservation Project, Zanzibar, and the Planning Process of the JFM Component of the CARE-FBD Misitu-Yetu Project, Tanzania.* Dar es Salaam/Zanzibar: CARE Tanzania.

Ducourtieux, Olivier, Jean-Richard Laffort, and Silinthone Sacklokham. 2002. La Politique Foncière au Laos: Est-elle Compatible avec les Pratiques Paysannes? Manuscript prepared for Institut National Agronomique de Paris-Grignon.

Edmunds, David, and Eva Wollenberg. 2001. A Strategic Approach to Multistakeholder Negotiations. *Development and Change* 32:231–53.

Edwards, M., and D. Hulme, eds. 1997. *NGOs, States, and Donors.* Basingstoke: Macmillan.

Eicher, C. K., and J. M. Staatz, eds. 1984. *Agricultural Development in the Third World.* Baltimore: John Hopkins University Press.

Elbow, K., and A. Rochegude. 1991. *Guide Pratique des Codes Forestiers du Mali, du Niger, et du Sénégal.* LTC Paper 139-F. Madison: Land Tenure Center, University of Wisconsin–Madison.

Elías, Silvel, and Hannah Wittman. 2004. State, Forest, and Community: Power Reconfigurations and Challenges for the Decentralization of Forest Administration in Guatemala. Paper presented at the Interlaken Workshop on Decentralization in Forestry, April 27–30, Interlaken, Switzerland. http://www.cifor.cgiar.org/int_ref/events/swiss/papers.htm (accessed 25 October 2004).

Environment News Service. 1999. Natives, Enviros, MacMillan Bloedel Sign Clayoquot Truce (June 17).

Escobar, Arturo. 1991. Anthropology and the Development Encounter: The Making and Marketing of Development Anthropology. *American Ethnologist* 18, no. 4: 658–82.

Etzioni, Amitai. 1996, Positive Aspects of Community and the Dangers of Fragmentation. *Development and Change* 27, no. 2: 301–14.

Fay, Chip, Martua Sirait, and Ahmad Kusworo. 2000. *Getting the Boundaries Right: Indonesia's Urgent Need to Redefine Its Forest Estate.* Bogor: International Centre for Research in Agroforestry.

FECOFUN Steering Committee. 1996. The Federation of Community Forestry Users in Nepal: A Federation with a Mission. *Forest, Trees, and People Newsletter* 31.

Fernow, B. E. 1913. *A Brief History of Forestry: In Europe, the United States, and Other Countries.* Toronto: University of Toronto Press.

Filer, C., and N. Sekhran. 1998. *Loggers, Donors, and Resource Owners: Papua New Guinea Country Study.* Policy That Works for Forests and People no. 2. London: International Institute for Environment and Development.

Firey, Walter. 1960. *Man, Mind, and Land: A Theory of Resource Use.* Glencoe, IL: Free Press.

Fisher, William. 1997. Doing Good? The Politics and Antipolitics of NGO Practices. *Annual Review of Anthropology* 26:439–64.

Flader, Susan. 1983. *The Great Lakes Forest: An Environmental and Social History.* Minneapolis: University of Minnesota Press.

Fortmann, Louise. 1995. Talking Claims: Discursive Strategies in Contesting Property. *World Development* 23, no. 6: 1053–63.

——, ed. Forthcoming. *Democratizing Science: The Practice and Politics of Participatory Research.*

Fortmann, Louise, and John Bruce, eds. 1988. *Whose Trees? Proprietary Dimensions of Forestry.* Boulder, CO: Westview.

Fowler, Alan F. 1998. Authentic NGDO Partnerships in the New Policy Agenda for International Aid: Dead End or Light Ahead? *Development and Change* 29:137–59.

French, H. 2000. *Vanishing Borders: Protecting the Planet in the Age of Globalization.* Washington, DC: Worldwatch Institute.

Fried, Stephanie Gorson. 2000. Tropical Forests Forever? A Contextual Ecology of Bentian Rattan Agroforestry Systems. In Charles Zerner, ed., *People, Plants, and Justice: The Politics of Nature Conservation,* 204–33. New York: Columbia University Press.

Friedmann, John, and Haripriya Rangan, eds. 1993a. *In Defense of Livelihood: Comparative Studies on Environmental Action.* West Hartford, CT: Kumarian.

——. 1993b. Introduction: In Defense of Livelihood. In John Friedmann and Haripriya Rangan, eds., *In Defense of Livelihood: Comparative Studies on Environmental Action.* West Hartford, CT: Kumarian.

Fruman, C. 1998. *Self-Managed Village Savings and Loan Banks in the Pays Dogon Region of Mali.* Washington, DC: World Bank/Sustainable Banking with the Poor.

García-Guadilla, María Pilar. 2002. Environmental Movements, Politics, and the Agenda 21 in Latin America: How to Build Consensus. Draft paper for the conference Political Economy of Sustainable Development: Environmental Conflict, Participation, and Movements. World Summit on Sustainable Development. Johannesburg: United Nations Research Institute for Social Development/University of Witwatersrand.

Gaunitz, S. 1984. Resource Exploitation on the North Swedish Timber Frontier in the Nineteenth and the Beginning of the Twentieth Centuries. In H. K. Steen, *History of Sustained Yield Forestry: A Symposium,* 134–44. Durham: Forest History Society.

Gautam, A. P., G. P. Shivakoti, and E. L. Webb. 2004. A Review of Forest Policies, Institutions, and Changes in the Resource Condition in Nepal. *International Forestry Review* 6, no. 2: 136–48.

Geist, H. J., and E. F. Lambin. 2001. *What Drives Tropical Deforestation? A Meta-Analysis of Proximate and Underlying Causes of Deforestation Based on Subnational Case Study Evidence.* Louvain-la-Neuve: University of Louvain, Department of Geography.

Ghai, D. 1991. *Conservation, Livelihood, and Democracy: Social Dynamics of Environmental Changes in Africa.* Geneva: United Nations Research Institute for Social Development.

Ghimire, Krishna B., and Michel P. Pimbert, eds. 1997. *Social Change and Conservation.* London: Earthscan.

Gibson, Clark, Elinor Ostrom, and Margaret McKean. 2000. Forests, People, and Governance: Some Initial Theoretical Lessons. In Clark Gibson, Margaret A. McKean, and Elinor Ostrom, eds., *People and Forests: Communities, Institutions, and Governance,* 227–42. Cambridge: MIT Press.

Gibson, Clark, Margaret A. McKean, and Elinor Ostrom, eds. 2000. *People and Forests: Communities, Institutions, and Governance.* Cambridge: MIT Press.

Glacken, C. J. 1967. *Traces on the Rhodian Shore: Nature and Culture in Western Thought from Ancient Times to the end of the Eighteenth Century.* Berkeley: University of California Press.

Gollin, Karin L., and James L. Kho. 2002a. Power to the Community? Philippine CBNRM Facing Globalisation. Abstract for International Association for the Study of Common Property biennial conference panel, Bloomington.

——. 2002b. *Rethinking Community, Participation, and Power in Philippine CBNRM.* Manila: Ford Foundation.

Gray, Gerald, Maia Enzer, and Jonathan Kusel. 2001. *Understanding Community-Based Forest Ecosystem Management.* New York: Haworth.

Griffiths, Tom, and Libby Robin, eds. 1997. *Ecology and Empire: Environmental History of Settler Societies.* Seattle: University of Washington Press.

Grinspoon, Elisabeth Julie. 2002. Socialist Wasteland Auctions: Privatizing Collective Forest Land in China's Economic Transition. PhD diss., University of California, Berkeley.

Grove, Richard H., Vinita Damodaran, and Satpal Sangwan, eds. 1998. *Nature and the Orient: The Environmental History of South and Southeast Asia.* Delhi: Oxford University Press.

Guha, Ramachandra. 1990. *The Unquiet Woods: Ecological Change and Peasant Resistance in the Himalayas.* Berkeley: University of California Press.

Guowuyuan Fazhan Yanjiu Zhongxin Zhongguo Nongdi Zhidu Keti Zu [State Council Development Research Center Working Group on Land Tenure in China]. 1993. *Zhongguo Nongcun Tudi Zhidudi Biange* [China's Rural Land Tenure Reform]. Beijing: Beijing Daxue Chubanshe.

Hale, Lynne Zeitlin, Mark Amaral, Abdulrahman S. Issa, and B. A. J. Mwandotto. 2000. Catalyzing Coastal Management in Kenya and Zanzibar: Building Capacity and Commitment. *Coastal Management* 28:75–85.

Hanscom, Greg. 2004. A Timber Town Learns to Care for the Forest. *High Country News* 36, no. 18 (September 27): 12–13.

Hardin, Garrett. 1974. Lifeboat Ethics: The Case Against Helping the Poor. *Psychology Today* (September). http://www.garretthardinsociety.org/articles/art_lifeboat_ethics_case _against_helping_poor.html (accessed 17 October 2004).

Harkness, James. 1998. Recent Trends in Forestry and Conservation of Biodiversity in China. *China Quarterly* 156 (December): 911–34.

Harper, Keith, Richard Guest, and John Echohawk. 2004. Native American Rights Fund (NARF) Case Updates, January 2004: Trust Fund Matters; Individual Indian Money (IIM) Accounts. http://narf.org/cases/index.html (accessed 12 February 2004).

Harrison, Elizabeth. 2002. The Problem with the Locals: Partnership and Participation in Ethiopia. *Development and Change* 33, no. 4: 587–610.

Hartley, Dawn, and Hamza Rijali. 2003. Final Project Review: Jozani–Chwaka Bay Conservation Project, Phase III (19th April–3rd May 2003). Report for CARE Tanzania, Zanzibar.

He, Jun. 2004. Globalized Forest Products: Commodification of Matsutake Mushroom in Tibetan Villages, Yunnan Province, Southwest China. Paper presented at the Tenth Biennial Conference of the International Association for the Study of Common Property, Oaxaca, Mexico. http://www.iascp.org/conference.html.

Hecht, Susanna, and Alexander Cockburn. 1989. *The Fate of the Forest: Developers, Destroyers, and Defenders of the Amazon.* London: Verso.

Henderson, A., C. Padoch, and J. M. Ayres. eds. 1999. *Ecology, Conservation, and Development of Amazonian Várzea.* New York: New York Botanical Garden Press.

Herman, John E. 1997. Empire in the Southwest: Early Qing Reforms to the Native Chieftain System. *Journal of Asian Studies* 56, no. 1: 47–74.

Herrold, Melinda K. 2002. Cranes and Conflicts: NGO Programs to Improve People-Park Relations in China and Russia. PhD diss., University of California, Berkeley.

High Court of Himachal Pradesh. 2000. Court Notice OMP no. 369/2000 in Civil Suit no. (N-2242/2000). Shimla: High Court of Himachal Pradesh.

Hiraoka, Mario. 1999. Miriti (*Mauritia flexuosa*) Palms and Their Uses and Management Among the Ribeirinhos of the Amazon Estuary. In Christine Padoch, José Márcio Ayres,

Miguel Pinedo-Vasquez, and Andrew Henderson, eds., *Várzea: Diversity, Development, and Conservation of Amazonia's Whitewater Floodplains*, 169–86. Advances in Economic Botany 13. New York: New York Botanical Garden Press.

Hoben, Alan. 1995. Paradigms and Politics: The Cultural Construction of Environmental Policy in Ethiopia. *World Development* 23, no. 6: 1007–21.

Hobley, M. 1996. *Participatory Forestry: The Process of Change in India and Nepal*. Rural Development Forestry Study Guide 3. London: Overseas Development Institute.

Holdcroft, L. E. 1984. The Rise and Fall of Community Development, 1950–65: A Critical Assessment. In C. K. Eicher and J. M. Staatz, eds., *Agricultural Development in the Third World*. Baltimore: John Hopkins University Press.

Homewood, Katherine, and W. A. Rodgers. 1987. Pastoralism, Conservation, and the Overgrazing Controversy. In David Anderson and Richard Grove, *Conservation in Africa: People, Policies, and Practice*. Cambridge: Cambridge University Press.

Honey, Martha. 1999. *Ecotourism and Sustainable Development: Who Owns Paradise?* Washington, DC: Island Press.

——. 2002. *Ecotourism and Certification: Setting Standards in Practice*. Washington, DC: Island Press.

Hosford, David, David Pilz, Randy Molina, and Michael Amaranthus. 1997. *Ecology and Management of the Commercially Harvested American Matsutake Mushroom*. Pacific Northwest Research Station, General Technical Report PNW-GTR-412. Corvallis, OR: U.S. Forest Service.

Hoskins, Marilyn. 2002. Decentralizing Community Forestry at FAO: An Institutional Analysis. Paper presented at the Workshop in Political Theory and Policy Analysis, Indiana University, Bloomington, November 11.

Huang Qinghe. 1993. Zhongguo Nongcun Tudi Zhengcedi Huigu Yu Mianlindi Wenti [A Review of China's Rural Land Tenure Policy and Current Issues]. In Guowuyuan Fazhan Yanjiu Zhongxin Zhongguo Nongdi Zhidu Keti Zu [State Council Development Research Center Working Group on Land Tenure in China], *Zhongguo Nongcun Tudi Zhidudi Biange* [China's Rural Land Tenure Reform], 13–28. Beijing: Beijing Daxue Chubanshe.

Huntsinger, Lynn, and Sarah McCaffrey. 1995. A Forest for the Trees: Forest Management and the Yurok Environment, 1850 to 1994. *American Indian Culture and Research Journal* 19, no. 4: 155–92.

Huntsinger, Lynn, Sarah McCaffrey, Laura Watt, and Michele Lee. 1994. A Yurok Forest History. Report presented to the Bureau of Indian Affairs, Sacramento.

Hyde, William F., Brian Belcher, and Jintao Xu, eds. 2003a. *China's Forests: Global Lessons from Market Reforms*. Washington, DC: Resources for the Future/Bogor: CIFOR.

——. 2003b. Introduction. In William F. Hyde, Brian Belcher, and Jintao Xu, eds., *China's Forests: Global Lessons from Market Reforms*, 1–21. Washington, DC: Resources for the Future/Bogor: CIFOR.

Igoe, Jim. 2003. Scaling Up Civil Society: Donor Money, NGOs and the Pastoralist Land Rights Movement in Tanzania. *Development and Change* 34, no. 5: 863–87.

Indigenous People's Forest Forum. 2003. *Wendake Action Plan*. Huron-Wendat Territory, Québec. Official Event of the Twelfth World Forestry Congress. www.nafaforestry.org/docs/WendakeActionPlanEnglish.pdf.

Inglis, Andrew, and Susan Guy. 1997. *Rural Development Forestry in Scotland: The Struggle to Bring International Principles and Best Practices to the Last Bastion of British Colonial Forestry*. Rural Development Forestry Network Paper 20b. London: Overseas Development Institute.

Jacobs, Nancy J. 2003. *Environment, Power, and Injustice: A South African History.* Cambridge: Cambridge University Press.

James, N. D. G. 1990. *A History of English Forestry.* Oxford: Blackwell.

Jeffery, Roger, and Nandini Sandar, eds. 1999. *A New Moral Economy for India's Forests? Discourses of Community and Participation.* New Delhi: Thousand Oaks/London: Sage.

Joshi, Anuradha. 1999. *Progressive Bureaucracy: An Oxymoron? The Case of Joint Forest Management in India.* Rural Development Forestry Network Paper 24a. London: Overseas Development Institute.

Junk W. J. 1997. *The Central Amazon Floodplain: Ecology of a Pulsing System.* New York: Springer.

Kaimowitz, David. 2003. Bad Loans and Lost Forests. CIFOR media release (March). http://www.cifor.cgiar.org/docs/_ref/media/release/2003/2003_01_15.htm (accessed 5 February 2005).

Kaimowitz, David, Cristian Vallejos, Pablo D. Pacheco, and Raul Lopez. 1998. Municipal Governments and Forest Management in Lowland Bolivia. *Journal of Environment and Development* 7, no. 1 (March): 45–60.

Kangra District Cooperative Forest Societies Union. 1993. Parawise Comments on Comments of Sh. G. C. Choudhary, C. F. Dharamsala. Trippal, District Kangra.

Kassibo, Bréhima. 2002. Gestion Participative et Décentralisation Démocratique: Étude de Cas: La Gestion de la Forêt du Samori dans la Commune de Baye, Région de Mopti (Mali). Paper presented at the Conference on Decentralization and the Environment, Bellagio, Italy, February 18–22. Washington, DC: World Resources Institute, Institutions and Governance Program.

Kepe, Thembela. 1998. *The Problem of Defining Community: Challenges for the Land Reform Programme in South Africa.* Programme for Land and Agrarian Studies Occasional Paper no. 6. Bellville: University of the Western Cape.

Klein, Kewin Lee. 1995. In Search of Narrative Mastery: Postmodernism and the People Without History. *History and Theory* 34, no. 4: 275–98.

Klooster, D. 1999. Community-Based Forestry in Mexico: Can It Reverse Processes of Degradation? *Land Degradation and Development* 10:365–81.

Kombo, Yussuf. 2000. Habitat Destruction Threatens the Endangered Wild Animals in Zanzibar. Paper presented at the Third Regional Session for Africa: Using Biodiversity to Strengthen Livelihoods, Gland, Switzerland, Global Biodiversity Forum, February 21–23.

Korten, David. 1980. *Community Organization and Rural Development: A Learning Process Approach.* New York: Ford Foundation (reprinted from *Public Administration Review*).

——, ed. 1987. *Community Management: Asian Experience and Perspectives.* West Hartford, CT: Kumarian.

Kosek, Jake. 2004a. Deep Roots and Long Shadows: The Cultural Politics of Memory and Longing in Northern New Mexico. *Environment and Planning D: Society and Space* 22:329–54.

——. 2004b. Purity and Pollution: Racial Degradation and Environmental Anxieties. In Richard Peet and Michael Watts, *Liberation Ecologies: Environment, Development, Social Movements,* 125–54. 2nd edition. London: Routledge.

Kramer, R. A., C. P. Van Schaik, and J. Johnson, eds. 1997. *Last Stand: Protected Areas and the Defense of Tropical Biodiversity.* New York: Oxford University Press.

Kumar, Niraj. 2000. All Is Not Green with JFM in India. *Forests, Trees, and People Newsletter* 42 (June): 46–50.

Kusel, J., and E. Adler. 2001. *Forest Communities: Community Forests: A Collection of Case Studies of Community Forestry.* Taylorsville, CA: Forest Communities Research.

La Duke, Winona. 1996. The Growing Strength of Native Environmentalism. *Sierra Magazine,* no. 11 (November/December) (special issue entitled "Native Americans and the Environment").

Landell-Mills, Natasha, and Ina T. Porras. 2002. *Silver Bullet or Fools' Gold? A Global Review of Markets for Environmental Services and Their Impact on the Poor.* London: International Institute for Environment and Development, Forestry and Land Use Programme.

Larson, Anne M. 2004. Formal Decentralization and the Imperative of Decentralization "from Below": A Case Study of Natural Resource Management in Nicaragua. *European Journal of Development Research* 16, no. 1: 55–71.

Larson, Anne M., and Jesse C. Ribot. 2004. Democratic Decentralisation Through a Natural Resource Lens: An Introduction. *European Journal of Development Research* 16, no. 1: 1–25.

Laungaramsri, Pinkaew. 1998. Reconstructing Nature: The Community Forest Movement and Its Challenge to Forest Management in Thailand. In M. Victor, C. Lang, and Jeff Bornemeier, eds., *Community Forestry at a Crossroads: Reflections and Future Directions in the Development of Community Forestry: Proceedings of an International Seminar,* 45–55. RECOFTC Report no. 16. Bangkok: Regional Community Forestry Training Center.

———. 2001. *Redefining Nature: Karen Ecological Knowledge and the Challenge to the Modern Conservation Paradigm.* Chennai: Earthworm.

Leach, Melissa, and James Fairhead. 2000. Fashioned Forest Pasts, Occluded Histories? International Environmental Analysis in West Africa Locales. In Martin Doornbos, Ashwani Saith, and Ben White, eds., *Forests: Nature, People, Power,* 35–59. Oxford: Blackwell.

———. 2001. Plural Perspectives and Institutional Dynamics: Challenges for Local Forest Management. *International Journal of Agricultural Resources, Governance, and Ecology* 1, no. 3/4: 223–42.

Leach, Melissa, and Robin Mearns, eds. 1996. *The Lie of the Land: Challenging Received Wisdom on the African Environment.* Oxford: International African Institute/Portsmouth, NH: Heinemann.

Lee, Robert, Donald R. Field, and William R. Burch Jr., eds. 1990. *Community and Forestry: Continuities in the Sociology of Natural Resources.* Boulder, CO: Westview.

Legge, James. 1960. *The Works of Mencius.* Hong Kong: Hong Kong University Press.

Lele, Sharachandra. 2002. *Godsend, Sleight of Hand, or Just Muddling Through: Joint Water and Forest Management in India.* Natural Resource Perspectives no. 53 (April 2000). London: Overseas Development Institute.

Levine, Arielle. 2004. Local Responses to Marine Conservation in Zanzibar, Tanzania. Paper presented at the Breslauer Symposium on Natural Resource Issues in Africa, April 19. Berkeley: Center for African Studies. http://repositories.cdlib.org/cas/breslauer/levine2004.

Li, Tania Murray. 1997. Boundary Work: A Response to Community in Conservation: Beyond Enchantment and Disenchantment by Arun Agrawal. In Arun Agrawal, *Community in Conservation: Beyond Enchantment and Disenchantment,* 69–82. CDF Discussion Paper. Gainesville, FL: Conservation and Development Forum.

———. 2001. Boundary Work: Community, Market, and State Reconsidered. In Arun Agrawal and Clark C. Gibson, eds., *Communities and the Environment: Ethnicity, Gender, and the State in Community-Based Conservation,* 157–79. New Brunswick: Rutgers University Press.

———. 2002. Engaging Simplifications: Community-Based Resource Management, Market Processes, and State Agendas in Upland Southeast Asia. *World Development* 30, no. 2: 265–83.

Lima, Deborah de Magalhães. 1999. Equity, Sustainable Development, and Biodiversity Preservation: Some Questions About Ecological Partnerships in the Brazilian Amazon. In A. Henderson, C. Padoch, and J. M. Ayres, eds., *Ecology, Conservation, and Development of the Amazonian Várzea*, 247–63. New York: New York Botanical Garden Press.

Lind, Jeremy, and Jan Cappon. 2001. *Realities or Rhetoric? Revisiting the Decentralization of Natural Resources Management in Uganda and Zambia*. Nairobi: African Center for Technology Studies.

Linden, Eugene, Thomas Lovejoy, and J. Daniel Phillips. 2004. Seeing the Forest: Conservation on a Continental Scale. *Foreign Affairs* 83, no. 4: 8–12.

Lines, William J. 1991. *Taming the Great South Land: A History of the Conquest of Nature in Australia*. Berkeley: University of California Press.

Little, Peter D. 1994. The Link Between Local Participation and Improved Conservation: A Review of Issues and Experiences. In David Western, R. Michael Wright, and Shirley C. Strum, eds., *Natural Connections: Perspectives in Community-Based Conservation*, 347–72. Washington, DC: Island Press.

Liu Dachang. 2001. Tenure and Management of Non-State Forests in China Since 1950: A Historical Review. *Environmental History* 6, no. 2: 239–63.

Liu Jinlong and Natasha Landell-Mills. 2003. Taxes and Fees in China's Southern Collective Forest Region. In William F. Hyde, Brian Belcher, and Jintao Xu, eds., *China's Forests: Global Lessons from Market Reforms*, 45–58. Washington, DC: Resources for the Future/Bogor: CIFOR.

Liu Shouying. 1993. Shandi Chanquan Zhidu Bianqian Yu Nonghu Xingwei Bianhua—Hunan Sheng Huaihua Ge'an Yanjiu [Changes in Rights to Mountain Land and Changes in Farm Household Behavior—a Case Study from Huaihua, Hunan Province]. In Guowuyuan Fazhan Yanjiu Zhongxin Zhongguo Nongdi Zhidu Keti Zu [State Council Development Research Center Working Group on Land Tenure in China], *Zhongguo Nongcun Tudi Zhidudi Biange* [China's Rural Land Tenure Reform], 99–114. Beijing: Beijing Daxue Chubanshe.

Lohmann, Larry. 1999. *Forest Cleansing: Racial Oppression in Scientific Nature Conservation*. Corner House Briefing no. 13. Sturminster Newton (Dorset). http://www.thecornerhouse .org.uk/item.shtml?x=51969 (accessed 2 February 2004).

Lund, H. Gyde. 2004. Definitions of Forest, Deforestation, Afforestation, and Reforestation. Gainesville, VA: Forest Information Services. http://home.comcast.net/~gyde/DEFpaper .htm (accessed 1 March 2005).

Lynch, Owen, and Kirk Talbott. 1995. *Balancing Acts: Community-Based Forest Management and National Law in Asia and the Pacific*. Washington, DC: World Resources Institute.

Maathai, Wangari. 2004. Nobel Lecture. Stockholm: Nobel Foundation.

Makarabhirom, Pearmsak. 2000. The Evolution of the Policy Making Process: Will There Ever Be a Community Forestry Bill? *Asia Pacific Community Forestry Newsletter* 13, no. 2 (December): 58–62.

Mamdani, Mahmood. 1996. *Citizen and Subject: Contemporary Africa and the Legacy of Late Colonialism*. Princeton: Princeton University Press.

——. 2001. *When Victims Become Killers: Colonialism, Nativism, and the Genocide in Rwanda*. Princeton: Princeton University Press.

Mander, Jerry. 1992. *In the Absence of the Sacred*. San Francisco: Sierra Club.

Mandondo, Alois, and Everisto Mapedza. 2003. *Allocation of Governmental Authority and Responsibility in Tiered Governance Systems: The Case of Environment-Related Laws in Zimbabwe*. Environmental Governance in Africa Working Papers no. 11. Washington, DC: World Resources Institute.

Manor, James. 2004. User Committees: A Potentially Damaging Second Wave of Decentralisation? *European Journal of Development Research* 16, no. 1: 192–213.

Marchak, P. 1983. *Green Gold: The Forest Industry in British Columbia.* Vancouver: University of British Columbia Press.

Marsh, George Perkins. 1864. *Man and Nature; or, Physical Geography as Modified by Human Action.* Reprinted Cambridge: Harvard University Press, 1965.

Marshall, George. 1990. The Political Economy of Logging: The Barnett Enquiry into Corruption in the Papua New Guinea Timber Industry. *The Ecologist* 20, no. 5: 174–81.

Martinez-Alier, J. 2003. *The Environmentalism of the Poor: A Study of Ecological Conflicts and Valuation.* Cheltenham, UK: Edward Elgar.

Marx, Karl. 1975 [1842]. Debates on the Law on Thefts of Wood. Published as a supplement to the *Rheinische Zeitung,* October 25, 27, 30, November 1, 3. In Karl Marx and Friedrich Engels, *Collected Works,* vol. 1:224–63. New York: International Publishers.

Mascarenhas, Michael, and Rik Scarce. 2004. "The Intention Was Good": Legitimacy, Consensus-Based Decision-Making, and the Case of Forest Planning in British Columbia, Canada. *Society and Natural Resources* 17:17–38.

Masoud, Thabit. 2003. Civil Society: Partners in Change: The Jozani–Chwaka Bay Conservation Project, Zanzibar. Paper prepared for the United Nations Development Program. Zanzibar: CARE Tanzania.

Mater, Catherine M. 1998. *Menominee Tribal Enterprises: Sustainable Forestry to Improve Forest Health and Create Jobs.* Washington, DC: Island Press.

Matthews, Kay. 1999. Sierra Club Hears from Minorities Locally and Nationally. Editorial in *La Jicarita News* (August) (Chamisal, New Mexico) IV (VII).

Maxwell, S., and R. Riddell. 1998. Conditionality or Contract: Perspectives on Partnership for Development. *Journal of International Development* 10:257–68.

May, Peter H., Emily Boyd, Fernando Veiga, and Manyu Chang. 2004. *Local Sustainable Development Effects of Forest Carbon Projects in Brazil and Bolivia: A View from the Field.* Markets for Environmental Services Series ME5. London: International Institute for Environment and Development.

Mayers, James, and Sonja Vermeulen. 2002. *Company-Community Forestry Partnerships: From Raw Deals to Mutual Gains?* Instruments for Sustainable Private Sector Forestry Series. London: International Institute for Environment and Development.

McCarthy, John F. 2000. The Changing Régime: Forest Property and Reformasi in Indonesia. In Martin Doornbos, Ashwani Saith, and Ben White, eds., *Forests: Nature, People, Power,* 89–128. Oxford: Blackwell.

McCay, Bonnie J. 2001. Community and the Commons: Romantic and Other Views. In Arun Agrawal and Clark C. Gibson, eds., *Communities and the Environment: Ethnicity, Gender, and the State in Community-Based Conservation,* 180–92. New Brunswick: Rutgers University Press.

McDermott, Melanie Hughes. 2001. Invoking Community: Indigenous People and Ancestral Domain in Palawan, Philippines. In Arun Agrawal and Clark C. Gibson, eds., *Communities and the Environment: Ethnicity, Gender, and the State in Community-Based Conservation,* 32–62. New Brunswick: Rutgers University Press.

McKean, Margaret A. 1992. Management of Traditional Lands (Iraichi) in Japan. In Daniel W. Bromley et al., eds., *Making the Commons Work: Theory, Practice, and Policy,* 63–98. San Francisco: ICS.

Mehta, Lyla, Melissa Leach, Peter Newell, Ian Scoones, K. Sivaramakrishnan, and Sally-Anne Way. 1999. *Exploring Understandings of Institutions and Uncertainty: New Direc-*

tions in Natural Resource Management. IDS Discussion Paper 372. Brighton: Institute of Development Studies.

Melone, Michelle. 1993. The Struggle of the Seringueiros: Environmental Action in the Amazon. In John Friedmann and Haripiya Rangan, *In Defense of Livelihood: Comparative Studies in Environmental Action,* 106–26. West Hartford, CT: Kumarian.

Menzies, Nicholas. 1988a. A Survey of Customary Law and Community Control over Trees in China. In Louise Fortmann and John Bruce, eds., *Whose Trees? Proprietary Dimensions of Forestry,* 51–62. Boulder, CO: Westview.

———. 1988b. Three Hundred Years of Taungya: A Study of Long Term Stability in an Agroforestry System. *Human Ecology* 16.

———. 1992. Strategic Space: Exclusion and Inclusion in Wildland Policies in Late Imperial China. *Modern Asian Studies* 26, no. 4: 719–33.

———. 1994. *Forest and Land Management in Imperial China.* London: Macmillan.

Menzies, Nicholas, and Nancy Peluso. 1992. Rights of Access to Upland Forest Resources in Southwest China. *Journal of World Forest Resource Management* 6, no. 1: 1–20.

Merchant, Caroline. 2004. Shades of Darkness: Race and Environmental History. *Environmental History* 8, no. 3: 380–95.

Michon, Geneviève. 2003. Ma Forêt, ta Forêt, leur Forêt: Perceptions et Enjeux Autour de l'Espace Forestier. *Bois et Forêts des Tropiques* 278, no. 4: 15–24.

Migdal, Joel S. 1977. *Peasants, Politics, and Revolution: Pressures Toward Political and Social Change in the Third World.* Princeton: Princeton University Press.

Miller, Byron. 1992. Collective Action and Rational Choice: Place, Community, and the Limits to Individual Self-Interest. *Economic Geography* 61, no. 1: 22–42.

Miller, Char. 2000. Back to the Garden: The Redemptive Promise of Sustainable Forestry, 1893–2000. *Forest History Today* (Spring): 16–23.

Miller, Char, and Rebecca Staebler. 1999. *The Greatest Good: 100 Years of Forestry in America.* Bethesda, MD: Society of American Foresters.

Ministry of Environment and Forests (India). 2003. MoEF Press Release, February 10, reported in *Community Forestry E-News* no. 2003.2 (February 19). Bangkok: Regional Community Forestry Training Center for Asia and the Pacific. http://www.recoftc.org/04resource/e-letter/e-letter.html (accessed 2 March 2003).

Moench, Marcus, and J. Bandyopadhyay. 1986. People-Forest Interaction: A Neglected Parameter in Himalayan Forest Management. *Mountain Research and Development* 6, no. 1: 3–16.

Molnar, Augusta, Sara J. Scherr, and Arvind Khare. 2004. *Who Conserves the World's Forests? Community-Driven Strategies to Protect Forests and Respect Rights.* Washington, DC: Forest Trends/Ecoagriculture Partners.

Moore, Donald S. 1993. Contesting Terrain in Zimbabwe's Eastern Highlands: Political Ecology, Ethnography, and Peasant Resource Struggles. *Economic Geography* 69, no. 4: 380–401.

Moore, Donald S., Jake Kosek, and Anand Pandian, eds. 2003. *Race, Nature, and the Politics of Difference.* Durham: Duke University Press.

Moore, Donald S., Anand Pandian, and Jake Kosek. 2003. Introduction: The Cultural Politics of Race and Nature: Terrains of Power and Practice. In Donald S. Moore, Jake Kosek, and Anand Pandian, eds., *Race, Nature, and the Politics of Difference,* 1–70. Durham: Duke University Press.

Moote, Ann. 2001. Community, Culture, and Forest Restoration. *Communities and Forests* (newsletter of the Communities Committee of the Seventh American Forest Congress) 5, no. 4 (Winter).

Morsello, Carla. 2004. New Forestry Régimes in Brazilian Amazonian Communities: Opportunities and Problems Caused by Corporate-Community Deals. Paper presented at the workshop on Community-Based Forestry in the Next Decade: Towards an "Agrarian" Approach? Berlin: Humboldt University, Junior Research Group on Postsocialist Land Relations, October 8–9. http://www.agrar.hu-berlin.de/wisola/ipw/plr/ (accessed 8 October 2004).

Mosse, David. 2004. Good Policy Is Unimplementable? Reflections on the Ethnography of Aid Policy and Practice. *Development and Change* 35, no. 4: 639–73.

Moyo, Sam. 1995. *The Land Question in Zimbabwe.* Harare: SAPES.

Mu Wenchun, Su Yufang, and Zheng Baohua. 2001. Study of Forest Land Tenure and Sustainable Forest Management in Taohua. In Brian Schwarzwalder, Li Ping, Zheng Baohua, Su Yufang, and Zhang Lichang, eds., *Tenure and Management Arrangements for China's Forestland and Grassland Resources: Fieldwork Findings and Legal and Policy Recommendations,* 197–216. Beijing/Seattle: Proceedings of the International Conference on Nonarable Land Tenure organized by CDS/Rural Development Institute (University of Washington, Seattle) and the Development Research Centre of the State Council.

Mukandala, Rwekaza S., and Haroub Othman, eds. 1994. *Liberalization and politics: The 1990 Elections in Tanzania.* Dar es Salaam: Dar es Salaam University Press.

Murombedzi, James. 2003. Devolving the Expropriation of Nature: The "Devolution" of Wildlife Management in Southern Africa. In William Adams and Martin Mulligan, eds., *Decolonizing Nature: Strategies for Conservation in a Post-Colonial Era,* 135–51. London: Earthscan.

Murphree, Marshall. 1993. *Communities as Resource Management Institutions.* Gatekeeper Series no. 36. London: International Institute for Environment and Development.

——. 2000. Community-Based Conservation: Old Ways, New Myths, and Enduring Challenges. Paper presented as the key address for theme no. 3 at the Conference on African Wildlife Management in the New Millennium, Mweka, Tanzania, College of African Wildlife Management.

——. 2004. Communal Approaches to Natural Resource Management in Africa: From Whence and to Where? Keynote Address to the Breslauer Graduate Student Symposium, Berkeley, March 5. http://repositories.cdlib.org/cas/breslauer/murphree2004a.

Myers, Garth Andrew. 2000. Narrative Representations of Revolutionary Zanzibar. *Journal of Historical Geography* 26, no. 3: 429–48.

——. 2002. Local Communities and the new Environmental Planning: A Case Study from Zanzibar. *Area* 34, no. 2: 149–59.

Namara, Aggripinah, and Xavier Nsabagasani. 2003. *Decentralization and Wildlife Management: Devolving Rights or Shedding Responsibility? Bwindi Impenetrable National Park, Uganda.* Environmental Governance in Africa, Working Papers no. 9. Washington, DC: World Resources Institute.

Namgyel, Phuntso. 2000. The Story of Buddha Mushroom: Tricholoma Matsutake. Manuscript, University of Reading.

National Association of Social Workers. 2003. *Tribal Business Contributions and Federal Mismanagement of Trust Funds.* http://www.naswdc.org/diversity/ntaive2003/tribal2003.asp (accessed 12 February 2004).

Nature. 1998. The Complex Realities of Sharing Genetic Assets. *Nature* 392, no. 6676 (April 9) (special issue on bioprospecting).

Nelson, N., and S. Wright, eds. 1995. *Power and Participatory Development: Theory and Practice.* London: IT Publications.

Newmark, William D., Stephen Mariki, and Joyce Bayona. 2004. After the Gold Rush. . . . *Swara* 27, no. 1: 22–25.

News Today (Chennai). 2004. Greener Pastures for Forest Tribals. Report filed on October 12 by G. Babu Jayakumar. http://newstodaynet.com/12OCT/SS3.HTM (accessed 2 November 2004).

Ng'weno, Bettine. 2001. Reidentifying Ground Rules: Community Inheritance Disputes Among the Digo of Kenya. In Arun Agrawal and Clark C. Gibson, eds., *Communities and the Environment: Ethnicity, Gender, and the State in Community-Based Conservation*, 111–37. New Brunswick: Rutgers University Press.

Noon, Barry R. 2003. Stakeholders in Social-Ecological Systems: Response to Walker et al. 2000 "Resilience Management in Social-Ecological Systems: A Working Hypothesis for a Participatory Approach." *Conservation Ecology* 7, no. 1, resp. 5. http://www.consecol .org/vol7/iss1/resp5.

Nugent, J. B. 1993. Between State, Markets, and Households: A Neoinstitutional Analysis of Local Organizations and Institutions. *World Development* 21, no. 4: 623–32.

Nugent, S. 1997. The Co-ordinates of Identity in Amazonia: At Play in the Fields of Culture. *Critique of Anthropology* 19, no. 1: 33–51.

Oates, J. F. 1999. *Myth and Reality in the Rain Forest: How Conservation Strategies Are Failing in West Africa*. Berkeley: University of California Press.

Ostrom, Elinor (Lin). 1992. The Rudiments of a Theory of the Origins, Survival, and Performance of Common Property Institutions. In Daniel W. Bromley et al., eds., *Making the Commons Work: Theory, Practice, and Policy*, 293–318. San Francisco: ICS.

——. 1993. Design Principles in Long-Enduring Irrigation Institutions. *Water Resources Research* 29, no. 7: 1907–12.

——. 1998. Self-Governance and Forest Resources. Plenary presentation at the International CBNRM Workshop, May 10–14, Washington, DC: World Bank. http://www.cbnrm .net/resources/literature/literature.html.

Ostrom, Elinor, Larry Schroeder, and Susan Wynne. 1993. *Institutional Incentives and Sustainable Development: Infrastructure Policies in Perspective*. Boulder, CO: Westview.

Padoch, Christine, José Márcio Ayres, Miguel Pinedo-Vasquez, and Andrew Henderson, eds. 1999. *Várzea: Diversity, Development, and Conservation of Amazonia's Whitewater Floodplains*. Advances in Economic Botany 13. New York: New York Botanical Garden Press.

Painter, Judith. 2000. Village Banking Performance: A Comparative Review, 1994–1998. *Nexus* (newsletter of Small Enterprises Education and Promotion Network) (September): 3–11.

Pankaj-Khullar. 1992. Forestry Programme: Need for Change in Approach. *Indian Forester* 118, no. 10: 736–43.

Parsons, Reginald, and Gordon Prest. 2003. Aboriginal Forestry in Canada. *Forestry Chronicle* 79, no. 4: 779–84.

Pecore, Marshall, and Larry Nesper. 1993. "The Trees Will Last Forever": The Integrity of Their Forest Signifies the Health of the Menominee People. *Cultural Survival Quarterly* 17, no. 1: 28–31.

Peet, Richard, and Michael Watts. 1993. Introduction: Development Theory and Environment in an Age of Market Triumphalism. *Economic Geography* 69, no. 3: 227–53.

——. 1996. *Liberation Ecologies: Environment, Development, Social Movements*. 1st edition. London: Routledge.

——. 2004. *Liberation Ecologies: Environment, Development, Social Movements*. 2nd edition. London: Routledge.

Peluso, Nancy Lee. 1992. *Rich Forests, Poor People: Resource Control and Resistance in Java.* Berkeley: University of California Press.

———. 1996. Fruit Trees and Family Trees in an Indonesian Rainforest: Property Rights, Ethics of Access, and Environmental Change. *Comparative Studies in Society and History* 38, no. 3: 510–48.

Peluso, Nancy Lee, and Jesse Ribot. 2003. A Theory of Access. *Rural Sociology* 68, no. 2: 153–81.

Peluso, Nancy Lee, and Peter Vandergeest. 2001. Genealogies of the Political Forest and Customary Rights in Indonesia, Malaysia, and Thailand. *Journal of Asian Studies* 60, no. 3: 761–812.

Perlin, John. 1991. *A Forest Journey: The Role of Wood in the Development of Civilization.* Cambridge: Harvard University Press.

Peyron, J. L., and J. Maheut. 1999. Les Fondements de l'Économie Forestière Moderne: Le Role Capital de Faustmann, il y a 150 Ans et Celui de Quelques-uns de ses Précurseurs et Successeurs. *Revue Forestière Française* 6:679–98.

Pimbert, Michel P., and Jules N. Pretty. 1997. Parks, People, and Professionals: Putting "Participation" into Protected Area Management. In Krishna B. Ghimire and Michel P. Pimbert, eds., *Social Change and Conservation,* 297–330. London: Earthscan.

Pinchot, G. 1947. *Breaking New Ground.* Reprinted Washington, DC: Island Press, 1998.

Pinedo-Vasquez, Miguel, C. Padoch, D. McGrath, and T. Ximenes-Ponte. 2002. Biodiversity as a Product of Smallholder Responses to Change in Amazonia. In H. Brookfield, C. Padoch, H. Parsons, and M. Stocking, eds., *Cultivating Biodiversity: Understanding, Analysing, and Using Agricultural Diversity,* 167–78. London: ITDG.

Pinedo-Vasquez, Miguel, Daniel J. Zarin, Kevin Coffey, Christine Padoch, and Fernando Rabelo. 2001. Post-Boom Logging in Amazonia. *Human Ecology* 29, no. 2: 219–39.

Poffenberger, Mark. 1990. *Keepers of the Forest: Land Management Alternatives in Southeast Asia.* West Hartford, CT: Kumarian.

Poffenberger, Mark, and Betsy McGean, eds. 1996. *Village Voices, Forest Choices: Joint Forest Management in India.* New Delhi: Oxford University Press.

Poffenberger, Mark, Betsy McGean, and Arvind Khare. 1996. Communities Sustaining India's Forests in the Twenty-first Century. In Mark Poffenberger and Betsy McGean, eds., *Village Voices, Forest Choices: Joint Forest Management in India,* chap. 1. New Delhi: Oxford University Press.

Poffenberger, Mark, and Steve Selin. 1998. *Communities and Forest Management in Canada and the United States: A Regional Profile of the Working Group on Community Involvement in Forest Management.* Berkeley: Working Group on Community Involvement in Forest Management.

Poffenberger, Mark, and Chhatrapati Singh. 1996. Communities and the State: Re-establishing the Balance in Indian Forest Policy. In Mark Poffenberger and Betsy McGean, eds., *Village Voices, Forest Choices: Joint Forest Management in India,* 56–85. New Delhi: Oxford University Press.

Poffenberger, Mark, and S. Singh. 1989. *Community Management for India's Forests: Emerging Experiences.* Delhi: Ford Foundation.

Pokorny, Benno, Guillhermina Cayres, and Westphalen Nuñes. 2004. Improving Collaboration Between Outsiders and Communities in the Amazon. In Carol J. Pierce Colfer, ed., *The Equitable Forest: Diversity, Community, and Resource Management,* 229–41. Washington, DC: Resources for the Future/Bogor: CIFOR.

Poonan, Unjinee. 2002. *An Overview of Land Claims in Protected Areas in South Africa.* Johannesburg: Ford Foundation.

Posey, Darrell A. 1996. Protecting Indigenous People's Rights to Biodiversity. *Environment* 38, no. 8: 6–45.

Poudel, Keshab. 2003. Nepal: Community Forestry in Nepal Under Threat. *Community Forestry E-News* no. 2003.13 (August 15). Bangkok: Regional Community Forestry Training Center for Asia and the Pacific. http://www.recoftc.org/04resource/e-letter/e-letter.html (accessed 15 September 2003).

Prance, G. T. 1979. Notes on the Vegetation of Amazonia, III: The Terminology of Amazonian Forest Types Subject to Inundation. *Brittonia* 31:26–38.

Pulido, Laura. 1996. *Environmentalism and Economic Justice: Two Chicano Struggles in the Southwest.* Tucson: University of Arizona Press.

Raffles, Hugh. 2002. *In Amazonia: A Natural History.* Princeton: Princeton University Press.

Rahnema, Majid. 1992. Participation. In Wolfgang Sachs, ed., *The Development Dictionary: A Guide to Knowledge as Power,* 116–31. Johannesburg: Zed.

Rajesh, Daniel. 2002. Thailand: Senate Blocks Draft Community Forest Bill. *World Rainforest Movement Bulletin* 57 (April). http://www.wrm.org.uy/bulletin/57/Thailand.html (accessed 5 October 2004).

Ramos, Alcida Rita. 1994. The Hyperreal Indian. *Critique of Anthropology* 14, no. 2: 153–71.

Rangan, Haripriya. 2000. *Of Myths and Movements: Rewriting Chipko into Himalayan History.* London: Verso.

Rangarajan, M. 1996. *Fencing the Forest: Conservation and Ecological Change in India's Central Provinces, 1860–1914.* Delhi: Oxford University Press.

Redford, K. H., and B. Richter. 1999. Conservation of Biodiversity in a World of Use. *Conservation Biology* 13:1246–56.

Reid, Hannah. 2001. Contractual National Parks and the Makuleke Community. *Human Ecology* 29, no. 2: 135–55.

Ren, Chentong (C. T. Jen). 1925. *Jingying Cunyou Lindi Haochu He Banfa* [Advantages and Methods of Managing Village Owned Forests]. Nanjing: Nanjing Jinling Daxue Senlin Xi (reprinted 1930, 1935).

Repetto, Robert C., and Malcolm Gilllis. 1988. *Deforestation and Government Policy.* San Francisco: International Center for Economic Growth.

Ribot, Jesse. 1999. A History of Fear: Imagining Deforestation in the West African Dryland Forests. *Global Ecology and Biogeography* 8:291–300.

——. 2001. *Science, Use Rights, and Exclusion: A History of Forestry in Francophone West Africa.* Drylands Issues Papers no. 104. London: International Institute for Environment and Development.

——. 2002. *Democratic Decentralization of Natural Resources: Institutionalizing Popular Participation.* Washington, DC: World Resources Institute.

——. 2004. *Waiting for Democracy: The Politics of Choice in Natural Resource Decentralization.* Washington, DC: World Resources Institute.

Richards, John F., and Richard Tucker, eds. 1988. *World Deforestation in the Twentieth Century.* Durham: Duke University Press.

Richards, Michael. 1997. *Tragedy of the Commons for Community-Based Forest Management in Latin America?* Natural Resource Perspectives no. 22. London: Overseas Development Institute.

Richards, R. T., and M. Creasy. 1996. Ethnic Diversity, Resource Values, and Ecosystem Management: Matsutake Mushroom Harvesting in the Klamath Bioregion. *Society and Natural Resources* 9, no. 4: 359–74.

Richardson, S. D. 1966. *Forestry in Communist China*. Baltimore: Johns Hopkins University Press.

——. 1990. *Forests and Forestry in China: Changing Patterns in Resource Development*. Washington, DC: Island Press.

Rist, G. 1997. *The History of Development: From Western Origins to Global Faith*. London: Zed.

Ritchie, Bill, and Mandy Haggith. 2004. The Push-Me-Pull-You of Forest Devolution in Scotland. Paper presented at the Interlaken Workshop on Decentralization in Forestry, April 27–30, Interlaken, Switzerland. http://www.cifor.cgiar.org/int_ref/events/swiss/papers.htm (accessed 25 October 2004).

Rodrigues, Edgar. 2003. Municipio de Mazagão. State of Amapá Web site: http://www.amapa.gov.br/municipios/municipio-mazagao.htm (accessed 25 December 2003).

Rodriguez, Sylvia. 1987. Land Water and Ethnic Identity in Taos. In Charles Briggs and John R. Van Ness, eds., *Land, Water, and Culture*, 313–403. Albuquerque: University of New Mexico Press.

Roe, Emery. 1991. Development Narratives; or, Making the Best of Blueprint Development. *World Development* 19, no. 4: 287–300.

——. 1995. Except—Africa: Postscript to a Special Section on Development Narratives. *World Development* 23, no. 6: 1065–69.

Romm, Jeff. 1981. The Uncultivated Half of India. *Indian Forester* 107, no. 1: 1–23; no. 2: 69–85.

——. 1982. A Research Agenda for Social Forestry. *International Tree Crops Journal* 2, no. 1: 25–29.

Roosevelt, Anna G. 1999. Twelve Thousand Years of Human-Environmental Interaction in the Amazon Floodplain. In Christine Padoch, José Márcio Ayres, Miguel Pinedo-Vasquez, and Andrew Henderson, eds., *Várzea: Diversity, Development, and Conservation of Amazonia's Whitewater Floodplains*, 371–92. Advances in Economic Botany 13. New York: New York Botanical Garden Press.

Rosa, Herman, Susan Kandel, and Leopoldo Dimas, with contributions from Nelson Cuéllar and Ernesto Méndez. 2003. *Compensation for Environmental Services and Rural Communities: Lessons from the Americas and Key Issues for Strengthening Community Strategies*. San Salvador: PRISMA.

Ross, Lester. 1988. *Environmental Policy in China*. Bloomington: University of Indiana Press.

Ross, M., and P. Smith. 2002. Accommodation of Aboriginal Rights: The Need for an Aboriginal Forest Tenure (Synthesis Report). University of Alberta Sustainable Forest Management Network. Edmonton: University of Alberta.

Rozmeijer, Nico. 2003. CBNRM in Botswana: Revisiting the Assumptions After 10 Years of Implementation. Background Paper for the World Parks Congress, Durban. Gaborone, Botswana: IUCN/SNV CBNRM Support Programme in Botswana. http://www.cbnrm.bw (accessed 21 April 2004).

Rozmeijer, Nico, and Corjan van der Jagt. 2000. Community Based Natural Resources Management (CBNRM) in Botswana. How Community Based Is CBNRM in Botswana? In S. Shackleton and B. Campbell, eds., *Empowering Communities to Manage Natural Resources: Case Studies from Southern Africa*. Lilongwe, Malawi: SADC Wildlife Sector Natural Resource Management Programme/CSIR/WWF.

RUPFOR (Resource Unit for Participatory Forestry). 2002. *Joint Forest Management: A Decade of Partnership.* Delhi: Ministry of Environment and Forests/Winrock.

Saberwal, Vasant. 1999. *Pastoral Politics: Shepherds, Bureaucrats, and Conservation in the Western Himalaya.* Delhi: Oxford University Press.

Sachs, Wolfgang, ed. 1992. *The Development Dictionary: A Guide to Knowledge as Power.* Johannesburg: Zed.

Sahlins, Peter. 1994. *Forest Rites: The War of the Demoiselles in Nineteenth-Century France.* Harvard Historical Studies 15. Cambridge: Harvard University Press.

Sampson, Gary P. 2000. *Trade, Environment, and the WTO: The Post-Seattle Agenda.* Washington, DC: Overseas Development Council/Baltimore: Johns Hopkins University Press.

San Francisco Examiner. 1999. Madame Butterfly. Editorial (December 21).

Sarin, Madhu, Manju S. Raju, Mitalee Chatterjee, Narayan Bannerjee, and Shyamala Hiremath. 1998. *Who Is Gaining? Who Is Losing? Gender and Equity Concerns in Joint Forest Management.* Delhi: Society for Promotion of Wastelands Development.

Sarin, Madhu, Neera M. Singh, Nandini Sundar, and Ranu K. Boghal. 2003. *Devolution as a Threat to Democratic Decision-Making in Forestry? Findings from Three States in India.* Working Paper 197. London: Overseas Development Institute.

Sato, Jin. 2000. People in Between: Conversion and Conservation of Forest Lands in Thailand. In Martin Doornbos, Ashwani Saith, and Ben White, eds., *Forests: Nature, People, Power,* 153–74. Oxford: Blackwell.

Saxena, N. C. 1992. Joint Forest Management: A New Development Bandwagon in India? In *Rural Development Forestry Network* Paper 14, 27–33. London: Overseas Development Institute.

——. 2003. From Monopoly to De-regulation of NTFPs: Policy Shifts in Orissa (India). *International Forestry Review* 5, no. 2: 168–76.

Saxena, N. C., and Madhu Sarin. 1999. The Western Ghats Forestry and Environmental Project in Karnataka: A Preliminary Assessment. In Roger Jeffery and Nandini Sandar, eds., *A New Moral Economy for India's Forests? Discourses of Community and Participation,* 181–215. New Delhi: Thousand Oaks/London: Sage.

Scherr, Sara J., Andy White, and David Kaimowitz. 2002. *Making Markets Work for Forest Communities.* Policy Brief 1. Washington, DC: Forest Trends/Bogor: CIFOR.

Schwartzman, S., A. Moreira, and D. Nepstad. 2000. Rethinking Tropical Forest Conservation: Perils in Parks. *Conservation Biology* 14:1351–57.

Schwarzwalder, Brian, Li Ping, Zheng Baohua, Su Yufang, and Zhang Lichang, eds. 2001. *Tenure and Management Arrangements for China's Forestland and Grassland Resources: Fieldwork Findings and Legal and Policy Recommendations.* Beijing/Seattle: Proceedings of the International Conference on Nonarable Land Tenure organized by CDS/Rural Development Institute (University of Washington, Seattle) and the Development Research Centre of the State Council.

Scott, James C. 1987. *Weapons of the Weak: Everyday Forms of Peasant Resistance.* New Haven: Yale University Press.

——. 1990. *Domination and the Arts of Resistance: Hidden Transcripts.* New Haven: Yale University Press.

——. 1998. *Seeing Like a State: How Certain Schemes to Improve the Human Condition Have Failed.* Yale Agrarian Studies/Yale ISPS Series. New Haven: Yale University Press.

Shackleton, Sheona E., and Bruce M. Campbell. 2001. *Devolution in Natural Resource Management: Institutional Arrangements and Power Shifts: A Synthesis of Case Stud-*

ies from Southern Africa. Lilongwe, Malawi: SADC Wildlife Sector Natural Resource Management Programme/Harare, Zimbabwe: WWF (Southern Africa).

Shackleton, Sheona E., Bruce M. Campbell, Eva Wollenberg, and David Edmunds. 2002. *Devolution and Community-Based Natural Resource Management: Creating Space for Local People to Participate and Benefit?* Natural Resource Perspectives no. 76. London: Overseas Development Institute.

Shah, Meera Kaul, Sarah Degnan Kambou, and Barbara Monahan, eds. 1999. *Embracing Participation in Development: Wisdom from the Field.* Atlanta: CARE.

Shapiro, Judith. 2001. *Mao's War Against Nature: Politics and the Environment in Revolutionary China.* Cambridge: Cambridge University Press.

Sharma, O. P. n.d. [1998?]. Co-operative Forest Societies in District Kangra. Dharamsala: Himachal Pradesh Forestry Department report.

Sheil, D., and S. Wunder. 2002. The Value of Tropical Forest to Local Communities: Complications, Caveats, and Cautions. *Conservation Ecology* 6, no. 2, art. 9. http://www.consecol.org/vol6/iss2/art9.

Sheriff, Abdul. 1987. *Slaves, Spices, and Ivory in Zanzibar: Integration of an East African Commercial Empire into the World Economy, 1770–1873.* Athens: Ohio University Press.

——. 1994. The Union and the Struggle for Democracy in Zanzibar. In Rwekaza S. Mukandala and Haroub Othman, eds., *Liberalization and Politics: The 1990 Elections in Tanzania,* 149–60. Dar es Salaam: Dar es Salaam University Press.

Shiva, Vandana, and J. Bandyopadhyay. 1986. Chipko: Rekindling India's Forest Culture. *The Ecologist* 17, no. 1: 26–34.

Shiva, Vandana, H. C. Sharatchandra, and J. Bandyopadhyay. 1987. Social Forestry for Whom? In David Korten, ed., *Community Management: Asian Experience and Perspectives,* 238–46. West Hartford, CT: Kumarian.

Sichuan Academy of Social Sciences. 2001. *Case Study on Conversion of Farmland to Forest and Grassland in Tianquan County, Sichuan Province.* Chengdu: Sichuan Academy of Social Sciences Cropland Conversion Task Force.

Sidney Morning Herald. 1998. Australian Greens to Decide on Forest Blockades (November 20).

Siex, Kirstin S., and Thomas T. Struhsaker. 1999. Colobus Monkeys and Coconuts: A Study of Perceived Human-Wildlife Conflicts. *Journal of Applied Ecology* 36, no. 6: 1009–20.

Singh, R. V. 2002. *Forest and Wastelands: Participation and Management: The Ford Foundation, 1952–2002.* Delhi: Ford Foundation.

Sithole, Bevelyne. 2004. Becoming Men in Our Dresses? Women's Involvement in a Joint Forestry Management Project in Zimbabwe. In Carol J. Pierce Colfer, ed., *The Equitable Forest: Diversity, Community, and Resource Management,* 171–85. Washington, DC: Resources for the Future/Bogor: CIFOR.

Sivaramakrishnan, K. 1999. *Modern Forests: Statemaking and Environmental Change in Colonial Eastern India.* Delhi: Oxford University Press.

Slater, Candace. 2002. *Entangled Edens: Visions of the Amazon.* Berkeley: University of California Press.

Smil, Vaclav. 1993. *China's Environmental Crisis: An Inquiry into the Limits of National Development.* Armonk: Sharpe.

Smith, Nigel J. H. 2002. *Amazon Sweet Sea: Land, Life, and Water at the River's Mouth.* Austin: University of Texas Press.

Snook, Laura K., and Citialli López. 2003. Regeneration of Mahogany (*Swietenia Macrophylla King*): Results of Seven Years of Collaborative Research. Results of a workshop held in Chetumal, Quintana Roo, Mexico, November 5–7. Bogor: CIFOR.

Snook, Laura K., V. A. Santos Jimenez, M. Carréon Mundo, C. Chan Rivas, F. F. May Ek, P. Mas Kantún, C. Hernández, A. Nolasco Morales, and C. Escobar Ruíz. 2003. Managing Natural Forests for Sustainable Harvests of Mahogany (*Swietenia Macrophylla*): Experiences in Mexico's Community Forests. *Unasylva* 54, no. 214/215: 68–73.

So, Alvin Y. 1990. *Social Change and Development: Modernization, Dependency, and World Systems.* London: Sage.

Soubies, F. 1979–80. Existence d'une Phase Sèche en Amazonie Brésilienne Datée par la Presence de Charbons dans les Sols (6.000–3.000 Ans B.P.). *Cahiers ORSTROM Sér. Géol.* 11:113–48.

Spence, Mark David. 1999. *Dispossessing the Wilderness: Indian Removal and the Making of the National Parks.* New York: Oxford University Press.

Springate-Baginski, Oliver. 2001. "A Boat That Cannot Reach Either Bank": Lessons from a Long-Term Analysis of the Cooperative Forest Societies of Kangra District, Himachal Pradesh. *Himalayan Research Bulletin* 21, no. 2: 46–53 (published April 2003).

——. 2004. Can CBFM Avoid Strengthening "Forestry Hegemony"? Patterns of Implementation and Livelihood Impacts in India and Nepal Compared. Paper presented at the workshop on Community-Based Forestry in the Next Decade: Towards an "Agrarian" Approach? Berlin: Humboldt University, Junior Research Group on Postsocialist Land Relations, October 8–9. http://www.agrar.hu-berlin.de/wisola/ipw/plr/ (accessed 8 October 2004).

Stebbing, E. P. 1922. *The Forests of India.* London: Lane. Reprinted New Delhi: A. J. Reprints, 1982–83.

Steen, H. K. 1984. *History of Sustained Yield Forestry: A Symposium.* Durham: Forest History Society.

Sundar, Nandini, and Roger Jeffery. 1999. Introduction. In Roger Jeffery and Nandini Sandar, eds., *A New Moral Economy for India's Forests? Discourses of Community and Participation*, 15–54. New Delhi: Thousand Oaks/London: Sage.

Surplus People Project. 2000. *Surplus People Project Report on the Community Facilitation and Education Project on Municipal Demarcation in the Act 9 Areas of Namaqualand.* Cape Town: Surplus People Project.

Suryanata, Krisnawati. 1994. Fruit Trees Under Contract: Tenure and Land Use Change in Upland Java, Indonesia. *World Development* 22, no. 10: 1567–78.

Suryanata, Krisnawati, and Jefferson Fox, eds. 2003. Issues of Decentralization and Federation in Forest Governance: Proceedings from the Tenth Workshop on Community-Based Management of Forestlands. Honolulu: East West Center/Bangkok: Regional Community Forestry Training Center. http://www.eastwestcenter.org/res-rp-publicationdetails.asp?pub_ID=1459 (accessed 30 April 2004).

Tapp, Nicholas, and Nicholas K. Menzies. 1997. Fallow Management Strategies Among Upland Cultivators of the Southwest China Borderlands: The Case of Cunninghamia lanceolata. Full text available as part VI, paper 43, in M. F. Cairns, ed., *Indigenous Strategies for Intensification of Shifting Cultivation in Asia-Pacific: Proceedings of a Regional Conference Held in Bogor, Indonesia, 23–27 June 1997.* Chiang Mai: International Centre for Research in Agroforestry, 2002. Abstract at http://web.idrc.ca/ev_en.php?ID=3306_201&ID2=DO_TOPIC.

Taylor, Bron Raymond. 1997. Earthen Spirituality or Cultural Genocide? Radical Environmentalism's Appropriation of Native American Spirituality. *Religion* 27, no. 2: 183–215.

Terborgh, J. 1999. *Requiem for Nature.* Washington, DC: Island Press/Shearwater.

Thompson, E. P. 1975. *Whigs and Hunters: The Origin of the Black Act.* London: Lane.

Thompson, Michael, and Michael Warburton. 1985. Decision Making Under Contradictory Uncertainties: How to Save the Himalayas When You Can't Find Out What's Wrong with Them. *Journal of Applied Systems Analysis* 12, no. 1: 3–34.

Thongchai Winichakul. 1994. *Siam Mapped: A History of the Geo-Body of a Nation.* Honolulu: University of Hawai'i Press.

Time Asia Magazine. 2002. Nagarahole Is a Lush Tropical Forest on the Edge of Coorg. Report filed on September 16 by Sarita Rai. http://www.time.com/time/asia/magazine/article/0,13673,501020916-349199,00.html (accessed 2 November 2004).

Toronto Globe and Mail. 1993. Activists Question Tactics in Clayoquot Protest (November 11).

Totman, Conrad. 1989. *The Green Archipelago: Forestry in Preindustrial Japan.* Berkeley: University of California Press.

Tucker, Catherine M. 2004. Community Institutions and Forest Management in Mexico's Monarch Butterfly Reserve. *Society and Natural Resources* 17:569–87.

Tucker, Richard P., and J. F. Richards, eds. 1983. *Global Deforestation and the Nineteenth-Century World Economy.* Durham: Duke University Press.

Tuma, Elias H. 1965. *Twenty-Six Centuries of Agrarian Reform: A Comparative Analysis.* Berkeley: University of California Press.

Turnbull, David, ed. 1991. *Knowledge, Land, and the Australian Aboriginal Experience.* Geelong: Deakin University Press.

Turner M. D. 1999. Conflict, Environmental Change, and Social Institutions in Dryland Africa: Limitations of the Community Resource Management Approach. *Society and Natural Resources* 12, no. 7: 643–57.

Uchida, Emi, Jintao Xu, and Scott Rozelle. 2004. Grain for Green: Effectiveness and Sustainability of China's Conservation Set-Aside Program. Manuscript.

Unasylva. 1998. Accommodating Multiple Interests in Forestry. *Unasylva* 49, no. 4 (special issue).

United Nations. 2004. Follow-up to the outcome of the Millennium Summit: Implementation of the United Nations Millennium Declaration. New York: United Nations General Assembly. Report of the Secretary General, August 27. http://www.un.org/millenniumgoals/ (accessed 13 October 2004).

United States National Parks Service. 2001. *Environmental Assessment: Proposed Rule: Religious Ceremonial Collection of Golden Eaglets in Wupatki National Monument.* Washington, DC: U.S. National Parks Service. http://data2.itc.nps.gov/parks/wupa/ppdocuments/ACF342.htm (accessed 19 October 2004).

Uphoff, Norman T. 1993. Grassroots Organizations and NGOs in Rural Development: Opportunities with Diminishing States and Expanding Markets. *World Development* 21, no. 4: 607–22.

Uphoff, Norman T., and Milton J. Esman. 1974. *Local Organization for Rural Development: Analysis of Asian Experience.* Rural Development Committee Special Series on Rural Local Government no. 19. Ithaca: Cornell University Press.

Uprety, Hima. 2003. Participation and Good Forest Governance Initiatives: The Experience of FECOFUN. In Krisnawati Suryanata and Jefferson Fox, eds., *Issues of Decentralization and Federation in Forest Governance: Proceedings from the Tenth Workshop on Commu-*

nity-Based Management of Forestlands, 100–109. Honolulu: East West Center/Bangkok: Regional Community Forestry Training Center.

Vandergeest, Peter. 1996. Territorialization of Forest Rights in Thailand. *Society and Natural Resources* 9:159–75.

Vandergeest, Peter, and Nancy Lee Peluso. 1995. Territorialization and State Power in Thailand. *Theory and Society* 24, no. 3: 385–426.

Van Ryneveld, Philip. 1996. Namaqualand District Planning and Management Project (Pre-planning Phase): A Draft Submission to the Northern Cape Land Reform Steering Committee. Cape Town: Surplus People Project.

Van Schaik, C. P., and R. A. Kramer. 1997. Toward a New Protection Paradigm. In R. A. Kramer, C. P. Van Schaik, and J. Johnson, eds., *Last Stand: Protected Areas and the Defense of Tropical Biodiversity*, 212–30. New York: Oxford University Press.

Varughese, George. 1999. Villagers, Bureaucrats, and Forests in Nepal: Designing Governance for a Complex Resource. PhD diss., Indiana University.

Vasan, Sudha. 2001. Community Forestry: Historical Legacy of Himachal Pradesh. *Himalayan Research Bulletin* 21, no. 2: 36–45 (published April 2003).

Vasavada, Shilpa, Abha Mishra, and Crispin Bates. 1999. How Many Committees Do I Belong To? In Roger Jeffery and Nandini Sandar, eds., *A New Moral Economy for India's Forests? Discourses of Community and Participation*, 151–80. New Delhi: Thousand Oaks/London: Sage.

Verdery, Katherine. 1996. *What Was Socialism and What Comes Next?* Princeton: Princeton University Press.

Victor, M., and Andrew Barash, eds. 2001. *Cultivating Forests: Alternative Forest Management Practices for Community Forestry: Proceedings of an International Seminar.* RECOFTC Report no. 17. Bangkok: Regional Community Forestry Training Center. http://www .recoftc.org/03region/materials/conference_reports/international2.html#Cultivating.

Victor, M., C. Lang, and Jeff Bornemeier, eds. 1998. *Community Forestry at a Crossroads: Reflections and Future Directions in the Development of Community Forestry: Proceedings of an International Seminar.* RECOFTC Report no. 16. Bangkok: Regional Community Forestry Training Center.

Voon, Tania. 2000. Sizing Up the WTO: Trade-Environment Conflict and the Kyoto Protocol. *Journal of Transnational Law and Policy* 10, no. 1: 71–107.

Vu Huu Tuynh. 2001. *Evaluation Report Documentation Study on Community Forest Management Model Yen Bai Province.* Hanoi: Ministry of Agriculture and Rural Development, Vietnam Sweden Mountain Rural Development Programme.

Wade, Robert. 1988. *Village Republics: Economic Conditions for Collective Action in South India.* Cambridge: Cambridge University Press.

Watkin, John. 2001. Community Based Conservation in East Africa: What Do Communities Think? Draft report on the East African Regional Workshop Series. Nairobi: African Conservation Centre.

Wéber, Jean. 1996. Conservation, Développement et Coordination: Peut-on Gérer Biologiquement le Social? Paper presented to the PanAfrican Symposium on Community Management of Natural Resources and Sustainable Development. Harare: IUCN.

Weber, Max. 1978. *Economy and Society: An Outline of Interpretive Sociology.* Berkeley: University of California Press.

Weiss, G. 2001. Mountain Forest Policy in Austria: A Historical Policy Analysis on Regulating a Natural Resource. *Environment and History* 7, no. 3: 335–55.

Western, David, R. Michael Wright, and Shirley C. Strum, eds. 1994. *Natural Connections: Perspectives in Community-Based Conservation*. Washington, DC: Island Press.

Westoby, Jack. 1987. *The Purpose of Forests: Follies of Development*. Oxford: Blackwell.

White, Andy, and Alejandra Martin. 2002. *Who Owns the World's Forests? Forest Tenure and Public Forests in Transition*. Washington, DC: Forest Trends.

Wilshusen, Peter R., Steven R. Brechin, Crystal L. Fortwangler, and Patrick West. 2002. Reinventing a Square Wheel: Critique of a Resurgent "Protection Paradigm" in International Biodiversity Conservation. *Society and Natural Resources* 15:17–40.

Winrock International. 2002. *Emerging Issues in Community Forestry in Nepal*. Kathmandu: Winrock.

Wollenberg, Eva. 1998a. A Conceptual Framework and Typology for Explaining Outcomes of Local Forest Management. *Journal of World Forest Resource Management* 9:1–35.

——. 1998b. Methods for Assessing the Conservation and Development of Forest Products: What We Know and What We Have Yet to Learn. In Eva Wollenberg and Andrew Ingles, eds., *Incomes from the Forest: Methods for the Development and Conservation of Forest Products for Local Communities*, 1–16. Bogor: CIFOR/IUCN.

Wollenberg, Eva, and Andrew Ingles, eds. 1998. *Incomes from the Forest: Methods for the Development and Conservation of Forest Products for Local Communities*. Bogor: CIFOR/IUCN.

Worldwide Fund for Nature. n.d. What Is a Sacred Gift to the Earth. http://www.panda.org/about_wwf/how_we_work/gifts_to_the_earth/about_sacred.cfm (accessed 13 November 2003).

Xu Jianchu, J. Fox, N. Lü, N. Podger, S. Leisz, and X. Ai. 1999. Effects of Swidden Cultivation, State Policies, and Customary Institutions on Land Cover in a Hani Village, Yunnan, China. *Mountain Research and Development* 19, no. 2: 123–32.

Xu Jianchu and Jesse Ribot. 2004. Decentralization and Accountability in Forest Management: Case from Yunnan, Southwest China. *European Journal of Development Research* 16, no. 1 (Spring): 147–64.

Xu Xiuli and Ting Zuo. 2003. Implementation Gap: A Critical Analysis of the County Forestry Bureau (CFB) in the Implementation of the Cropland Conversion Program (CCP). In Krisnawati Suryanata and Jefferson Fox, eds., *Issues of Decentralization and Federation in Forest Governance: Proceedings from the Tenth Workshop on Community-Based Management of Forestlands*, 26–30. Honolulu: East West Center/Bangkok: Regional Community Forestry Training Center.

Yeh, Emily. 1998. *Forest Products and Foreign Markets: Community Forestry in Northwest Yunnan Province*. Working Paper Series. Berkeley: Asia Forestry Network.

——. 2000. Forest Claims, Conflicts, and Commodification: The Political Ecology of Tibetan Mushroom-Harvesting Villages in Yunnan Province, China. *China Quarterly* 161 (March): 212–26.

Zerner, Charles, ed. 2000. *People, Plants, and Justice: The Politics of Nature Conservation*. New York: Columbia University Press.

Zhao Yaqiao. 2004. Sustainable Forestry as an Alternative to the Logging Ban: Findings from Policy Experiments. Paper presented at the Tenth Meeting of the International Association for the Study of Common Property, Oaxaca, Mexico. http://www.iascp.org/conference.html.

Zhu, Haijiao. 2004. Participation of Community Associations in Watershed Management in Jiang Jia Qing Village, Yunnan Province, China. Paper presented at the Global Workshop for Community-Based Forestry Practitioners, Lake Tahoe CA, September 24–26. Providence, RI: National Network of Forestry Practitioners.

Zingerli, Claudia. 2003. Changing the Rules of the Game: Forest Management in the Mountain District of Ba Be, Vietnam. *European Tropical Forest Research Network News* no. 38: 45–47.

Web Sites

African Conservation Centre (ACC): http://www.conservationafrica.org/Reports.htm

Associación Coordinadora Indigena y Campesina de Agroforesteria Comunitaria Centroaméricana (ACICAFOC): http://www.acicafoc.net

Consultative Group to Assist the Poorest (CGAP): http://www.cgap.org/keyprinciples.html

Ecotourism Society of Kenya (ESOK): http://www.esok.org/?q=node/view/26

Eudafano: http://www.thebodyshop.com.au/upload/CT_Marula.doc

First Nations Forestry Program (Canada): http://www.fnfp.gc.ca/

Global Caucus on Community-Based Resources Management, country profile for Canada: http://www.forestsandcommunities.org/Country_Profiles/canada.html

Global Environmental Facility (GEF)/United Nations Development Program (UNDP) programs in Uganda: http://www.undp.org/biodiversity/biodiversitycd/practiceUganda .htm

Il Ngwesi Group Ranch and Lewa Downs Conservancy: http://www.lewa.org/ilngwesi .php

International Ecotourism Society (TIES): http://www.ecotourism.org

Maisons Familiales Rurales (MFR): http://www.mfr.asso.fr/

PhytoTrade Africa: http://www.phytotradeafrica.com/

Redlodge Clearing House: Collaborative Management, story profile on Maidu Stewardship Project: http://www.redlodgeclearinghouse.org/stories/maidustewardship.html#contact (accessed 5 November 2004)

Southern African Natural Products Trade Association (SANProTA): http://www.sanprota .com

TRAFFIC: http://www.traffic.org/

United Nations Department of Economic and Social Affairs, Division for Sustainable Development, World Summit on Sustainable Development, Johannesburg: http://www .un.org/esa/sustdev/documents/WSSD_POI_PD/English/POIChapter4.htm

World Tourism Organization—International Year of Ecotourism: http://www.world-tourism .org/sustainable/IYE-Main-Menu.htm

Personal Communications

Asseid, Bakari. Director of the Department of Commercial Crops, Fruits, and Forestry, Zanzibar. Interviews in November 2002.

Gombya-Ssembajjwe, William. Department of Forest Biology and Ecosystem Management, Makerere University, Kampala, Uganda. Informal discussion in April 1996 about the impact of AIDS on rural Ugandan communities.

Kumar, Ajit, and Rajeev Ahal. Cooperative Transformation Initiative (CTI), Navrachna, Kangra. Discussion on 14 July 2002 about the history of the cooperative movement in Kangra and surrounding districts.

Lesage, Louis. Coordinator of Forest and Wildlife Activities, Conseil de la Nation Huronne-Wendat. Wendake, Québec, Canada. 29 September 2003.

Masoud, Thabit. CARE, Zanzibar. E-mail communication on 21 August 2003.

May, Harry. Surplus People Project, Cape Town, South Africa. E-mail communication on 13 July 2004 updating the status of the Transformation of Certain Rural Areas Act (TRANCRAA) consultation process and referendum results.

Pinedo-Vazquez, Miguel. Columbia University, New York. Discussions on 22 April 2003 in Macapá, Brazil, following field visit to Mazagão.

Stauffer, Renée. Karuk Indigenous Basketweavers' Association, Orleans, CA. Conversation on 24 September 2004 at Lake Tahoe, CA.

Zweede, Johann. Fundacão Floresta Tropical (FFT), Belém, Brazil. Discussion on 24 April 2003 about alternative timber harvesting technologies in Amazonia and private sector/community partnerships in forestry.